REBEL COLUMNS

REBEL
COLUMNS

Danny Morrison

First published 2004
by
Beyond the Pale
BTP Publications Ltd
Unit 2.1.2 Conway Mill
5-7 Conway Street
Belfast BT13 2DE

Tel: +44 (0)28 90 438630
Fax: +44 (0)28 90 439707
E-mail: office@btpale.com
Website: http://www.btpale.com

British Library Cataloguing-in-Publication Data.
A catalogue record for this book is available from the British Library.

ISBN 1-900960-27-3

Front cover photograph by kind permission of Bill Rolston.
Back cover photograph of Danny Morrison by kind permission of Bobby Hanvey

Also by Danny Morrison:

Novels

West Belfast
On The Back of The Swallow
The Wrong Man

Letters

Then The Walls Came Down

Memoir

All the Dead Voices

Play

The Wrong Man

DEDICATION

To Leonard Peltier.
On the 28th year of his imprisonment.
Activist, writer, poet.
A symbol of the suffering of his people.

Contents

Acknowledgements   12

Prologue

     A Tale of Two Cities   15

From Armalites to Ballot Boxes

     The Belfast Agreement – The Good Friday Signing   19
     A Long History   22
     The Visit   25
     Never Going Away   27
     The Cause of Violence   28
     30,492   31
     Futility of the Real IRA   33
     Wonderful World, Beautiful People   35
     Arms Beyond Use   37
     Now You See 'Em, Now You Don't!   39
     The Issues of Assent and Consent   41
     Like a Tube of Toothpaste   43
     Helloes and Goodbyes   45
     IRA Apologises   47
     An Impossible Demand   49
     Stealing Votes – the British Way!   51
     IRA Will Not Be Humiliated   54
     One More IRA Statement   56
     SDLP – No Problem!   58
     One Extreme   60
     Spies, Spinners and Spoofers   62
     IMC Land   65
     Rosy Future for Sinn Féin   67
     The Real Slow Learners   69

Unionism Misunderstood – Some Clarifications

The Beliefs of Mahatma Taylor 75
If I Were a Political Correspondent… 77
The Siege of Finaghy Road North 79
Giving a Dog a Bad Name 81
Willie Wonky 85
Unionism in a State 87
Shame on Them 89
Bending the Rules 91
Let's Not Talk 93
Let There be a Referendum 95
Enough Is Enough 97
'I am what I am' 99
Tell us the War is Over! 102
The Next 'D' Word 104
Targeting the Unionist Community 106
Transparent Reminders 108
145 Divis Street 110

Collusion and the Dirty War

Nairac's Dirty War 115
Massacre on the New Lodge 117
Suspicion Over Omagh 120
The Crime of Castlereagh 122
Poor Souls Didn't Know What They Were Doing 124
The Perfect Form of Collusion 126
A Shameful Story 128
The Stakeknife Affair 131
The Politics of Terror 134

The Media

The Nun's Car 139
A Right Paean in the Ass 141
The Politics of Condemnation 143
We Now [Don't] Have a Party Political Broadcast on Behalf of… 145
For the Cause of Liberty 147
'Ireland – Bobby Sands!' 149

After September 11

After September 11   155
Terror Spotting   157
Heil, Adolf Sharon!   159
Remembering All of the Dead   161
Our Silence is Not for Sale   163
Lying Time Again   165
Some Will Be Innocent   167
Yours Sincerely, Tony Blair   169
Prisoners of War   171
WMD   173
The Disappeared   175
A Proud Tradition   178

People

The Life of Demitrios Tsafendas   183
Crucifying Jesus Christ   185
The Man in Black   187
Rodolfo Walsh – The Writer as Freedom Fighter   190
In the Simplicity of His Defiance   192
Terence 'Cleeky' Clarke   194
A Story of Revenge   196
Simple Song of Freedom   198
Spike Milligan   200
Mayor Alec Maskey Pays Tribute   203
'A Spiritual Act, A Holy Deed'   205
Mary Robinson – 'An awkward voice'   208
Said and Frankl – Race and Belonging   210
Resting in Peace – Le Père Lachaise   212
Marwan Barghouthi – A Palestinian Hero   214
Proud to be an American   217
Yes, Prime Minister   219

Acknowledgements

With thanks to Bill, Mike and Agnieszka at Beyond the Pale Publications.

The features included in this book originally appeared in several publications – the *Andersonstown News*, *The Examiner*, *The Guardian*, *An Phoblacht/Republican News* and *The Irish Times*. All of the pieces, apart from a small number of grammatical corrections or elisions, appear here as they were originally submitted, and some are thus longer than when first published.

Prologue

A Tale of Two Cities

Andersonstown News, 12 January 2004

Danny McCooey was taken into the hotel through the back.

Baha Mousa was taken out of the hotel through the front.

Earlier, Danny had his dinner with his family at their Falls Road home, got spruced up – it was a Saturday night – and went into Belfast city centre for a drink with his friend Michael Masterson.

Baha was working as a receptionist in the Haitham Hotel in Basra city centre, along with his friend Kifah Taha and other staff.

It was April 30, 1977.

It was September 14, 2003.

Danny and Michael left the bar and were walking along Castle Street when they ran into a British army patrol.

Baha was on the desk when a British army patrol ran into the hotel and ordered everyone to lie on the floor. Soldiers went to the safe and discovered two rifles and two pistols. The owner of the hotel, Haitham Vaha, the man who had hidden the weapons, had fled in the confusion of the raid.

Michael Masterson said, 'As we passed, a soldier said, "Go on, you Irish bastards!" I stopped and said, "Pardon; I can't understand what you're saying". He kept calling me an "Irish bastard". He took a swing at me with his fist and I threw a punch back. Danny grabbed me by the shoulder and said, "Na, don't get involved with them".

'I saw another rifle butt getting swung but it missed me and must have hit Danny about the stomach because he fell to the ground, screaming, "My stomach, my stomach!" I went to his aid and asked the Brits for a doctor but they arrested me. The cops had arrived by now. I was put in the back of a jeep. Two Brits went to where Danny was lying, picked him up, half-dragged him to the jeep and then threw him in the back next to me. He was crying about his stomach.'

A workmate of Baha said, 'We were taken to a barracks. We were put in a big room with our hands tied and with bags over our heads. But I could see through some holes in my hood. Soldiers would come in – ordinary soldiers, not officers, mostly with their heads shaved but in uniform – and they would kick us, picking on one after the other. They were kickboxing us in the chest and between the legs and in the back. We were crying and screaming.'

The men were held for three days.

'They set on Baha especially, and he kept crying that he couldn't breathe in the hood. He kept asking them to take the bag off and said that he was suffocating. But they laughed at him and kicked him more. One of them said, "Stop screaming and you'll be able to breathe more easily". Baha was so scared. Then they increased the kicking on him and he collapsed on the floor.'

Michael Masterson said, 'We were taken to the barracks at the Grand Central Hotel. Danny was dragged away. About ten minutes later I heard him screaming. I never saw Danny again.'

Twenty-year-old Danny McCooey was taken from the barracks to the City Hospital but because of the seriousness of his injuries it wouldn't admit him and he was rushed to the Royal Victoria Hospital. He was bleeding internally, his stomach collapsed and there was a hole in the base of his lungs. He died twenty days later.

Twenty-two-year old Baha Mousa died in the barracks and was taken to a British army field hospital. The death certificate stated that he had died from 'cardiorespiratory arrest: asphyxia'. His nose had been broken, two of his ribs were broken, the skin had been ripped off his wrists by the handcuffs and his torso was covered in bruises.

Michael Masterson was released without charge in the early hours of 1 May.

Kifah Taha was released without charge from hospital in late September, having suffered severe bruising to his upper abdomen, which led to acute renal failure.

A 20-year-old British soldier was charged with the manslaughter of Danny McCooey but was acquitted. The judge said that the soldier 'did what he instinctively thought was necessary in the moment of the threatened attack'.

No soldier has been charged with killing Baha Mousa, though the British have offered his family £4,500 in compensation provided the Mousa family do not hold British forces liable for his death. The family refused to sign the settlement and plans to take the Ministry of Defence to court.

Last week in Basra Tony Blair declared that the prestige and reputation of the British armed forces, a party to the Iraqi 'peace process', had never been higher.

Last week in Belfast Tony Blair's government gave itself powers outside of the terms of the Good Friday Agreement and established the Independent Monitoring Commission, which will scrutinise and judge potential breaches of the peace process. These powers allow the British to exclude Sinn Féin from a power-sharing executive if the Commission were, for example, to find the IRA guilty of a punishment beating.

That is the policy.

'We do not accept admission of guilt. That is the policy', an MoD spokesperson said last week, in relation to the beating to death of Baha Mousa. The British army carried out the inquiry into itself. There was no Independent Monitoring Commission, yet the British exercised the power of exclusion.

The lawyer representing the family of Baha Mousa was banned from the hearing.

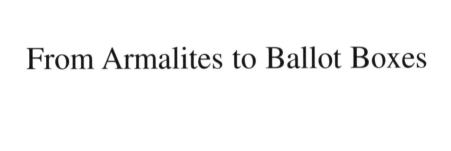

From Armalites to Ballot Boxes

The Belfast Agreement – the Good Friday Signing

The Guardian, 11 April 1998

Letitia Fitzpatrick from Ulster Television says to me, 'I am so thirsty. Would you?'

'Okay', I say. 'Once more I'll trudge off and get you coffee.' It is 11.55pm, Stormont, Government Buildings, and at midnight, if the parties to Senator George Mitchell's talks haven't agreed and gone home, they'll all turn into pumpkins. Just at midnight I arrive back into the press conference hut with the coffee. Behind me the aroma has seemingly attracted several suspicious-looking men in suits, some more in denim jackets, and, to my left, women with non-Catholic perms. Then I hear the booming voice of Ian Paisley and realise that I am at my first DUP press conference and have no flak jacket.

'I have here in my hand,' he begins, 'a delegate's badge which gives me the right to attend all meetings of the Forum on one side, and the right to attend all meetings of the Talks, on the other hand.'

'Why didn't you use it for two years!', shouts a man to my left.

'The people wanted you in here to fight for them. You wouldn't do it! You hadn't got the balls!', shouts a man to my right.

Oh dear, I think. I'm with the UVF.

'You're not pressmen,' declares a most perspicacious Mr Paisley. 'You belong to parties that are opposed to my party, so just shut up!'

'Your days of telling people to shut up are gone!'

'Yeh! You don't even care about the people. You don't give a shit, with your big fucking house!'

Uh-oh. I'm now in the middle of the UDA.

'You are all fascists! Adams lovers!', shouts Ginger Spice at me and them, and which is partially true. At any moment I am awaiting them to zero in on the common enemy – me, the Armalite-and-Ballot-Box-Kid – but the division between them is palpable. And where now is Paisley to go, because his muscle, the people who accuse him of rolling the snowballs for them to throw, back in 1972, back in the DUP/UDA strike of 1977, are no longer with him, but have their own representatives here in the talks. Unionism in change is dynamic: Unionism is interesting.

Earlier in the evening we were told by Tony Blair's coiffeur, Alistair Campbell, described affectionately, I think, by one British newspaper as the Spindoctor-General, that the deadline of midnight is having a powerful effect of focusing the parties on concluding. He is received by journalists from London with just a teeny-weeny bit too much sycophancy for my liking. Two hours later and no one from the government is telling us what is happening, though we have had Sinn

Féin's Mitchel McLaughlin come out and declare bleakly that there is no agreement because unionists are blocking the agreement.

Time passes. The press people get bored. A woman runs in. 'There's a rumour that Sinn Féin are walking out!'

'Who started that?'

'God knows. But it's a good one.'

An hour later a journalist from Dublin says, 'Heard anything?'

'No. What about you?'

'Can't say, but just wanted to check if anybody had a better rumour than me.'

Some people are reading, others are snoring. I asked Letitia to name her favourite film, favourite book, favourite song and favourite poem, and at the prompt of the latter she launches into Eliot's 'Journey of the Magi':

> A cold coming we had of it,
> Just the worst time of the year
> For a journey, and such a long journey:
> The ways deep and the weather sharp,
> The very dead of winter...

It was an eerie rendition, given our circumstances.

In one of the press huts I met with Frank Millar, London Correspondent of the *Irish Times*. Years ago we couldn't speak to each other because he was the general secretary of the Ulster Unionist Party and I was the National Director of Publicity for Sinn Féin. But now that we were covering the talks for newspapers we had a cover for talking. People have to talk – it is the way forward.

As the night progressed the rumours that Sinn Féin was feeling shafted by the SDLP and the Dublin government increased to the point where I was predicting that Sinn Féin could not go along with the re-negotiated Mitchell paper, which also proposed an Assembly (probably based at Stormont). Sinn Féin, an abstentionist party in the North, is implacably opposed to a return to Stormont, because of its connotations of sectarian, 'majority' rule, its de facto recognition of partition. Yet, Sinn Féin had contributed to the Mitchell paper and made amendments to it, proposals to which it has to remain faithful if it is to be consistent. The biggest difference between Stormont and the new Assembly is the crux issue of consent: the combined strength of Sinn Féin and the SDLP gives the nationalist community a powerful veto. Can Sinn Féin adapt to this fairly scary, new challenge and, if so, can Sinn Féin persuade its supporters that there is a case for entering a parliament in the North?

Driving up to Stormont on Thursday was a strange experience. But, confession to make, it wasn't my first time there. I took my seat a long time ago. The summer of 1962, to be precise. My father took my two older sisters and myself on one of those bus tours around the city that included a visit to the Stormont Parliament, which was a wholly uncharacteristic act for nationalists back in those days. During the fifty years of one-party unionist rule at Stormont, nationalists initiated one single piece of legislation – an Act for the Preservation of Wild Fowl! I sat in the speaker's chair. All I can remember is the smell of leather and pine.

In 1979, when editor of *An Phoblacht/Republican News*, much to the horror of the NIO press officer, David Gilliland, I got past several RUC security checkpoints and into Stormont Castle, thanks to Peter Fearon of the Press Association, a wild and lovable man. He brought me into a press conference where the late Humphrey Atkins, the Secretary of State, was announcing a new initiative, a round-table conference. A month earlier the British government launched the Lancaster House talks between Robert Mugabe's outlawed Patriotic Front and Ian Smith's National Party. I asked Atkins what was the difference between the Patriotic Front and the IRA, and shouldn't the government be talking to the Republican Movement to end the conflict. He replied, 'Don't be ridiculous!'

I wasn't allowed to ask another question but an American reporter repeated my question. Atkins hesitated, stuttered and said, 'I … I … I don't know what the difference is,' after which the press conference erupted in laughter. For helping me, Peter Fearon didn't remain too long at the PA! He moved to New York, where he still lives and works, and found infamy. Tom Wolfe in *The Bonfire of the Vanities* based the character of the English journalist, Peter Fallow, on Mister Fearon.

It's fine going to Stormont for a stunt, but would one's attendance there, as a republican, copper-fasten partition, undermine one's republicanism or, could it, through example and reconciliation, undermine the sectarianism and opposition to Irish unity of one's erstwhile opponents? Who knows?

By 4am those of us still alive are watching James Cagney in 'Public Enemy' followed by a programme ironically titled, 'Living With Violence.' This vigil reminds me of barricade duty back in 1969, when you wished that the loyalists would hurry up and attack so that you could get it over with and go to bed. Bored out of his mind, one hack begins singing, to a Dr Hook air, the words, 'If I said I had a Cross-Border body would you hold it against me…' Several other appalling plagiarisms follow.

There is a new rumour that Sinn Féin is preparing to walk out. Then, at 7.10am Mitchel McLaughlin arrives to read out a short statement but not to answer questions. In confident tones he declares that Sinn Féin has, during negotiations, clawed back a considerable amount of ground which it believed had been lost earlier. Suddenly, the atmosphere changes. There is no rush of Ulster Unionist MPs out to contradict him. The impossible begins to seem possible. Everyone is in great form. There is a buzz. This could genuinely be a new beginning. Of course, there are still problems. Of course, there are issues outstanding, and we can forget about it all if Orange feet get marching down Garvaghy Road this July.

In late afternoon the document has still not been finalised. There are rumours of dissent within the Ulster Unionist Party.

But as I drive out of Stormont, past the statue of Lord Edward Carson, down

Prince of Wales Avenue, I feel that something fundamental has shifted. My view of East Belfast is always from the west of the city, my home. Stormont lies in the Castlereagh Hills, foreign. On this evening, I look from this Avenue across to Black Mountain above West Belfast, distinct and familiar, and realise that it is not that far away, after all.

A Long History

On the last days of Long Kesh

From 'A Long History', *Irish Examiner*, 28 July 2000 and
'Always Going to Fail', *Andersonstown News*, 20 November 2000

For most working-class nationalists in the North, Long Kesh has been part of their lives for almost 30 years, since it was converted from an RAF base in 1971 into a 'temporary' camp for republican internees.

Most of its inmates were released last Friday and though it must be difficult for those few who remain, it will be a relief to see Long Kesh close, to see a line drawn through a strife-torn past (even though there will still be political prisoners in Maghaberry as a result of dissident loyalist and republican activities). The impact of this jail on Irish and British politics has been immense. It was during a protest against internment that British paratroopers killed fourteen people on Bloody Sunday – an event that broke hearts in Derry and across Ireland and fuelled at least another decade of conflict.

And it was to deflect international opprobrium, earned through its torture of 'the hooded men', among others, that in November 1972 the British government changed the name of the camp to 'the Maze', renamed the prisoners 'detainees' and announced to the world that it had ended internment and closed Long Kesh! But it will always be Long Kesh and the H-Blocks of Long Kesh to those who came through it.

Among the internees, and those sentenced republicans who were later moved from the Crum to the Cages, were many who would become legendary figures, years down the line. The Cages were compounds of four Nissan huts, a Portakabin for recreation, a toilet block and an exercise yard, surrounded by British army watchtowers and an ocean of barbed wire. The huts were regularly searched for tunnels and for the 'jungle juice' brewed sometimes in the fire extinguishers. During raids, handicrafts were often destroyed, personal photos and letters stolen, petrol poured into water tanks, and the food sent in by relatives tampered with – sugar sprinkled over meats, salt over sweet things.

Of course, as far as the soldiers were concerned the prisoners were the enemy whose mates on the outside were killing their mates, over 100 of who were shot dead or blown up in 1972 alone.

When an escape was successful prisoners didn't care about the revenge assaults that usually followed. But there were also tragedies. Mark Graham was paralysed for life when he hid under a bin lorry but was crushed going over ramps. And in October 1974 Hugh Coney from County Tyrone emerged from an escape tunnel only to be shot dead by a British soldier. I also remember the Sunday when news came across to our Cage that Paddy Crawford, suffering from depression, hanged himself. Other prisoners were to die from medical neglect, including Paddy Teer when warders refused to answer the emergency bell.

Powerful friendships were forged in these adverse conditions, lasting comradeships established between countrymen and city men. Young people were politicised by older prisoners, and older prisoners converted by the young. Every Cage had its wags. Listening to the Craddocks (Dominic O'Neill and Andy Fennell) jointly cooking dinner over an open fire was like listening to an extremely Odd Couple!

In 1976 Long Kesh was again transformed when the H-Blocks were opened and a British Labour government announced the end of political status. Penologists and seasoned observers advised the government not to make the prison a battleground (up until then no prison warder had lost his life). But the British government thought it could do on the inside what it had failed to do on the outside – bring the IRA to heel by criminalising its prisoners.

And so the blanket protest began.

Most of those young people who from 1976 onwards resisted the policy of criminalisation had already been arrested under special laws, had suffered ill-treatment whilst being interrogated, were convicted by judges sitting in special, non-jury courts, using special rules of evidence, only to be told when they arrived in the H-Blocks (and Armagh) that they weren't special and that they had better put on a criminal uniform and obey orders. One third of the prison officers had been imported from Britain on special bounties. Most of them had a military background.

Republicans served years in solitary confinement or in bare cells wearing only a blanket, without access to books or newspapers or writing material. They lived in cells floating with urine and covered in their own excrement. On punishment diets they were given one slice of bread a day. 'One would hardly allow an animal to remain in such conditions, let alone a human being,' said Archbishop (later Cardinal) Ó Fiaich, when he visited there in 1978.

Mrs Thatcher said they were common criminals who had no public support but their leader, Bobby Sands, became an MP. And when the story of the peace process was to be written it was acknowledged that the contribution and support of those prisoners was crucial to its success, whereas Thatcher's only success in life was in waging war and impoverishing her subjects.

Thatcher once asked Ó Fiaich why it was that Britain could be at peace with Germany and France despite their ancient enmities but still in conflict with Ireland. 'Well, Madam,' he replied, 'it's because you don't occupy the Ruhr.'

Long Kesh was a jail built on a lie – that lie being that there was a system of justice in the North, that fifty years of grievances under sectarian rule, the odd pogrom and curfew, the torture and internment of nationalists, the shooting of civil rights demonstrators, was tolerable and didn't justify shots being fired back.

Ten prisoners died in 1981 on hunger strike but on the outside over sixty others lost their lives in incidents linked to the prison, including women and children killed by plastic bullets and almost 30 prison warders. Fifty other warders – according to Chris Ryder in his book, *The Untold Story of the Northern Ireland Prison Service* – committed suicide, including the chief medical officer at the time of the hunger strike.

IRA Volunteer Bobby Sands died the people's own MP, and Kieran Doherty, in his election as TD for Cavan/Monaghan, breached partition and opened up the future which is now unfolding for Sinn Féin in the South. By the time Mickey Devine died in mid-August all had changed utterly.

The truth always comes out and had the truth been told earlier, many lives would have been spared. A former governor of the H-Blocks, speaking about the role of prison officers, told Ryder: 'They were used as cannon fodder by governments and put in the frontline of a battle for the false aim of criminalisation that was always going to fail.'

In 1991 I was sentenced to eight years and spent four of those in the H-Blocks. By then, political status had been conceded as the authorities realised they couldn't run such a unique prison without the co-operation of the inmates. During this period, with men serving Mandela-like sentences, the most difficult aspect of life was in maintaining with wives or girlfriends meaningful relationships, the vast majority of which broke down.

Conflict produces irresolvable inequities and injustices all around. Understandably, the early release of prisoners has been highly distressing for many relatives of the dead. On the other hand, for hundreds of mostly nationalist and republican families the killers of their loved ones – British soldiers and RUC men, protected by the state – never served a day in jail for the lives they took, the homes they destroyed.

You learn nothing if you choose to forget history and that is why I think the prison hospital, a H-Block and a Cage should be preserved as some sort of testimony to what was suffered and endured. Nor is there any reason why the story of those prison officers who died should not also be remembered in monument or tribute, so that each side is reminded that there were other sides to the conflict. For some, the line-of-duty was the meaning of their life; for others, it was the struggle for freedom and justice and major sacrifices.

It couldn't be done back in those fraught and emotional times, but now at a time of – albeit, fragile – peace, it would be a powerful symbol of understanding and an act of reconciliation to recognise humanity in one's adversaries.

The Visit

Back to an empty Long Kesh

Andersonstown News, 13 August 2001

The minibus dropped us off at the hospital. Among our delegation were a mix of ex-prisoners, Sinn Féin representatives, and a former member of the Relatives Action Committee. Gerry Adams, as an MP, had organised the visit. On the road up to the hospital, all the gates were lying open, there were no checks, and I noticed a plaque on the side of the road in memory of those prison officers killed by republicans.

The hospital is divided into two wings: one, to the left where the cells are; the other, to the right, has surgeries for the doctor, the dentist, the optician's and an X-ray room. An administrative section divides the two wings. I had been down the right side of the block on several occasions since 1991 as a prisoner. But this was the first time in twenty years that Jim Gibney and I had come back to the place where the ten hunger strikers had spent their agonising last days.

There was a chill about the wing. The two prison officials stayed away and allowed us to enter the cells, one by one. Jim Gibney pointed out Bobby's cell. We huddled in and closed the door. It was terrible. This is where his great spirit left the earth. It was a tomb. Surrender or die had been the only option open to him and his comrades. We stood for a minute's silence in honour of Bobby, Frank, Raymond, Patsy, Joe, Martin, Kevin, Kieran, Tom and Mickey. I bit my tongue and I could see that Marie Moore – 'an bean uasal' [literally, honoured lady] to the prisoners whom she visited throughout the blanket protest and hunger strike – was visibly upset.

We went into the room where, separately, Gerry Adams and I had met groups of hunger strikers. We told our stories. We were amazed at how small the room was. In my memory it had been like a big canteen. Here, I had met Tom McElwee, Kieran Doherty TD, Kevin Lynch and Mickey Devine, among others.

Joe McDonnell, who had two days to live, was brought in on a wheelchair and kept joking throughout the visit. He smoked several cigarettes in between sipping water. I had been there to bring them up to date with our contacts with the British and the ultimately forlorn attempts to resolve the political status issue.

I can see their faces still.

They had been through too many beatings, had witnessed too much British deceit and treachery, to allow false hope undermine their resolve.

I pointed out the cell in which I visited Sean McKenna on the eve of the ending of the 1980 hunger strike. Then I pointed out Brendan Hughes' cell. Jim Gibney said that that was where Raymond McCreesh died and I felt a fresh rush of emotion knowing that this is exactly where it had happened, where his mother and father and family members had stood and suffered with their son and brother.

We also visited H-5, which along with H-3 and H-4 is still maintained. We went down its wings and into clean, newly painted cells. I looked out the slatted windows and noticed a total absence of those black crows which used to wheel in the sky over the camp and which Bobby wrote so often about in his prose and poems.

We also visited the 'old' Kesh and stood in the ruins of the internees' cages, some completely gone but for their slightly raised concrete bases. Rabbits were running about everywhere, terrified, as if this was their first sight of human beings. Jim Gibney could only find the collapsed fencing around Cage 3 where he had lived for two years. Looking from here towards the wall which hides the M1 in the distance, with Cages 4 and 5 having vanished, you can see the shape of the old RAF runway begin to re-emerge from the past.

Cage 2, where I spent a year, still had its Nissan huts, with the odd, bedraggled curtain blowing in the winds that swept through its cold interior. I took a 'boul' around the Cage on my own and closed my eyes to take in the sensations of the past. Walking a winter's night underneath the copper tones of security lights. The irony of fond memories of the place, of chucking water around each other on a hot summer's day. But I was overwhelmed with the sense of loss, of those who suffered most. Who died trying to escape, or died of medical neglect or from suicide.

I pointed out the spot in Hut 17 where John Stone's bunk and mine was. After he was released, John was killed in January 1975 on active service with Bap Kelly. The next bed to ours belonged to John Davey, from Bellaghy, a 'ninth of August man', who had been picked up in the original internment swoop. John, a Sinn Féin councillor, was assassinated in February 1989.

Looking up the hut I could imagine the aisle of lockers, beds and tables, the overhead lights dulled by hanging wet towels, the boiler bubbling away at one end of the hut, the backs of thirty or forty heads watching 'M.A.S.H.' on the black and white TV at the other end. And this scene repeated wherever republicans were jailed: in the other Cages of Long Kesh, in Magilligan, in Armagh, in Crumlin Road, on the Maidstone, in England and Scotland and the Free State. All those jails, all those prisoners, all that personal suffering, all those years … which never stopped the march of republicanism, only temporarily hindered it.

Never Going Away

Andersonstown News, 19 February 2001

Ilove St Valentine's Day. But with it come sad memories, especially of the year 1976. In subsequent years there were other sad memories, such as hearing, just two days after the killing of Pat Finucane, about the assassination of Sinn Féin Councillor John Davey, with whom I had been interned.

I think it was in the early morning of 12 February 1976 that we heard about the death of Frank Stagg on hunger strike in an English jail. He and his comrade Michael Gaughan had been on hunger strike in 1974 demanding to be transferred to a prison in the North. Michael Gaughan died in June of that year and, unfortunately, the solidarity protest movement on the outside was nothing of the order of the protests that we witnessed in 1980 and 1981.

This had been Frank Stagg's fourth hunger strike and he died in Wakefield Prison, blind, weighing four stones after sixty-two days, his wife and mother at his bedside. There were some protests on the streets, but not many, some rioting and some IRA operations. I was standing at the corner of Brighton Street that night with a friend, Seando Moore, when we heard a muffled explosion from the direction of Iveagh. About half an hour later we learnt that a small bomb had exploded in a house in Nansen Street and that our friend and comrade, Sean 'Stu' Bailey, was seriously injured, along with several young people.

I wrote 'young people' there and it has just occurred to me that Stu himself was just eighteen. He had been in the IRA for over a year and had been very close to Paul Fox who had been killed on active service two months earlier. Stu had been shot and wounded by the Sticks in that disastrous feud of October 1975 and was still recovering.

That night of the explosion I went around to tell his wife, Geraldine, that he had been seriously injured and taken to the Royal. On the mantelpiece was a Valentine's card from Geraldine and their young daughter, Seaneen, which Stu was never to see. Geraldine and, I think, Stu's mother, Mrs Bailey, rushed to the hospital where he died a few hours later. He was a very funny fellow with an infectious laugh and I can still see his spirit in his daughter. It is hard to believe that that was twenty-five years ago. But all of us, from whatever walk or persuasion, carry around inside us these evocative reminiscences, with the images and voices of our dead friends asserting themselves, and not just on anniversaries.

Frank Stagg had made a will requesting that he be buried in the republican plot in Leigue Cemetery, Ballina, beside his comrade, Michael Gaughan. Before his remains were released, several other people lost their lives, including 17-year-old IRA Volunteer James O'Neill in North Belfast and 15-year-old Anthony Doherty on the Falls Road.

As Frank Stagg's body was being flown home, and as the aeroplane was approaching Dublin airport, the Fine Gael/Labour coalition government ordered Aer Lingus to fly on to Shannon where the Special Branch seized the coffin. To this day I can still see Frank Stagg's mother standing at Dublin airport, completely bewildered, but absolutely dignified. The government had split the family, with one son, Emmet, who is now a Labour TD, agreeing to the intervention.

And so the Special Branch buried IRA Volunteer Frank Stagg and poured six feet of concrete on top of his grave to prevent republicans from re-interring his body alongside Michael Gaughan's. The following day, republicans gathered in Leigue Cemetery where they heard Joe Cahill make a promise to Frank Stagg. He said: 'I pledge that we will assemble here again in the near future when we have taken your body from where it lies. Let there be no mistake about it, we will take it, Frank, and we will leave it resting side by side with your great comrade, Michael Gaughan.'

For six months the gardai were stationed in the cemetery watching the grave but eventually they gave up and left. And when they did, the IRA disinterred Frank Stagg's remains and reburied them with Michael Gaughan, thus carrying out his last request.

When you consider all the state and loyalist violence, all the laws, all the sermons, all the editorials, all the censorship, that were used to stop republicans from being republicans and practising republicanism, what is left is mountain after mountain after mountain of failure, and thousands upon thousands upon thousands of republicans who haven't gone away and never will.

The Cause of Violence

Andersonstown News, 14 January 2002

International opinion, the British public and the people of the twenty-six counties were assured for decades that the cause of violence in the North was the IRA campaign. If it were not for the IRA, we were told, there would be no need for the British army, for repressive powers, for state censorship. Loyalist paramilitary violence was explained away by the RUC, Secretaries of State, and unionists of every hue, including those cutting their victims' throats, as a tit-for-tat response to the provocative republicans, as reprisals.

Indeed, even high nationalist unemployment, the preponderance of low skilled workers in that community, the location of industries in unionist areas, the general poor showing of the economy and the lack of investment, the collapse of the tourist industry, the reason why enough houses were not built, why buses didn't run, why the RUC had to beat up prisoners and fire plastic bullets, were all the fault of republicans and the IRA's armed struggle.

Republicans, on the other hand, insisted that their campaign was an ultimate response to fifty years of unionist misrule, then British direct rule in support of unionism. The fact that the IRA campaign was bloody, ferocious and tenacious, masked, in a crucial sense, the ultimate truth of the matter. Furthermore, the fact that there could never be a real peace process until the IRA called an enduring ceasefire also implied IRA causation of conflict.

It is one of the ironies of the conflict that unionists, the British, most Irish governments and most sections of the media hid behind the IRA campaign. Former Ulster Unionist leader, James Molyneaux's famous slip of the tongue, shortly after the first IRA ceasefire announcement in August 1994, that the ceasefire represented 'the greatest threat to the union' in sixty years, was just such an admission.

For thirty years, but actually for eighty years, the British government, and successive Dublin governments for their own reasons, chose to ignore the ugly nature of the state established by partition and the Government of Ireland Act. They chose to ignore nationalist appeals for justice, and continued to ignore the situation even when nationalist violence was in its infancy and the state, its police force and its supporters, began shooting Catholics and burning them in their thousands out of their homes in response to the campaign for civil rights. All intentions by London to introduce reforms were always primarily circumscribed by concerns for unionist sensibilities, not for nationalist rights.

And that preoccupation continues to this day because the raison d'être of the 'Northern Ireland' state was unionist primacy. In defence of unionists and the union Britain itself became ensnared (thanks to its gung-ho militarists) and depraved through its involvement in the 'dirty war', details of which are only beginning to emerge and will ultimately reveal the magnitude of the scandal. Number 10 Downing Street cleared these assassinations of nationalists and republicans by its army and in collusion with its various agents. It had already cleared the torture of detainees when it derogated from the European Convention on Human Rights.

Although implicit in the Belfast Agreement was that unionism, the British and republicanism all shared some culpability (with unionists and the Brits in public denial, and through their demand for 'IRA decommissioning' still attempting to occupy the moral high ground), the Agreement was meant to create a balanced situation, a new beginning. All parties have, to some extent or another, been in breach of its terms. That is hardly surprising.

Republicans made major compromises but still haven't realised even their limited goals (especially in relation to new policing). But it is the unionists who have balked most at the terms of the new dispensation. The Ulster Unionists, under pressure from Ian Paisley's DUP, sometimes appear to be two or three different parties. The Agreement guaranteed the unionists that they would not be frogmarched into a united Ireland and in return they were to agree to share power with those whom they and the British have oppressed and abused.

The loyalist violence against Catholic schoolchildren in North Belfast,* whilst having a sectarian fervour, is directly related to the political process. Those attacks, and the ongoing pipe-bomb campaign, are aimed at provoking the IRA into breaking its ceasefire. If the IRA breaks its ceasefire then the unionists, the British and the media can revert to the myth that republicans are responsible for causing the violence and they can deny the injustices at the heart of the northern state.

The British government is being duplicitous when – as in Secretary of State, Dr John Reid's recent speech about unionist alienation – it panders to unjustified and exaggerated unionist claims that they are being made second-class citizens, and that justice and equality issues are somehow a threat. The only threat such changes pose is psychological.

In my opinion, the IRA ceasefire was the best thing to have happened here in decades. It cleared the air, created a breathing space, granted relief, and opened up certain political possibilities, which have to be intelligently and courageously pursued outside of any reliance on, or thoughts of a return to, armed struggle.

Republicans – because of their opposition to the RUC and because the changes outlined in the policing legislation fall short of what they are demanding – are caught in a bind. They refuse to recognise the PSNI because it still looks too much like the old RUC, still has the corrupt Special Branch pulling strings. Yet there is no contradiction in demanding action from the British, including impartial policing. Indeed, there is even an advantage to be making certain demands of the police force by way of testing its capacity to change (and to acknowledge such change when it occurs).

The loyalist violence in North Belfast and elsewhere is aimed at provoking the IRA into breaking its ceasefire so that the Belfast Agreement can be destroyed and the clock turned back to old times. Despite nationalist anger and feelings of helplessness at the sight of school children being attacked by thugs, republicans should remain patient, mobilise international opinion and hold Britain to its responsibilities.

* *Catholic schoolchildren attending Holy Cross primary school for girls were repeatedly attacked by loyalists at Glenbryn, North Belfast.*

30,492

On the election of Bobby Sands

Andersonstown News, 9 April, 2001

Twenty years ago today, 9th April, the people of Fermanagh and South Tyrone went to the polls in a by-election to fill the seat held by the late Frank Maguire, an Independent MP, who died just five days after Bobby Sands began his hunger strike. Upon hearing of his death I doubt if any of us involved in the H-Block/Armagh campaign thought in terms of an election with a prisoner candidate.

Firstly, the death of an MP does not automatically give rise to a by-election. A writ must be moved by an MP in the House of Commons to cause a by-election. Although republicans were friendly with some left-wing MPs, relations weren't of the nature that they would do your bidding. Besides, such a call would have presupposed the existence of a concrete plan or strategy – when there was none. Bobby Sands' entry into Fermanagh and South Tyrone was an accident of history, and if there is one person who can be 'credited' with allowing that intervention then it is James Molyneaux, leader of the Ulster Unionist Party in 1981, and arguably one of that party's most stupid.

Molyneaux thought that the nationalist vote would be split between the SDLP and an Independent candidate and that a single unionist candidate, in the form of former party leader, Harry West, would take the seat. It was only when the election was called that the idea was suggested that the Smash H-Block/Armagh campaign should make an intervention. Around about the same time that Bernadette McAliskey let it be known that she was prepared to stand but would stand aside for a prisoner candidate, others, most notably, Jim Gibney from Sinn Féin, were suggesting that Bobby Sands should be put forward.

A meeting was held in Monaghan and, incredibly, a small minority of Fermanagh republicans actually favoured the candidature of Noel Maguire, the former dead MP's brother. However, at the end of the meeting it was decided to stand Bobby Sands, provided he got a clear run against West.

Noel Maguire, under tremendous emotional pressure, eventually withdrew his name and the SDLP, fearing a backlash, decided not to put up a candidate, though Austin Currie threatened to stand and SDLP councillor Tommy Murray, who signed Bobby Sands' nomination papers, was dismissed from the party.

I have never seen an election campaign like it. Thousands of activists were mobilised from across Ireland to go to Fermanagh and South Tyrone to help out in the postering and canvassing. In Dungannon and Enniskillen offices were opened round-the-clock. Some of us from Belfast went up, thinking we were going to teach the locals how to run an election. What we discovered was that working quietly away in the background for decades were people who had dedicated themselves to the electoral registers, ensuring that everyone of voting age was on the rolls, that the sick or those overseas were registered for postal votes, that people were trained in the science of organising an election and supervising the count. They were brilliant.

At after-Mass meetings people would emerge from chapel, stand and listen, applaud and then make generous contributions to the fighting fund. I remember a group of Belfast women return to the election office in Dungannon totally despondent about Bobby's chances after they got an extremely cold reception outside a church on the Ballygawley Road. Francie Molloy asked them to describe exactly where they had made the speeches. It turned out they had been addressing and leafletting parishioners leaving a Church of Ireland service!

In Enniskillen on the day of the count we felt in our bones that Bobby was going to win. You just knew it from the atmosphere, the people flocking to the polling stations, queueing to vote. In the afternoon when the returning officer declared the vote I couldn't contain myself and let out a huge yell.

For years the British government had been denigrating republicans, declaring they had no support, challenging them to go to the ballot box. Bobby Sands got 30,492, with a majority twice as large as Thatcher's in her constituency of Finchley. Bobby's election agent, Owen Carron, made Bobby's acceptance speech and called for dialogue to resolve the hunger strike. Harry West got up and began to make his victory speech, then appeared confused, then realised that the unthinkable had happened – Bobby Sands had won!

That night I came back to Belfast with Mr and Mrs Sands and Bobby's sister, Marcella, and went into town to do more interviews. In the car we discussed the impact of Bobby's victory and the hope it gave that his life might be saved, that Thatcher would be compelled to recognise his mandate. But that was not to be. Her reaction was to amend the Representation of the People Act so that no Irish political prisoner in any jail in the world could contest a Westminster election. British governments were later to continually amend electoral rules – on identification, on deposits, on local government oaths – all with the objective of excluding republicans, and all of which failed because Sinn Féin circumvented all obstacles by simply adopting a pragmatic approach.

Republicans and electoralism could have ended there in 1981, had not James Molyneaux, again inexplicably, moved another writ for another by-election! Because of the exclusion of prisoner candidates, this time Owen Carron, a member of Sinn Féin, standing on an anti-H-Block/Armagh political prisoner ticket, was nominated and was elected, increasing Bobby's vote, in yet another dramatic election. Owen's election took place on 20th August, the day on which Mickey Devine became the last hunger striker to die.

In voting for Bobby Sands and Owen Carron the people of Fermanagh and South Tyrone rejected British rule and asserted the integrity of the prisoners and the cause of Irish independence. They provided the springboard for the electoral rise of Sinn Féin and the empowerment of the general nationalist population in its unrelenting challenge to unionist and British misrule.

Futility of the Real IRA

The Observer, 22 April 2001

Last Sunday the ongoing foot and mouth crisis meant that there were a limited number of Irish republican marches commemorating the 1916 Easter Rising.

The media was interested in the turn-out in Dublin for the 32-County Sovereignty Movement because of its alleged links to the Real IRA (there had been an explosion in London the night before), and to see if it would attract significant numbers (two hundred people showed up), and if a threatened picket by relatives of the Omagh bomb victims materialised.

But the largest number of commemorations with the highest attendance were those organised by the National Graves Association addressed by Sinn Féin speakers. At these marches were relatives of dead IRA Volunteers, former hunger strikers, ex-escapees, former prisoners in abundance, as well as thousands of supporters.

The speaker at the 32-CSM commemoration in Dublin said that they had small numbers and were being vilified just like the men and women of 1916. On other occasions dissidents have likened their splitting from mainstream republicans in Sinn Féin and the IRA as a re-run of the split in 1969. At that time the Republican Movement divided into the 'Officials' (who imploded several times before quickly bowing out of the struggle) and those colloquially referred to as 'the Provisionals' (today's Sinn Féin and IRA).

However, the Real IRA has not flourished in the way the IRA did after the split from the Officials. It will never be able to replicate the IRA's firepower and thus bring the British to the negotiating table. The 32-CSM has no popular support, has failed to produce a cogent leadership that can articulate a position beyond its obsession with Sinn Féin, and lacks a credible political programme.

Whereas the Officials went into decline after they cease-fired in 1972, Sinn Féin's popularity, North and South, has risen remarkably since the IRA's cessation of August

1994, to the extent where the party in the South may hold the balance of power after the next election. Dissidents rely on exploiting growing republican disquiet at Britain's mishandling of the peace process, but that anger is unlikely to be directed at the Sinn Féin leadership or be channelled into substantial support for dissidents.

In its constitution the 32-CSM pompously states: 'We hold that all administrations and assemblies purporting to act as lawful government for the Irish people, or otherwise functioning as partitionist entities, to be illegal...' But how can its leaders square this belated purism with the fact that for eleven years – from 1986 until 1997 – they remained part of the Republican Movement, which had dropped its policy of abstentionism towards that 'partitionist' entity, the Dáil? At least former president Ruairi Ó Bradaigh had the honesty to leave and form Republican Sinn Féin.

If the 32-CSM and the Real IRA really believe in the 1916 analogy then they should go back to first principles, should contest elections on an abstentionist ticket and set up an all-Ireland assembly in opposition to what the electorates, North and South, have overwhelmingly voted for – the Good Friday Agreement. Similarly, its members should refuse to recognise the courts. Of course, that would be absurd, and they know it.

Those who split from the Republican Movement in 1997 to form the Real IRA and the 32-CSM did so because they refused to go along with or respect the opinion of the majority of their comrades whom they categorise as 'stooges' of the leadership. As if activists and supporters are incapable of evaluating strategy and making up their own minds or have no right to defend the opinions they have reached.

The 32-CSM's principal alternative to the Sinn Féin project of bringing about a new Ireland is remarkably naïve: pressing Ireland's right to sovereignty and independence at the United Nations. Ask the Palestinians about UN Resolution 242 and what it has done for their freedom. Just last week Hizbollah guerrillas who attacked Israeli soldiers in a disputed border region were condemned by the UN because 'the UN has determined the territory was conquered by Israel from Syria'. I wouldn't trust the UN with my back garden never mind my country.

Tragically, the Real IRA will continue with its sporadic campaign, continue to kill innocent people and lose its own Volunteers to cemetery and jail until some member has the guts to face up to the futility of the campaign. They and the 32-CSM have no message for the unionist people, do not understand that the building of trust, the normalisation of relations with the unionists, preparatory cross-border social and economic harmonisation, the building of a strong, all-Ireland republican party, are all part of the struggle for Irish re-unification.

Wonderful World, Beautiful People

The 2001 Westminster election results

Andersonstown News, Monday, 11 June 2001

Whilst I was more than pleased with Sinn Féin's increased vote in all the constituencies, and with Pat Doherty's stupendous victory in West Tyrone, it was the final result in Fermanagh and South Tyrone at twenty past ten on Friday night that moved me the most and made me feel immensely proud to be an Irish republican and part of a brilliant community.

On this, the twentieth anniversary of the hunger strike, it was like a rendezvous with history. I had heard Michelle Gildernew at the re-launch of Bobby Sands' *One Day In My Life* in April speak about being eleven years old in 1981 when Bobby died and being astonished and humbled at his and the other hunger strikers' sacrifice. You could hear the raw emotion in her voice, a memory come alive as she relived those heart-breaking days.

Eleven years of age!

And now, with 17,700 votes, she is the first woman republican abstentionist MP since the election of Countess Markievicz with 7,835 votes in December 1918. When you hear the words 'Fermanagh and South Tyrone' you always think of Bobby Sands and 1981 long before you think of Churchill's 'dreary steeples'. 1981 changed our lives and those of our young and I predict that the rally in Belfast this August to commemorate the memory of those ten dead men and their comrades Michael Gaughan and Frank Stagg will see the biggest turn-out of republicans in a hundred years.

What are we to make of the highest ever republican electoral performance since the foundation of this state, Sinn Féin's outpolling of constitutional nationalists, its effect on the peace process, and the drive for Irish independence?

Firstly, at a national level Sinn Féin has proved to be spot on. In the twenty-six counties it was castigated by that coalition government luminary, Tanaiste Mary Harney of the 'Regressive' Democrats, not solely for being inextricably linked to you-know-who, but for having crazy world politics! Yet, Sinn Féin and the Green Party won the referendum opposing the Nice Treaty, and demonstrably refuted – in the words of John Hume and Alex Attwood – that 'we are in a post-nationalist era'.

The people who came out and voted 'No' in the South form the real conscience of the Irish nation and are saying that despite the purported benefits of membership of the European Union their souls, their sovereignty, are not up for sale. The world has to remain a rainbow coalition of independent and good people, and if 'nationalism' means denying the bad people the authority to aggrandize power, and in our name to bomb people and nations we do not know or understand, who are of no threat, then 'nationalism' has to be for us.

Secondly, at a six-county level, Sinn Féin's rise has changed everything – even more than the DUP's increase in seats. Sinn Féin taps into a mood for freedom and generosity, the DUP into fear and intolerance. Working-class Gerry Adams now has more clout than John Hume in London, Dublin, Washington and Brussels – though those powers may well be in denial for a while.

Not all Sinn Féin's votes came solely from young people. Thus, it is a great tribute to former SDLP voters and households that they had the maturity to change, to ditch the Gerry Fitt-ism and the nonsense of Alex Attwood, and embrace a party which will robustly defend their interests on policing, equality, justice and freedom.

I sat in an RTÉ studio on Friday with Carmel Hanna of the SDLP and I said to her that Attwood had made a major blunder by describing West Tyrone as the party's 'Stalingrad'. She tetchily corrected me and said that it wasn't the SDLP but the BBC's political correspondent, Stephen Grimason, who invented the comparison. I made the point that not only had they not demurred from the analogy but that their spokespersons were enthusiastically quoting it on a number of occasions. Of course, you can't blame the SDLP alone. They had their confederates in the media, east of the Bann, part of a campaign machine which undoubtedly also sorely felt the loss, except that after the election these hypocrites had the temerity to say that they knew all along that Doherty would take West Tyrone!

On the unionist side David Trimble's UUP lost Strangford to the DUP's Iris Robinson, regained South Antrim from Willie McCrea, lost East Derry to Gregory Campbell (who could yet turn out to be a pragmatist), and gained North Down from Bob McCartney. The Ulster Unionists' vote overall was up but it is the perception that counts, those lost seats. Trimble asserted himself in North Down where he opposed the candidature of Peter Weir and successfully replaced him with pro-Agreement candidate Lady Sylvia Hermon.

However, not all votes for the Ulster Unionist Party can be said to be votes for the Good Friday Agreement. The only thing missing from the rabid David Burnside in his acceptance speech in South Antrim was a Free Presbyterian dog collar. He demanded IRA decommissioning.

And there will never, ever, be IRA decommissioning, an IRA surrender.

What there is, is a republican commitment to peace, and a commitment to put the guns beyond use.

So, David Trimble says he will resign on July 1st when the guns aren't melted down, and the man who may hold the reins for a very short time, is a man upon whom the Newry and Armagh sun is setting, Seamus Mallon.

For years the coming of a 'political vacuum' has been predicted and that such a scenario would spark widespread community violence. Look at the election.

Absolutely no support for dissident republicans; the unionists confused, split, disillusioned, and, even with the DUP's successes, without any real focus or authority.

In a few years Ian Paisley will know whether there's a God, his charisma-challenged son will be MP for North Antrim, Peter and Iris will be a double-act on 'Have I Got News For You', David Burnside will be leader of the Ulster Unionists, Tony Blair will be in his third term, and we republicans will be strong, united and confident, and in control of much of our country and our lives.

Arms Beyond Use

Against all expectations, the IRA decommissions

Irish Examiner, 24 October 2001

L ast Tuesday's announcement from the IRA that it had verifiably put 'arms beyond use' is unprecedented in the 200-year history of Irish republicanism and the physical-force tradition. At the conclusion of all campaigns – which usually ended in defeat or demoralisation or splits – wounds were licked, the remains of the organisation picked up the pieces, and the pike, literally and figuratively, was hidden in the thatch in the certainty that 'there will be another day'.

Many republicans find the IRA's decision extremely difficult to accept in the light of British hypocrisy and double standards on the morality of the use of violence. Even now, British and US forces are killing children, women and men in Afghanistan. Republicans also view unionist attempts over the last few years to use the arms issue to frustrate political progress as cynical. Unionist politicians courted loyalist paramilitaries and engaged in extra-parliamentary action when it suited them. More recently, they have balked at intervening in North Belfast, and elsewhere, to curb the wave of loyalist paramilitary attacks against nationalists.

Nationalists remain vulnerable and concerned about their safety, given the absence of an impartial and representative policing service which unionists still resist coming into being. It can be assumed that the IRA, which in a very real sense, 'arose out of the ashes of Bombay Street', has taken these concerns on board.

Though there is palpable disquiet and unease, most republicans have their eye on the bigger picture and understand that the peace and political processes, once underpinned, will lead to a material transformation in the lives of the people, to stability, progress and prosperity, and, through real engagements with former foes, a degree of reconciliation. The majority of the Republican Movement – made up of IRA activists, former prisoners, Sinn Féin activists and support and solidarity organisations – accepted the need for a pragmatic approach to the struggle once a military stalemate had been conceded by both the British military and the IRA – despite the subsequent provocative resistance to change from some British securocrats.

Sinn Féin's overtaking of the SDLP (historically, the darlings of the British and Irish establishments) is indicative of a buoyant nationalist mood that has placed its faith in the direction given by a radical republican leadership. In elections in the South Sinn Féin is likely to receive further endorsement of a major national role in Irish politics.

Dissident republican organisations have failed to attract any popularity, to articulate a rational or viable strategy, or to wage an effective armed struggle that has any potential to positively influence events. Indeed, there are reports that they are actually engaged in a re-think of their position and, if so, this should be welcomed and embraced, their prisoners released.

The IRA leadership have made a courageous decision. Right is on its side. The onus is now on the British government and the Ulster Unionist Party. The British must live up to the commitments they made under the Belfast Agreement, including those on demilitarisation, policing, equality and justice issues. The IRA's action also represents a momentous opportunity for Ulster Unionists to leave the past behind and enter into partnership with a community that they once victimised and which in turn rose up against them. This is an opportunity for them to face down Paisleyism and sectarianism and no doubt the DUP will be putting their hands up for their two ministries once they realise the game's up.

There will be those among unionists and in the media who will crow or gloat to provoke republican confusion or disunity. Ignore the ignoramuses because it is progress that they really fear and republicanism is on the rise. The challenge now is on the Ulster Unionists to lead their people into a historic partnership with representatives of the Irish electorate, North and South, in the Assembly, the Executive and the all-Ireland bodies.

Twenty years ago at the end of this month, during a crucial Sinn Féin ard fheis debate on whether the party should enter into electoral politics after the hunger strike, I made a speech about a twin strategy of going forward with an armalite in one hand and a ballot box in the other. The debate was won and Sinn Féin began its tentative steps into mainstream politics.

During the conflict the British boasted that they had the IRA on the run, that they were 'squeezing the IRA like a tube of toothpaste' and that 'the hunger strike was the IRA's last card'. They got it spectacularly wrong because the IRA was a force representative of an alienated community with amassed grievances. The British wasted many years, changing the rules of electoral engagement, refusing to recognise mandates and to talk, demonising republicans and perpetuating the war.

The IRA cessation of August 1994 was the real initiative which broke the stalemate and which ultimately led to this week's IRA announcement which, paraphrased, declares that the war is over and there is no longer any need for the armalite.

Now You See 'Em, Now You Don't!

Andersonstown News, 12 November 2001

In an unprecedented exclusive for the *Andersonstown News* the DUP has supplied us with that confidential John de Chastelain report on IRA decommissioning which was leaked to the party. It was this report which led to the Ulster Unionists returning to the Assembly, David Trimble's re-election as First Minister, and Frank Warren's bid for the franchise to stage future boxing matches (after last week's DUP/UUP punch-up) in the Great Hall of Parliament Buildings.

SECRET REPORT OF GENERAL JOHN DE CHASTELAIN TO PRIME MINISTER TONY
BLAIR, 10 DOWNING STREET, LONDON.
(For Your Eyes Only, not Cherie's, or that drunken kid of yours.)

Sir.

As arranged by our IRA interlocutor we all met up outside Hoppy Dobbins pub on the Andersonstown Road, myself, Martti and Cyril on Friday last. We were told to wear shorts and football boots so that we could be easily recognised. It was also explained to us that if we were stopped by the British army or the RUC we were to say that we played for St John's and had just been beaten by St Gall's. We were told that the police would believe this.

Two men came up the street, disguised in work clothes, and addressed us. 'What about ya! Are ya not headin' in?' As directed we went upstairs. Someone set up three pints of Guinness and three whiskies on the counter and told us to 'get them into ya!' After three hours it was my turn to sing. Some girl, taken by Martti's accent, said he looked like a good lumberer. Cyril was up on a table, leading the chorus to *Something Inside So Strong*. As an encore he sang *Diamonds on the Soles of her Shoes*, and the crowd were delirious. It was a truly historic occasion.

Somebody shouted, 'Where's the party?' and next we know we've a carry-out and a girl on each knee, there's six of us in a taxi and we're all heading for The Ardoyne. We clubbed till four in the morning, got up at ten, and had an Ulster Fry. On Saturday afternoon the club organised a bus-run to the beautiful Glens of Antrim, followed by the Giants Causeway, then over to Carrickmore where during dinner the boys put on a show of strength, then announced that they were heading off to put their weapons beyond use. Cyril, Martti and I were very impressed and somebody popped the champagne. Before we knew it, we were back in Hoppy Dobbins, three pints of Guinness and three whiskies on the counter, the drink flying, I'm being called for a song, Cyril's up on the table, tap-dancing and singing, *Me Little Armalite*, and somebody shouts, 'Where's the party?'

Sir, next we know we're back in The Ardoyne, but the club's all a-hush, watching a fantastic play about decommissioning, written, composed, produced, directed and acted by Martin and Briege Meehan, called *The Guns of Navarone*. Standing ovation, standing orders, standing a round, Cyril standing on stage singing, *Something Inside So Strong*, Martti standing at the bar. It was momentous.

Sir, I'm not sure of my days but I think it was Sunday night, closing time in Caffreys when somebody shouts, 'The Ballroom! We'll get a drink in The Ballroom!'

Taxi it is. None of the ten of us has to even tell him where to take us. A huge magnet draws the all-nighters towards its core. Into The Ballroom we go; everybody seems to know and love us, despite the fact that I haven't been out of my office in three years. The lights are flashing, the speakers pounding, I'm handed a gallon of cider, told to get it into me, clapped on the back, told I'm a great guy. Through the smoke, Cyril and Martti are bopping on the floor with two hundred others, including a number of guys wearing electronic tags. They turn out not to be escapees but just some husbands. Somebody shouts, 'Where's the party!' and next we know we're in some flat in Lenadoon or Bawnmore. It's as if we're doing shift work – you know, one party finishes and another begins, except it's only the decommissioners who are on the 138-hour week.

The dope and drink were flying so we're not sure if the next part really happened or was a film on the TV in the flat where the party was but, Sir, there were guns and explosives destroyed in large numbers before our very eyes, albeit in black and white. When I came back from the toilet the French were still destroying them, so that'll give you an idea of what numbers we're talking about. Also, I can confirm without fear of contradiction that over those few days I saw an enormous number of rounds put away.

There is no doubt, hic, in my mind, hic, that weapons and my liver have been put permanently beyond use, and I would like a year off.

Yours Sincerely,

General John de Chastelain.

The Issues of Assent and Consent

In New York Gerry Adams states that
nationalists cannot force unionists into a united Ireland

Andersonstown News, 11 February 2002

Within days of the IRA's declaration of a cessation of activity in 1994 loyalists responded by painting on the walls of the Shankill the boast that the IRA had surrendered. In interviews they claimed that it was their ruthless campaign of assassination of Catholic civilians, Sinn Féin representatives and their relatives that had brought republicans to their knees.

We know, of course, where the weaponry and intelligence for that campaign came from – the British government's secret services.

Sections of the media, if it meant they could divide and undermine republican support for the leadership's peace strategy, were only too glad to propagate the myth that loyalist paramilitaries had saved the Union. And who knows how many out there in the unionist chattering classes privately felt the same glow of satisfaction, that 'our boys beat the IRA scum into the ground'?

The hollowness of the claim was never challenged: that is, how come the Republican Movement didn't end its campaign earlier when Catholics were being slaughtered in greater numbers and when active service units were regularly arrested or wiped out? And if the IRA was thus defeated, why are unionists and loyalist paramilitary spokespersons telling us daily and solemnly that the IRA remains armed to the teeth and could fight on for another thirty years?

That the republican leadership freely (and responsibly) changed tack because of the military stalemate with British forces and decided to go on a major political offensive is an unpalatable truth for loyalists. Loyalists badly needed their claim to fame to cover up for their grubby, un-heroic sectarian campaign (not that the IRA's armed struggle was snow white).

Contrast their boasts of an IRA surrender in 1994 with their current constant complaints: the RUC has been destroyed, Sinn Féin/IRA is in government, Ulster has become 'a cold house for unionists', nationalists are getting all the jobs, we can't march our traditional routes, Sinn Féin's politics are offensively 'in your face', the British government is doing side deals with the IRA, there's going to be 'a united Ireland within fifteen years' (according to UDA leader Jackie McDonald), etc., etc.

Unionists coming to terms with equality (and we are by no means there yet) have been traumatised. To sympathise, try to understand or to offer an analysis is to be rebuffed, accused of cynicism or of strategically increasing unionist division and difficulty. (Incidentally, their war – be it the loyalist paramilitary war or the UUP/DUP propaganda one – against nationalism and republicanism continues unapologetically.) Thus, to them, every hand of friendship is suspect, every reassurance is a booby trap, and every offer to engage in discussion or debate has to be undermined or distorted.

Moreover, any concession or any agreement is immediately appropriated and often turned against one. The SDLP learnt this to their cost this week when John Taylor was quick to use the unanimity of the Police Board's decision not to singularly back Nuala O'Loan's report into the RUC's handling of the Omagh bomb inquiry as an Ulster Unionist/SDLP rebuff to Nuala O'Loan and support for Ronnie Flanagan.

Look at the unionist campaign to undermine Martin McGuinness as Minister of Education because of his IRA background. Unionists uphold as their heroes former illegal gunrunners who threatened the British government with a civil war, and a premier who presided over pogroms against Catholics in 1921. Unionists have never accepted that their discriminatory practises and state violence were a major factor in the IRA campaign. Fifty years of misrule, the pogroms against Catholics in 1969, the curfew, internment and Bloody Sunday, all took place under the auspices of Ulster Unionist governments.

Gerry Adams' recent speech in New York (that nationalists could not force the unionists into a united Ireland which did not have their 'assent or consent') was seized upon by David Trimble, not in the reconciliatory spirit in which it was offered, but to score cheap points about the alleged futility of the IRA campaign. (There is a basic contradiction here. In the mornings unionists claim that the Belfast Agreement and nationalist gains couldn't have been achieved without the IRA's campaign. In the afternoons they claim that the IRA campaign achieved nothing.)

The IRA campaign was aimed at bringing about a British withdrawal (not a unionist withdrawal), which would lead to the reunification of Ireland. The IRA, clearly, did not physically drive the British out of the North but, equally clearly, the British commitment to unionism is in terminal decline. Republicanism was never defeated nor thwarted, and republicans have successfully kept a united Ireland on the agenda.

In New York Adams said, 'Unionism now needs to begin seriously thinking about, discussing and engaging with nationalists and republicans about the nature and form a new and acceptable united Ireland might take. A united Ireland will not be a cold house for unionists if it guarantees their rights and entitlements, if they have their own place, their own stake in it and a sense of security and ownership.'

No one knows what form a united Ireland will take. If peace and demilitarisation can be consolidated, the PSNI changed, and with ongoing social and economic harmonisation (which will intensify when Britain inevitably joins the Euro), in a few years there will be no palpable border. There will still be two Assemblies, two political cultures, suspicion and resistance to change from many quarters (including from some in the twenty-six counties!) but there will slowly, very slowly be emerging, one people.

Like a Tube of Toothpaste

Election fever in the South

Andersonstown News, 11 March 2002

How can you be full of moral outrage and orgasmic at the same time? Easy. Join the Progressive Democrats. Write for the *Sunday Independent* or re-write history (much the same thing). Immigrate to Munster. Then wait until your favourite opinion poll comes along and, Hey Presto, who needs Viagra!

Yes, the election campaign has started in the Free State, the hormones are pumping, the brains have been put on wraps, and it's 'Bash Sinn Féin' time!

First off was Michael 'Zorro' McDowell, who left home that morning as the Attorney General, then at a Progressive Democrat convention turned into an election candidate for Dublin South East and was not the Attorney General, left the convention and was the Attorney General! As he launched his bid for a seat in Leinster House he accused Sinn Féin of having no loyalty to the state and its institutions, and that the Republican Movement was 'still involved in torture, mutilation… smuggling, racketeering, protection rackets and taxing the drug trade in our cities'.

Zorro, unfortunately, is one donkey short of a derby, as he is trailing the Sinn Féin candidate, Daithi Doolan, in an opinion poll and perhaps should consider staying on as Chief Marshal until peerages are reintroduced.

After Michael, the *Sunday Independent* brought out its pea-shooters – Ruth Dudley Edwards, Conor Cruise O'Brien, John A. Murphy – an awesome, intellectual triumvirate that had Adams begging for mercy. Nobody knew it was going to be this dirty. No one could have predicted from Ruth such a piercing piece of pretty prose – 'Ten Thorns in Shinners' Side', in which she approvingly quotes 'republican dissidents (intellectual)', that is, Anthony McIntyre, Thorn Number Five, as proof of her thesis that Sinn Féin is reeling.

But it was the RTÉ/*Irish Independent* opinion poll taken in Kerry North that boosted the morale of the establishment parties and media. In a TG4 poll taken last year, the Sinn Féin candidate Martin Ferris had 23 per cent support and was in line to take the third seat, a factor which influenced former Labour leader Dick Spring to declare that he would stand again. However, the most recent poll put Ferris standing at 16.8 per cent.

Ferris's director of elections had been arrested by the Gardai and questioned about vigilantism in the constituency, as had five others of his election team, and he complained that the arrests were politically motivated and an attempt to frighten people away from voting for Sinn Féin. The government also has made attractive promises to the area and pumped in finance to boost Fianna Fáil's prospects of retaining the seat, though this should not be read as 'buying votes' – since only TDs and councillors can be bought, which we've learnt from the ongoing Tribunals.

Sinn Féin TD, Caoimhghín Ó Caolain, was being interviewed by Vincent Brown on RTÉ last week and was asked if he would urge members of the public who might have information about the killing of gardai by the IRA or know the whereabouts of IRA arms dumps to inform. He replied: 'I am not going to urge people to take a particular position that challenges them individually and, indeed, within their own communities.'

In other words, people should be their own judges and follow the dictates of their conscience.

For recognising the continuing complexities of a transitional situation – one which has its roots in a conflict that arose out of partition and British repression; in which, out of necessity, the IRA used the south as a base; and the state, and its forces, cooperated with the British, introduced repressive laws, ill-treated detainees, imprisoned people, often on dubious information, using special courts, extradited and censored a political view – all of which conditioned the republican response, Ó Caolain was savaged by the media and the other parties which threatened him with suspension from Leinster House.

That was the kick off for a tirade that continues as we drink.

'The seemingly relentless march of Sinn Féin has been halted,' declared Alan Ruddock, again in the paper in which Sinn Féin inadvertently keeps in employment several peashooters. 'Ferris and his Sinn Féin colleagues are in reality dreary and largely unimpressive people who are no strangers to donkey jackets and socialist babble,' he continued.

For me, I hadn't appreciated the gravity of the situation until I heard the comments of a former swimmer. Who can forget the wettest press conference the North ever witnessed when in 1987 the then leader of the Alliance Party, John Cushnahan, left Belfast wreathed in tears, because he had to get away from politics and be with his family – only two years later, on dry land, to go back into politics as Fine Gael Euro MP for Munster?

John was 'appalled' – very strong language – by Ó Caolain's comments, as was Brid Rogers, the MP for West Tyrone in theory.

Many years ago – 1978 in fact – an old friend of mine, Secretary of State Roy Mason, declared that he was squeezing the IRA like a tube of toothpaste. Unfortunately, the IRA was not in that particular tube of toothpaste. Nor is Sinn Féin in the tube presently being squeezed.

Helloes and Goodbyes

The general election in the South

Andersonstown News, 20 May 2002

The Sinn Féin triumph in the twenty-six counties is a major endorsement of the party's leadership and strategy, places Sinn Féin in a major position of influence for the first time in sixty years and is set to change the face of politics in the South for the better, especially for the poor and dispossessed.

The election of Martin Ferris in Kerry has made international headlines and is reminiscent of the election of IRA Volunteer Bobby Sands in 1981 when politicians, the media and the forces of the state ganged up to interfere in the electoral process and thwart the popular will of the people.

When the opinion polls began indicating that Sinn Féin might hold the balance of power in the South the anti-Sinn Féin campaign began in earnest. Thus, whilst the Dublin government insists that unionists must share power with Sinn Féin on the basis of its electoral mandate and the IRA's ceasefire, Bertie Ahern refuses to accept the same criteria in the South and makes impossible demands of Sinn Féin in relation to its commitment to constitutional politics and the disbandment of the IRA. How can Sinn Féin prove its commitment to constitutional politics if it is excluded, through discrimination, from its entitlement to take part in constitutional politics?

The message directed at the electorate was simple: a vote for Sinn Féin is a wasted vote since they will not be allowed in government.

In April, the former O/C of IRA prisoners in the H-Blocks, Brendan McFarlane, who has been on bail and waiting for a trial for an unprecedented four and a half years in connection with the Don Tidey abduction in 1983, was suddenly informed by the State Solicitor's Office that his trial was being scheduled for April 15th. Expected to last several weeks, it would have been running in parallel with Sinn Féin's election campaign. We are expected to believe that the timing had nothing to do with the election. As it turned out, McFarlane's legal team, who are still awaiting disclosure of certain documents, had the trial postponed.

Just after the election was called the Garda announced that, on foot of anonymous information, it was resuming the search for missing Crossmaglen man, Charlie Armstrong, who disappeared twenty years ago. The Garda has claimed that the IRA was involved but the IRA has denied any responsibility for his death. Obviously, nothing should stand in the way of expediting the recovery of this man's remains, and their return to his family for a Christian burial. However, even Chris Thornton of the *Belfast Telegraph* wrote that the dig in the constituency of Sinn Féin TD, Caoimhín Ó Caoláin, which lasted for three weeks before being abandoned, 'is said to have been timed pointedly'.

Michael McDowell, while in the allegedly neutral role of Attorney General, but himself a candidate, joined in the attacks with allegations about IRA involvement in Colombia, in the Castlereagh raid, in compiling a hit list of Conservatives.

Perhaps the best example of state interference in the electoral prospects of Sinn Féin were the arrests of Martin Ferris and his director of elections on the eve of the election. They were questioned and publicly linked by the Garda to a vigilante incident that occurred four months before. Again, we are supposed to believe that the timing had nothing to do with the election.

Ten years ago the IRA shot dead Tom Oliver in County Louth, alleging that he was a Garda informer. Recently, his son sent a letter to the local paper, *The Argus*, taking the Sinn Féin candidate, Arthur Morgan, to task for calling for a public inquiry into the death of Seamus Ludlow in 1976 but not into the death of his father.

However, *The Argus* sat on the letter for two weeks and only published it when the election was in full swing and Arthur Morgan was riding high in the polls. That is, the newspaper published it when it believed the timing could do maximum electoral damage. Arthur Morgan replied, explaining that he understood the distress of the family but pointed out that in the case of Tom Oliver's death there was no doubt who had carried out the killing whereas in Seamus Ludlow's death the authorities had been involved in a cover-up, with the Garda actually suggesting to the family that he had been killed by the IRA. It is now believed that two UDR soldiers and another man, all members of the Red Hand Commandos, whose names are known to the Garda, carried out the murder, yet the case has not been pursued.

Several tabloid newspapers, as well as *The Sunday Times* and the *Sunday Independent* picked up *The Argus* story and gave it prominent coverage. That was last weekend. Then, on Wednesday, two days before the election, the *Irish Times*, usually loath to re-print another newspapers' copy, re-ran the Louth story, exploiting it to the full by illustrating it with a photograph of guess who? Yep. Kerry North candidate, Sinn Féin's Martin Ferris!

During the campaign RTÉ gave Sinn Féin scant television and radio coverage but interviewed independents more often.

During the week the bodies of two men were found near Warrenpoint, County Down. This gave rise to headlines in the Dublin *Evening Herald*: 'Provo beatings linked to discovery of ditch bodies'; and in the *Star*: 'Provos are blamed for double drug killings.' The papers also managed to squeeze in that the bodies were found close to the scene where (twenty-three years ago!) the IRA killed eighteen Paratroopers. The bodies were actually those of two Lithuanians believed to have been killed by other Lithuanians.

In contrast, none of the papers, tabloid or broadsheet, published the photograph of Padraig Devenney from the nationalist Short Strand who had to undergo brain surgery last weekend after he was definitely and viciously beaten unconscious by the RUC/PSNI, following a loyalist blast bomb attack on his mother's home. The reason for the omission? Well, that just might have triggered some sense of solidarity from people in the South towards beleaguered nationalists and resulted in votes for Sinn Féin.

Given the mountains that Sinn Féin has had to climb, the black propaganda campaign against the party, the many slurs cast, it is sweet to know that there are people on this island, and not only in the six counties, who just cannot be morally blackmailed, intimidated or bullied by the establishment parties and misled by the media.

And so it's goodbye to Dick Spring, Austin Currie, Alan Dukes and Nora Owens.

And it's hello to Martin Ferris, Arthur Morgan, Sean Crowe, Aengus Ó Snodaigh and Caoimhghín Ó Caolain!

IRA Apologises

On the thirtieth anniversary of Bloody Friday, the IRA apologises to those non-combatant and innocent bystanders killed by the organisation and acknowledges the grief and pain of the relatives of those whom it considered combatants and whose lives it took.

Andersonstown News, 18 July 2002

Anniversaries provide us with a particular focus on past events outside of the daily preoccupation of simply living and getting on with our lives. For many people who have lost loved ones in a conflict situation they are highly emotional occasions and relatives are particularly wrought and sensitive at these times.

The conflict in the North didn't simply start as a result of a split in the IRA in 1969 and the formation of what the media called 'The Provisional IRA'. The violence was fifty years in the making, if not centuries. What responsibility had the unionist businessmen whose discrimination against Catholics fuelled the eventual emergence of the Civil Rights Association? Did unionist supporters really fear (and mistakenly) that the CRA was a front for the IRA, as Stormont government ministers claimed? How much did state repression, especially from 1969 onwards, contribute to the decision by the IRA to restart, or provide the context for it to restart its campaign? How much did IRA actions, such as Bloody Friday or the killing of RUC and UDR men and women (viewed simply from within their own community as Protestants defending their British way of life) spark a backlash, in addition to the loyalist sectarianism that already existed?

Clearly, there will never be agreement on the cause of the conflict, of what might have been done to avoid it, or how to apportion blame.

Last Tuesday's statement from the IRA, apologising to the families of those people, non-combatants, innocent bystanders, running into many, many hundreds, was issued, appositely, a few days before the thirtieth anniversary of Bloody Friday, when IRA bombs killed nine people and injured dozens more. Some of the relatives of the dead welcomed the apology; others were, understandably, lukewarm or hostile.

The IRA also acknowledged the grief and pain of the relatives of those whom it considered combatants (including, presumably, members of the establishment – judicial and political – who were involved in the campaign to repress republicanism or who were cheerleaders of the dirty war) and whom it wilfully killed. Some commentators have taken exception to their exclusion from its apology when, clearly, the IRA, whilst regretting the loss of life, feels that no apology is required. IRA Volunteers took risks on operations understanding that the consequence could be imprisonment or death and the British soldier knew that one consequence of occupying Crossmaglen or the Creggan could be death (but rarely imprisonment, even when they murdered unarmed civilians, as on Bloody Sunday).

Of course, most unionist representatives (whom no republican can ever please, bar converting to unionism and accepting total responsibility for everything that has happened) once again spurned the IRA gesture and said that the statement was not enough. Yet no unionist has ever apologised to the nationalist community for fifty years of social and economic discrimination. One can hardly call Trimble's observation that the North was 'a cold house' for Catholics an apology. After all, he quickly forgot it and is once again threatening to pull down the Executive if Sinn Féin, the majority nationalist party, is not put out of government. No unionist has apologised for the RUC attacks on the Civil Rights Movement, the deaths of Francis McCloskey or Samuel Devenney as a result of RUC beatings in early 1969, or young Patrick Rooney at his home in Divis Flats, to mention but a few.

Under a unionist government the nationalist community experienced the pogroms of August 1969; the Falls curfew of 1970 when children, women and men were gassed in their homes; internment and the torture of detainees; and Bloody Sunday.

No apology and don't expect one.

On a visit to Africa in 1998 US President Bill Clinton apologised to African nations for the slave trade and the suffering and death it caused. Apart from one Church of England minister a few years ago, who said that he prayed Ireland would forgive England for all the misery it inflicted on its people, not one person in authority has thought it fit to say sorry for Britain's numberless malevolent deeds in Ireland.

No apology and don't expect one.

The IRA has apologised to the relatives of the people it accidentally or carelessly killed. It will not bring back the dead, it will not ease the suffering, it will not be the last word, but at least the words 'we are sorry' have been spoken, and it means that the Republican Movement and republican supporters are facing up to the consequences of their actions.

It is another move towards closure of conflict, another indication of the republican commitment to permanent peace and a desire never to go back to those dark, deadly days.

An Impossible Demand

On 15 October 2002, following PSNI raids on Sinn Féin's offices at Parliament Buildings and allegations of a republican spy-ring 'at the heart of government', the British government suspends devolution and reinstates direct rule. Two days later, Tony Blair visits Belfast and calls for 'acts of completion', that is, disbandment of the IRA.

Andersonstown News, 21 October 2002

In 1953 when Tony Blair was born Joe Cahill was still serving a life sentence, and in England IRA Volunteers were carrying out the arms raid on Felstead barracks in preparation for the next campaign. When Blair's father was born in 1923 Ireland had just been partitioned. In the twenty-six counties eleven thousand IRA Volunteers were in jail, hundreds of republicans on all sides had been killed in the civil war and the Free State government had executed seventy-seven prisoners. In the six counties thousands of IRA Volunteers, whose main role (the Republic having been lost) was the defence of vulnerable nationalist areas, were interned without trial by the unionist government.

When Blair's grandparents were born the Fenian Brotherhood was active, and, before them, the Young Irelanders, and, before them, the United Irishmen.

Irish republicanism is over two hundred years old.

Only a fool could fail to see the link between the recurrence of physical force republicanism and Britain's continued interference in Ireland.

Only a British prime minister, who is all-out for war with impoverished Iraq, could stand in Belfast and tell the IRA that it can't be half-in on peace, has to disband, and is to blame for the impasse.

For close on a century it has been illegal to be in the IRA. It has been a prison sentence or a death sentence to be in the IRA. Prisoners have faced firing squads or been hanged for being in the IRA. Republicans have died long and agonising deaths on hunger strike upholding their political status, refusing to bow to Britain's harsh prison regimes.

If the British couldn't defeat the IRA in a quarter of a century of armed conflict, if they couldn't break the blanket men – couldn't get them to 'disband' – why in heaven's name would the IRA disband in the current circumstances at the behest of a British prime minister?

This is the issue: is the IRA chiefly responsible for the attitude of unionists towards the Belfast Agreement or has unionism as part of its legacy an ingrained resistance to change and reform?

IRA meetings, reviews, discussions, are private activities that do not impact on the peace or political process. IRA mediation in disputes in nationalist areas causes little or no damage. Because of the absence of an acceptable police service there is a degree of tolerance for IRA actions against local criminals. But these and any other IRA activities, which are of an overt or more serious nature, are obviously going to be viewed as a challenge to authority and to the state or states on a sliding scale of outrage.

Sinn Féin has no control over the IRA but the two governments punish the party for the discovery of IRA activity (though the nationalist electorate views this punishment as yet another injustice).

For a large section of the British security and intelligence services, and for most unionist politicians, the war has never been over. They know that IRA disbandment is synonymous with IRA surrender. The double advantage for the unionists is that after all the hurdles the republicans have unexpectedly jumped through, here, at last, is a demand they cannot meet, and an excuse for unionists to halt political progress without being blamed.

On the same day that Blair flew in to Belfast to make his speech the BBC locally published a survey that showed that 58 per cent of unionists did not want to share power with either the SDLP or Sinn Féin. One did not need a poll to know that. It is a historic fact but a fact that Tony Blair did not focus on.

But he knows it and he chose to ignore it, just as he chooses to ignore the history of British rule in Ireland and how fresh in nationalist memory is their suffering, just as the devastation wreaked on the unionist community by the IRA has created bitter memories.

Tony Blair concedes that republicans fear that if the IRA disappears, nationalists would lose leverage, British interest in the treatment of nationalists would wane and that they would be ignored. On the one hand, Blair gives a guarantee that he is committed to the implementation of the Agreement, and, on the other, he contradicts himself by making its implementation conditional on IRA disbandment ('it makes it harder for us to respond to nationalist concerns', were his exact words).

Blair himself created distrust, reneged on promises he made at Weston Park, and destroyed a major opportunity for republicans to support a new police service – and for the IRA to move away from the past – when he gutted the Patten proposals on policing in order to appease unionists.

There will always be a republican response to British interference in Ireland. Currently, it is not in the form of armed struggle. Few believe that the IRA is preparing for a return to armed struggle, nor do republican supporters want it to, nor do unionists think it shall (which means their present stance is a sham). Fewer still believe the IRA will disband.

Linking the rights of the nationalist community to a demand on Sinn Féin that the IRA must dissolve is counter-productive. The IRA will retire from the scene and disappear through time but will do so speedier if Britain stops interfering in the affairs of the Irish people or gives a credible commitment to that end.

Stealing Votes – the British Way!

Andersonstown News, 27 January 2003

In 1999, a year before the controversial presidential elections in the USA, Katherine Harris, George Bush's presidential campaign co-chairperson and Florida secretary of state in charge of elections, called in researchers from Database Technologies to sift through Florida's electoral rolls. Its brief was to systematically remove anyone 'suspected' of being an ex-felon.

Thirty one per cent of all black men in Florida have a felony on their record and they were immediately struck off, as were thousands of other blacks that had had their voting privileges reinstated (after misdemeanours). Black people overwhelmingly vote Democrat – that is, would have been potential Al Gore supporters. But, as Michael Moore points out in his book *Stupid White Men*, the brief to Database Technologies went further and it was instructed to include not just felons, but those blacks who shared similar names to those of felons or had similar social security numbers.

To contest and reverse this mass disenfranchisement would – as the architects, of course, knew – take years, wading through a bureaucratic quagmire for which few people would have the patience or energy. As a result, 173,000 registered voters were placed on the ineligible list, 66 per cent of those who were removed in Miami-Dade, Florida's largest county, being black.

So, long before all those arguments about 'hanging chads', and what were the voters' true intentions, Al Gore was robbed off the presidency even though across the USA he received 539,898 more votes than George Bush. Perhaps, there would have been no difference between Gore's foreign policy and Bush's, and he too would have impatiently sidelined the work of UN weapons inspectors in Iraq. Perhaps, he too would have rushed us to war. We'll never know.

What Katherine Harris did for the voters of Florida the new Electoral Fraud Act 2002 is doing for 'democracy' in the North. The right to vote and to exercise one's vote is critical in determining just who goes into government, opposition or retirement. Mary Harney knows what it is like to sweat for a quota. In the last Westminster election Sinn Féin's Michelle Gildernew took Fermanagh and South Tyrone from the Ulster Unionists by a majority of just fifty-three.

Long before Sinn Féin stood for elections in the North electoral malpractice was common – 'Vote Early, Vote Often' being the legendary catchphrase of campaigners who correctly assumed 'the other side' was equally engaged in impersonation.

However, when republicans entered the electoral fray and enjoyed success, much of their success was written off as the results of mass impersonation. It was in Fermanagh and South Tyrone in 1981 that IRA Volunteer Bobby Sands, whilst on hunger strike, was elected MP and unwittingly initiated Sinn Féin's embracing electoral politics. Up to then, republicans had been accused by the British government of being a mere criminal conspiracy without popular support and had been repeatedly challenged to seek a mandate.

However, Mrs Thatcher's reaction to Sands' election was the first of many moves to manipulate the political process. In her case she amended the Representation of the People Act, barring any other prisoner from standing for election, rather than negotiate an end to the prison crisis.

In 1982 when five Sinn Féin candidates were elected to the Assembly, Northern Ireland Office ministers were instructed not to meet them on constituency matters and to cut them off from receiving salaries and expenses, government publications and press releases. Every time Sinn Féin made inroads the rules were changed: candidates were required to make declarations repudiating the use of violence for political ends; council election deposits were increased from £100 to £1000; former prisoners were barred from standing for five years after their release; and, finally, voter ID was introduced to stamp out what was alleged to be widespread impersonation.

But the Sinn Féin vote continued to increase and in 2001 the party outpolled the SDLP.

Still, the myth was perpetuated that the vote was down to impersonation and multiple registration, even though the only candidate to be brought before an electoral court and found guilty (on an overspending charge) was Joe Hendron of the SDLP.

Last year the British government introduced a new law that required every individual voter to fill out a form, supply his or her National Insurance Number, date of birth and sign it personally. To vote, an elector has to produce photographic ID: a British or Irish passport, a driving licence, a Senior SmartPass (for pensioners) or the new Electoral Identity card.

The Electoral Office began distributing forms and canvassing last September but when the new electoral register was published in December it showed a drop of 130,000 voters from the previous register. All the main parties in the North had voted at Westminster for the new restrictions and so they couldn't really raise objections. But when Sinn Féin complained that thousands of people were being disenfranchised, it was upon Belfast West, seat of Sinn Féin President Gerry Adams MP, where the drop was most dramatic with 11,000 voters gone missing, that the media and unionists zeroed in. The implication was that the Sinn Féin impersonation conspiracy was exposed at long last.

This story received wide coverage but was never balanced by the fact that every constituency registered a drop. In fact, Belfast South, with 10,000 missing voters wasn't far behind Belfast West.

Privately, the Ulster Unionists have been expressing concern with the inefficiency of the registration, while there is anecdotal evidence that the reason for the gung-ho attitude of Paisley's DUP (which accuses David Trimble of trying to avoid an Assembly election in May) is that it is confident it has registered its supporters.

The Electoral Office, which initially congratulated itself on compiling a list of over one million voters, has been forced to take on board some of the criticisms. How, for example, could there be such a discrepancy between their returns and the official census returns which show that, actually, not 130,000 voters have gone missing, but closer to 187,000? Have they all died in a year, emigrated or were they all impostors?

There is little voter apathy in the North. But there is considerable evidence that forms were not distributed, that homes were not canvassed, that the new forms were not explained to either the elderly or those with learning difficulties, that many forms were not collected, in addition to the fact that those without official ID would find it inconvenient and time consuming to go to the electoral office to be photographed for their Electoral Identity card.

Sinn Féin cites example after example. In one ward in nationalist Newry consisting of over 900 households, almost one hundred (including entire families) have been disenfranchised. In Gerry Adams' constituency, an entire side of one street (houses 1-80) in Cullingtree Road, did not appear in the December register.

A comparison of the census returns and the electoral returns show that at least 50,000 first-time voters (and young nationalists tend to vote for Sinn Féin) are not registered.

The restrictive nature of the new legislation, the failure of a more pro-active and cooperative approach from the Electoral Office, and unevenness in the distribution and collection of completed forms have left registration in a mess, with little time left to correct that mess if there are Assembly elections in May. And come May, many people will arrive at polling stations to discover not that their vote has been stolen but that their ID, which once sufficed, is no longer acceptable.

Katherine Harris must look jealously at the Westminster architects of the ironically, well-named, Electoral Fraud Act. She herself could not have devised a better way of eliminating voters from the register.

IRA Will Not Be Humiliated

The Guardian, 29 April 2003

As an Irish republican who joined the IRA in my teens in the early 1970s, and as someone who has been arrested and imprisoned in my own country a score of times by the British, I take great exception to the moral high tone often adopted by commentators when they turn their attention to the north of Ireland.

Now is the 'moment of finality', *The Guardian's* editorial declared on Saturday, for example, for Sinn Féin in relation to the existence of the IRA. Why not a 'moment of finality' for Britain in implementing all the promises it made five years ago about justice, equality and policing?

The British government will never have any right to be in Ireland. That basic premise never disturbs the thinking of British commentators, but every day in the North we live with the consequences of British interference in Irish affairs. Hundreds of nationalists, including our political representatives and our lawyers, were assassinated as a result of collusion between the British state and loyalist paramilitaries in a scandal which will now be swept under the carpet, if issuing the Stevens Report the day after parliament went into recess is anything to go by.

It is too simplistic to blame the IRA for current difficulties in the peace process. The real crisis is that unionists do not want to share power with nationalists, particularly Sinn Féin, and are attempting to turn the peace process into a surrender process, though the IRA was never defeated.

Our experience and our relationship with Britain, which informs our judgments, have been forged by British military might. When we compare what Britain has done in Ireland, including partitioning the country and handing power to the Ulster Unionist Party, which discriminated against nationalists for 50 years; when we consider the revelations of the Stevens Report (just the tip of the iceberg of 'the dirty war'), and then examine what republicans have given, things take on a different perspective.

David Trimble's Ulster Unionist Party has never acknowledged the part those decades of discrimination and oppression played in fuelling the outbreak of violence. We can live with that denial. What we cannot abide is the demand that the IRA prostrate itself so that David Trimble can present a triumphalist manifesto in his election battle against Ian Paisley.

The British government and the unionists say clarity and certainty from the IRA is needed. How about this?

The IRA's declaration of a cessation in 1994 was welcomed with obstacles and demands from day one. Sinn Féin was demonised and excluded from talks until Labour came to power in 1997. When it came to negotiations, republicans compromised on several key issues. In the Belfast Agreement they supported a unionist demand for devolved government to 'the hated' Stormont Assembly, and for the amendment of the Irish territorial claim on the North. They were promised a new beginning to policing and that the grievances surrounding justice, human rights and equality would be addressed.

For the first 18 months of the Assembly, David Trimble, as First Minister, refused to allow the nomination of the rest of the Executive. Power sharing lasted some 70 days before he brought it down on the issue of IRA decommissioning. Loyalist paramilitaries, in collusion with British intelligence, imported thousands of weapons from the South African apartheid regime. Loyalists refuse to disarm, have continued to kill Catholics (and each other) without any sanctions from Mr Trimble, whereas the IRA has twice put large numbers of arms beyond use.

Our experience of the peace process has been one of unionists repeatedly making humiliating demands of republicans which they think cannot be met, or, if met, might create a crisis within republicanism.

One of the more ridiculous proposals is that the IRA would be in breach of its ceasefire if there were any rioting in nationalist areas. Before that it was that the destruction of IRA weapons had to be filmed. Last year it was that if Sinn Féin continued to show solidarity with the banned Basque party, Herri Batusuna it would be expelled from the Executive.

And now, the IRA has to use words written by David Trimble along the lines that the war is over and it is going to disband, the clear subtext of which is 'republicans lost, unionists won'. If the IRA refuses, unionists want new rules if the Assembly elections go ahead (which look unlikely). In the Belfast Agreement the application of sanctions against a party, because of traditional unionist abuses, requires the support of a majority within both unionist and nationalist blocs.

Trimble now wants the power of sanction to be vested in a mere 40 per cent of the representatives, a return of the unionist veto and gerrymandering. Which is, interestingly, where the Provisional IRA first came into the picture over thirty years ago.

One More IRA Statement

The Examiner, 7 May 2003

The IRA should issue one more statement,' said the man next to me. I was at the annual Bobby Sands Lecture, which is held around May 5th, the anniversary of Bobby's death in 1981 after sixty-six days on hunger strike. Before the main address, a film had been shown, outlining the background to the hunger strike in the H-Blocks of Long Kesh Prison.

It was quite emotional, watching footage of a heavy metal door being yawned open and the television camera surprising the ghostly figures of two long-haired, bearded, skinny young men, dressed only in blankets, living in excrement-filled cells. They, and hundreds, had been deprived of exercise, letters, books, pen and paper, of their own clothes for four years and had been regularly beaten.

The two squint and stare with ghostly jail eyes before they realise that here is an opportunity and one shouts, 'We are political prisoners! We are political prisoners! Victory to the blanket men!' and then it goes blank.

All of us in that hall felt our dander rise as past and present coalesced, as parallel piled on parallel.

The film showed how the British government reneged on a deal made with republicans during the IRA truce of 1972 by withdrawing political status for IRA prisoners from March 1976 onwards. Imprisoned republicans were not to associate together as the IRA, not to organise, not to parade, not to stand for a minute's silence to honour dead comrades, otherwise they would be punished and placed in solitary confinement on a bread and water diet. The British government demanded the prisoners wear a criminal uniform, do menial prison work, that they use certain language (address the warders as 'Sir', answer to a number and come to attention).

We were thinking: the British government do a lot of demanding of Irish republicans.

'The IRA should issue one more statement,' my tablemate had begun.

The film recalled the 1980 hunger strike, which ended without death after fifty-three days. The prisoners were told they could wear their own clothes but within twenty-four hours the British double-crossed them: to get your own clothes you have to wear prison clothes first, they said.

The film showed the British government and Margaret Thatcher ridiculing republicans and challenging them to test their support at the ballot box.

The film showed Bobby Sands doing just that by standing for election in Fermanagh and South Tyrone, asking for a mandate, a position from which he could negotiate a peaceful end to the prison crisis. It showed him being elected and it showed the British government ignoring and deploring the results of the ballot box.

My tablemate, in his opening remark, unwittingly, presaged a similar call by Paul Murphy, the northern Secretary of State, the following day. In relation to the cancellation of the Assembly elections, and having rejected Gerry Adams' explication of the IRA statement, Murphy said that the IRA would need to provide a new statement if there was to be progress with an election in the autumn.

Perhaps the British government is just plain stupid and doesn't know when to shut up. If, on the other hand, it knows what makes the Republican Movement tick, then its demands on the IRA are an attempt to humiliate the Republican Movement, sow division and thus weaken it – something the British strove to achieve, but failed, in the course of conflict.

It was also the strategy and response of John Major's government to the initial offer of peace back in 1994.

It failed. Spectacularly.

'The IRA should issue one more statement,' said my tablemate, 'after they bomb Canary Wharf, and tell the Brits to come back when they are interested in peace.'

It was more an expression of anger and frustration than a desire to return to armed struggle, yet among many in the republican heartlands across the North this is the primary emotion stirred not simply by Tony Blair's cancellation of the Assembly elections but by the accumulation of endless demands and tests on the IRA – and only the IRA.

I am sure many people in the Republic also feel insulted. Together, North and South, in 1998 we voted overwhelmingly in the referenda for the Belfast Agreement. In the twenty-six counties this included the provision to amend Articles 2 & 3 of the Constitution as a gesture to unionists. But it was linked to Assembly elections to a power-sharing Executive – which David Trimble has now brought down four times over allegations of ongoing IRA activity.

The IRA's commitment to the peace process, the compromises it has made, its engagements with the international decommissioning body are beyond doubt. It is fanciful to think that they are reversible, that the IRA could resume the armed struggle where it left off, or that there is any desire on the part of the IRA to return to its campaign.

It may be that the calculation that the IRA cannot go back to armed struggle is behind the arrogance of the British government, which thinks it can treat Irish voters with impunity. Despite the provocation republicans should not deviate from their immensely successful peace strategy, which continues to expose and highlight the true nature of the problem.

I used to privately think that there might come a day when, without impeaching its past efforts and without prejudice to its ultimate objectives, the IRA could say the war is over.

But not now.

As a result of British and unionist demands, the expression 'the war is over' has taken on greater significance than any putative value it may have had as a reassurance to unionists. Besides, unionists say they don't trust the IRA so why the pressure to prise such a statement out of the 'untrustworthy' IRA unless it is but to symbolise defeat and confer triumph on unionism?

Why would the IRA now agree to such a statement? To satisfy the blessed peacemaker, the besmirched Tony Blair? To help pro-Agreement unionists, whose difficulties I can understand, but most of whose weaknesses are not of our making? To satisfy David Trimble so that he can crow and parade the IRA feather in his cap in an electoral contest with the DUP?

Nationalists feel cheated by the British government and ashamed of Dublin, the junior poodle in the Anglo-Irish relationship. Nationalists were expected to vote overwhelmingly for pro-Agreement candidates, for peace and progress and confirm Sinn Féin as their voice. Unionists were expected to vote substantially for anti-Agreement candidates from the DUP and within the Ulster Unionist Party. It is not hard to work out where the intransigence lies and why the British cancelled the elections.

We need another IRA statement, says the British government.

Who believes that next week or next autumn the IRA – to use an analogy – will don the criminal uniform implied by the words, 'the war is over', will call the British prime minister, 'Sir'? And, more to the point, why should it?

SDLP – No Problem!

A review of the SDLP on the eve of the 2003 Assembly elections

Andersonstown News, 3 November 2003

If I was in the SDLP and had worked hard all my political life for the party I would be angry and frustrated at the way Sinn Féin has 'stolen' the limelight and is predicted by media commentators as being on the verge of opening up the gap between it and the SDLP.

However, blaming the media or 'the problem parties', as Mark Durkan has done, is actually ignoring the fact that it is the people in secret ballot who are responsible for the changing fortunes of a party. In its case, the SDLP needs to ask itself why things have turned out this way.

The SDLP itself was born out of opportunism in 1970 when various independents and small, nationalist parties, coalesced after the traumas the nationalist community experienced in 1968 and 1969. It was never an ideologically focused party and the only 'history' it could call on was the various ineffectual attempts by constitutional nationalists to work the old Stormont. There, they were regularly humiliated – which then led to walkouts and years of boycotts.

Nevertheless, the SDLP was in an admirable and unassailable position: no other party was organised to represent the interests of nationalists. Sinn Féin was banned until 1974 and devoted itself to street politics and prisoners' welfare. The Workers' Party was to the right of the Alliance Party on the national question and never represented an alternative. By the time the largely rural Irish Independence Party enjoyed a ripple of support in May 1981 Sinn Féin was just about to burst onto the political scene.

SDLP leaders tended to be teachers, doctors or lawyers and mirrored middle-class values. It had close links to the Catholic Church and the provincial nationalist press. A party merely looking for reforms, not an end to partition, it was a blessing for Dublin governments, allowing them to orient their deficient policies around a constitutional party, which didn't make huge demands of Dublin. Meantime, Dublin could get on with demonising and suppressing the Republican Movement.

In July 1971 Ulster Unionist Prime Minister Brian Faulkner offered the SDLP a few positions on various Stormont committees. The SDLP's Paddy Devlin declared it Faulkner's 'finest hour'. Yet, within two years the SDLP was able to argue for a power-sharing Executive and an Irish 'dimension'. What had changed in the intervening period? Clearly, the IRA campaign, which had at its core the more fundamental demand for a British withdrawal, had created a new threshold that increased the negotiating position of the nationalist community and gave muscle to the SDLP.

The subtext of the SDLP position was that reforms that included the SDLP would undermine the IRA campaign. After the ceasefire this position was transmuted into a strategy of expecting help from Dublin and London in undermining Sinn Féin. In the current election they are receiving help from strategists in the British Labour Party, the Irish Labour Party, Fianna Fáil and the Progressive Democrats. Have they no strategists of their own or do they not trust local constituency associations? Furthermore, the SDLP believes that it is not only vulnerable to Sinn Féin in Newry and Armagh, and South Down, but even in Foyle, party leader Mark Durkan's home base!

Sinn Féin's history could not have been more contrasting. It emerged from a different tradition – a tradition of struggle and sacrifice, comradeship, discipline and loyalty.

My experience of the SDLP during the hunger strikes was that they were always looking for the prisoners to compromise more than the authorities. In other words, they were in awe of the British, never believed that they could break the Brits and would, therefore, unlike the republicans, never even make the attempt. One consequence of this mentality is the SDLP's obsession with Sinn Féin, with whom for electoral purposes it should be in alliance, actively seeking transfers. It surfaces at its most extreme in the intemperate outbursts of Alex Attwood, but others aren't too far behind, given the flavour of the following examples.

Gerry Adams goes to a fund-raiser in the USA, during which he meets the US special envoy Richard Haas to discuss the peace process, and Carmel Hanna accuses him of being a 'money grabber'! Patricia Lewsley attacks Martin McGuinness, falsely accusing him of not making children with special educational needs one of his priorities as a minister. An SDLP councillor in South Down launches an attack on Sinn Féin's Caitriona Ruane, linking her with 'The Cocaine Three' (the three innocent Irishmen in a Bogota prison, who were never charged with any cocaine offences and whom this SDLP councillor has found guilty before even the trial judge delivers his verdict).

A fortnight ago, when SDLP leader Mark Durkan, miffed at being excluded from the talks in Downing Street between Gerry Adams, Tony Blair and David Trimble, referred to Sinn Féin and the Ulster Unionists as the 'problem parties', he actually spoke volumes about the weakness of the SDLP.

For 'problem' read 'relevant'. In fact, the Paddy Devlin tradition of welcoming, embracing and hyping every morsel offered to nationalists (without having an eye to the bigger picture) is exactly what is wrong with the SDLP. When asked to join the policing board and district policing partnerships the SDLP declared, 'No problem!' and leaped in.

Increasingly perceived by many former supporters as a 'No Problem' party is just one explanation why the SDLP will remain in second place to Sinn Féin after the election.

One Extreme

The DUP after the Assembly Elections, November 2003

Andersonstown News, 1 December 2003

In February 1974, in a Westminster general election, eleven out of the North's then twelve constituencies returned anti-Agreement unionists. They were opposed to the Sunningdale Agreement, which had been negotiated a few months earlier between the Ulster Unionist Party, under Brian Faulkner, and the SDLP, under Gerry Fitt.

The eleven MPs were opposed to the power sharing Executive at Stormont, disrupted its meetings, and were opposed to what was called the 'Irish Dimension' in the shape of a Council of Ireland which actually never met.

Sinn Féin had yet to adopt an electoral strategy and the IRA was committed to armed struggle (though by Christmas of that year it would call a ceasefire).

The new MPs, made up of dissident Ulster Unionists and Ian Paisley, then collaborated with the Ulster Workers' Council and organised a general strike in May of that year. To bring the North to its knees the UWC had to rely on loyalist paramilitaries, mainly the UDA, but also the UVF, to hijack vehicles at gunpoint, close down roads and prevent people from going to work. The UDA commander, Andy Tyrie, and UVF leaders were on the UWC Co-ordinating Committee.

During this period loyalist paramilitaries killed six Catholics in the Rose and Crown bar on the Ormeau Road, a husband and wife in Donaghmore, several Catholic workers, and two Catholic brothers who ran a bar in Ballymena. On the third day of the UWC strike loyalists, almost certainly helped by elements of British intelligence, planted car bombs in Dublin and Monaghan and slaughtered 33 children, women and men.

When power and petrol supplies were cut Brian Faulkner was forced to resign and the power-sharing Executive collapsed. The alliance of anti-Agreement paramilitaries and politicians triumphantly marched to Stormont. In the intervening 30 years, to the top of the hill, then down again to the bottom, is the only place these politicians have ever taken their people.

Then, as now, the real issue wasn't about the IRA, or 'Sinn Féin/IRA', but was about sharing power, equality and parity of esteem – principles which are alien to the raison d'être of the six-county state and its culture of a 'Protestant Parliament for a Protestant People'.

Last week on television the DUP's Gregory Campbell inadvertently admitted this when he said that even had the IRA decommissioned its weapons 'with transparency' in October it still wasn't the issue. The issue was the terms of the Good Friday Agreement, which 'had given nationalists everything' – that is, some of their democratic entitlements.

The whole issue of the IRA is just an excuse for unionists not to engage with the nationalist community.

Some commentators have described the current deadlock as having been exacerbated by 'the election of the two extremes', as if Sinn Féin is refusing to share power with unionists or doesn't recognise unionist aspirations.

Sinn Féin has genuinely pursued a dialogue with unionism. However, most unionists still adhere to the myth that the conflict in the North was one-sided, that the IRA was responsible for all violence. The DUP and its supporters need reminding of its history.

In 1977 the DUP once again allied themselves to the UDA during another UWC strike. The stoppage lacked support and so the UDA turned to intimidation, shooting dead a Citybus driver in Belfast, Protestant Harry Bradshaw, in an attempt to stop public transport.

The DUP set up a 'Third Force', a vigilante organisation in 1981, which operated illegal checkpoints and held rallies. In 1986 the DUP helped found Ulster Resistance, a paramilitary-style force whose members marched in military formation wearing red berets. There was the famous incident when Peter Robinson, armed with a firearm, led a loyalist mob in an attack on Clontibret garda station. He was found guilty of unlawful assembly and fined fifteen thousand punts.

Members of Ulster Resistance were involved in industrial espionage and were caught selling details of Shorts' blowpipe missile technology to the South African apartheid regime. Ulster Resistance, in collaboration with British Intelligence, smuggled into the North a large shipment of weapons that were used to kill several hundred nationalists in the 1990s.

The DUP and other unionist representatives for decades have acted as cheerleaders for British army and RUC violence and have justified repression, torture, shoot-to-kill operations, exclusion orders, censorship and discrimination.

Extremists were certainly elected last Wednesday but they were unionists.

At the most, 34 or 35 unionist representatives out of a potential assembly of 108 members are opposed to the Belfast Agreement. The Agreement still has the support of a majority of people in the North, was endorsed in referenda, was passed as legislation in both Britain and Ireland and is lodged at the United Nations as an international binding Treaty.

However, the very provision, which was written into the Agreement to prevent abuse – that the Executive and Assembly require the consent of a majority of both unionist and nationalist elected representatives – gives the DUP, as the leading party of the unionist community, the power to prevent an inclusive Executive from being formed.

Ultimately, Britain is to blame for the supremacist mentality within unionism, which came with partition. That is not to say that things haven't changed. Things have changed and many unionists are prepared to share power and recognise the compromises that nationalists and republicans have made in the interests of reconciliation.

Sinn Féin, having emerged as the leaders for the nationalist community, has to face down the DUP. The DUP has declared that it will not share power with Sinn Féin and thinks that it can renegotiate the Agreement. It has yet to learn that there can be no assembly, no Executive and no power for the DUP without the consent of Sinn Féin, and that the nationalist community is not about to give up or dilute rights that it took eighty years to secure.

Spies, Spinners and Spoofers

Andersonstown News, 26 April 2004

The Independent Monitoring Commission has to be congratulated for its economy in fining Sinn Féin and allowing the £120,000 fine to offset IMC costs.

The IMC is of course a totally independent and impartial anti-Sinn Féin body. It demonstrated its independence when it was asked by the British to report two months in advance of its original deadline. No problem.

It demonstrated its independence when it forgot to report on the British government reneging on its responsibility to implement the Belfast Agreement and on the commitments it made were the IRA to take part in a process of putting its arms beyond use.

It demonstrated its independence when it wrote in partisan terms: 'All political parties with people elected to public positions, or aspiring to election, must play a full and constructive part in the operation of all criminal justice institutions. This includes working co-operatively with PSNI and active participation in the Policing Board and District Policing Partnerships.'

All talk of acts of completion is a one-way street. The most significant unresolved issue of the entire conflict, the issue of British collusion with unionist paramilitary organisations in which hundreds of people were murdered is a festering issue bigger than stealing cigarettes or bigger than vigilantism. Of all the deaths associated with allegations of collusion in the North, Pat Finucane's is the one with potentially the most profound repercussions for the British state.

Sir John Stevens' heavily censored report into that death recommended that charges be brought against several police and army officers. No one was ever charged.

Under intense pressure the British government eventually called in Judge Cory from Canada to investigate a number of controversial killings and it promised to act if he recommended inquiries.

Judge Cory did just that.

Before Cory's report was completed the DPP charged a loyalist with killing Pat Finucane and the British government now says that there can be no inquiry because the case is sub judice. No date has been set for trial. If there is a conviction the likelihood is that appeals to the High Court, the House of Lords and the European Court would last for another fifteen years. In other words, there will never be an inquiry and the issue will be submerged in a so-called Truth and Reconciliation process.

The British government at the request of Ulster Unionists set up the IMC last year. The International Decommissioning Body was also set up at the request of the Ulster Unionists, but General John de Chastelain's report on the IRA's third and most significant act of decommissioning last October was dismissed by David Trimble. Tony Blair then reneged on his side of the agreement with Sinn Féin in regard to a Bill of Rights, criminal justice reforms and the status of 'on the run' republicans.

David Trimble was never comfortable sharing power with Sinn Féin and for some time had wanted to bypass the weighted safety mechanisms in the Belfast Agreement. Under those mechanisms a party could only be punished for being in breach of the Mitchell Principles' anti-violence pledge of office if there was cross-party support for putting it out of office (that is, if the SDLP voted with the unionists). Instead, Trimble wanted a mechanism outside of the Assembly to facilitate the exclusion of Sinn Féin from government over the continued existence of the IRA. Note 'existence', not just alleged IRA activity.

London and Dublin acceded to that request only for Dublin to discover that the British unilaterally amended its powers of scrutiny. In other words, whilst the Dublin representative and the US nominee (a former director of the CIA) are allowed to investigate Irish republicans they are not allowed to investigate alleged unionist or British government breaches of the terms of the Belfast Agreement and its implementation. And who are the British nominees, chosen for their objectivity? The former head of Scotland Yard's anti-terrorist unit and the unelectable former head of the Alliance Party! And their sources? The securocrats, of course.

Spies, Spinners and Spoofers.

Sinn Féin's rejection of the IMC as being established outside of the terms of the Agreement and as being a sop to unionists has proved correct. Indeed, the IMC's scrutiny and reporting of loyalist violence has the appearance of an afterthought, despite a relentless sectarian campaign against nationalists, including murder, long pre-dating the Tohill affair.

In that incident PSNI Chief Constable, Hugh Orde, immediately declared that it was an attempted IRA kidnapping (of a dissident republican). The IRA denied responsibility. Orde's precipitance is in marked contrast to how his force – and unionism generally – understates or excuses loyalist violence. And it is those double standards that gall nationalists.

We are told that there can be no investigation of alleged British security involvement in the murder of Pat Finucane because a man has been charged but British government appointees can carry out an investigation into the alleged abduction of Bobby Tohill, despite four men being charged and it being *sub judice*.

Next week Sinn Féin faces the withdrawal of the public funding it uses to administer its Stormont offices and service its electorate. It faces further sanctions of the salaries of its Assembly members being withdrawn should they be named by the IMC as being members of the IRA.

All of this might be grist-to-the-mill for unionists opposed to power sharing with Sinn Féin, or for those in the South trying to stem the electoral rise of Sinn Féin.

But it does absolutely nothing for the peace process – as the cancellation of next week's 'proximity talks', involving all the parties, shows. Instead, it presents a one-sided picture of the cause of the impasse and allows the British government to evade its responsibility to address the issues of implementing equality, justice and accountable policing as promised in the Belfast Agreement.

IMC Land

Andersonstown News, 3 May 2004

Within just a week of publishing its findings the fallibility of the Independent Monitoring Commission became easily demonstrated if one considers how it would have reported had it been established in 2001, with the same punitive powers and using the same jaundiced criteria it was to use in the Tohill affair.

Once Jim Monaghan, Martin McAuley and Niall Connolly were arrested and charged in Bogota on 11 August 2001 the British would have asked for a report and the IMC would have swung into action and contacted the Colombian paramilitary police and the CIA. It would have spoken to President Alvaro Uribe of Colombia and General Fernando, the Chief of the armed forces, who would have told the commissioners that the men were absolutely guilty as charged.

It would have spoken to the American embassy official that carried out the forensic tests, which 'showed' that at the time of their arrest the men were covered in traces of cocaine and numerous types of sophisticated explosives. It would have consulted many lurid sources, and journalists such as the Colombian-based Jeremy McDermott of the BBC or the then 'security expert' for the *Irish Times*, Jim Cusack. It would have noted from these sources that there were satellite photos of the trio making 'barrack busters' and there were in existence taped radio transmissions between FARC commanders about the 'three gringos being on their way'. Had they checked out the *Daily Telegraph* they would have found that it was actually a small nuclear-type device that Jim Monaghan was working on for use in London.

It would have taken evidence from the Minister of Justice and former Irish attorney general Michael McDowell to the effect that his sources – impeccable but, understandably, anonymous – had told him that the three were definitely passing on their terrorist know-how.

Within weeks of its investigation – for why wait two and a half years for a trial to confirm only what we already know! – the IMC would have told us that the IRA was involved in training FARC guerrillas in 'terrorist acts, the handling and manipulation of explosives and the fabrication of non-conventional weapons'.

The IMC would have faithfully repeated what journalists and unionists had said, that no foreign traveller would dare go into FARC territory for fear of being kidnapped (except, that is, an envoy from the Pope, the deputy head of the New York Stock Exchange, the Queen of Jordan and, eh, Mo Mowlam, amongst many hundreds).

And based on all these sources, the Independent Monitoring Commission would have got it absolutely, totally wrong, when one considers the actual 'not guilty' verdict of a casehardened Colombian judge, operating within a tainted judicial system where the conviction rate is around 100 per cent.

The IMC would have done its job of ignoring government and unionist breaches of the Agreement whilst providing the pretext for fining Sinn Féin and driving Sinn Féin out of the executive and handing its two ministerial posts over to unionists.

Given the context in which the IMC was established it has one purpose and one purpose only. Given that it reports to the British government (let's cut the nonsense that Dublin is an equal in this relationship), given that the British nominated two of the IMC's appointees and that they are the more senior of the quartet, only a fool would think that the IMC is ever going to report then act on the failure of the British government to live up to its responsibilities.

Its sole purpose is to concentrate on Irish republicans and provide propaganda for the British. Make no mistake about it, the war goes on: the actions and demands of the British and the unionists illustrate how both lust for the symbols of victory where they failed to attain the substance, failed to defeat the IRA and the republican cause.

Republicans are the target because – unlike the SDLP and Dublin – they refuse to back down on the issue of accountable, proper policing and refuse to kowtow to the British reneging on the full implementation of the Belfast Agreement. The SDLP becomes more pathetic by the day – acting out the logic of its stance, best illustrated by the Fitt-like speech of Seamus Mallon in the House of Commons where he derided the IMC fine imposed on Sinn Féin.

The aloofness of the IMC report shows that its authors have no understanding of the political culture within the nationalist community. The IMC's McCarthyist edict has rightly alarmed community groups, many of whose best workers are ex-prisoners and often members of Sinn Féin. The report said:

> No organisation, statutory, commercial or voluntary, should tolerate links with paramilitary groups or give legitimacy to them. In particular, societies and other similar organisations should make every effort to satisfy themselves that none of their members are linked to paramilitary groups. If there is any suspicion that they might be, then the onus should be on the person concerned to show there is no basis for that suspicion, not on the organisation to act only if it is proved. We will examine this whole issue in future reports.

In IMC land we are all guilty even when, like the Colombia Three, proven innocent.

Rosy Future for Sinn Féin

Andersonstown News, 14 June 2004

If the 2004 European and Irish local authority election results augur well for the future of one party above all others throughout Ireland, that party is Sinn Féin. Both North and South its vote has continued to increase and Bairbe de Brun's victory over the SDLP confirms the party's leadership of northern nationalists.

Throughout the twenty-six counties its representation at local government level has risen dramatically.

What a story! From IRA prisoner Bobby Sands - a 'blanket' man from Belfast, endorsed by nationalists in Fermanagh and South Tyrone in 1981 – to Sinn Féin rising nationally to become a force for change for the working class of this island and an example, internationally, of the fruits of struggle, the power of conviction and idealism.

For unionists it means that the nationalist community, historically neglected, then berated for seeking justice and equality, has never been more stoutly represented. And with confidence comes a generosity of spirit that the DUP, the other winner in the European election, will ignore to the political detriment of its community. As is its wont it will continue to perpetuate sectarian divisions, will serve a perverse and fundamentalist interpretation of life, and will test not only the mettle of nationalists but their goodwill and their patience.

For the Dublin government it means - the success of its citizenship referendum aside – that its northern policy has to shift away from the 'softly, softly' approach of the SDLP which unionists now look back at nostalgically, banked and exploited, to a more robust nationalist approach.

Politics (and with electoral endorsement comes responsibility) has superseded physical force, though we in the North continue to live in a society in a state of flux, a society which lacks legitimacy and consensus, and which is why there is continued ambivalence towards the role, status and future of the IRA.

The result in the North, combined with the vote for Sinn Féin in the South, is truly of historic proportions. It is a defiance of partition and the partitionist mentality. It unites political activists from Kerry to Kerrykeel, from Ballymun to Ballymurphy.

What happened to the SDLP, which once had a monopoly over the nationalist vote? Its candidate Martin Morgan is personable, did an excellent job as Belfast's Lord Mayor, yet was never in the running. The SDLP's politics, not its candidate, are to blame. The nonsense about us now living in a 'post-nationalist' era, at a time when nationalists were being assassinated and burnt out of their homes because of their religion and convictions, has left its residue. The SDLP's premature endorsement of the PSNI has also complicated matters and slowed down the momentum for change within policing

In the twenty-six counties Sinn Féin captured almost 12 per cent of the European vote and nearly doubled its local government vote, finishing as the fourth party at council level. Only a lack of sufficient organisation in other areas prevented it from tapping into a tangible sentiment for change. Its overall vote is set to translate into increased Dáil representation after the next election and the possible attainment of its objective of holding the balance of power.

This is clearly a remarkable success given how the mainstream parties in the South have ganged up against Sinn Féin, continuing to demonise the party and treating it as second-class. Nowhere is this more in evidence than in the double-standard of insisting that in the North unionists have to share power with nationalists (that is, Sinn Féin) whilst proclaiming that no constitutional party in the South will participate in coalition government with Sinn Féin. The electorate is not stupid. It will be interesting to see how long that position is maintained when Sinn Féin becomes the 'king' maker.

The charge against Sinn Féin was led by Minister of Justice, Michael McDowell. He specifically attacked the party for calling for the release of those in Castlerea prison convicted in relation to the killing of Garda Detective Jerry McCabe in Limerick, Munster, eight years ago. The release of prisoners under the terms of the Belfast Agreement was extremely difficult and emotional for many families who had lost loved ones in the conflict. But the release of political prisoners was a necessary component of conflict resolution and an attempt to draw a line through the past.

Two British soldiers convicted of murdering a young Belfast Catholic, Peter McBride, were freed several years ago without any comment or objection from McDowell. Yet in relation to the Castlerea prisoners, who qualify for release under the Belfast Agreement but remain behind bars, he stirred up public emotion in a partisan way aimed at undermining Sinn Féin's attraction to new voters. Remarkably, his campaign had only a limited, tangible effect on Sinn Féin's vote, even in Munster where the party increased its number of councillors.

The Fianna Fáil/PD coalition's other recent contribution to the peace process, and to the resumption of negotiations in Belfast on Tuesday, was to seriously weaken the integrity of the Belfast Agreement and strengthen the hand of the anti-Agreement DUP. For years the DUP has been told that the Belfast Agreement, an international treaty that was massively endorsed in referenda by the Irish people in 1998, is non-negotiable. One aspect of that Agreement, in light of amending Articles Two and Three as a gesture towards unionist sensibilities, was, as a gesture towards nationalist sensibilities, to define anyone born in the six (and twenty-six) counties as having the right to Irish citizenship.

But by hastily pushing through the citizenship referendum (without sufficient debate and consideration), which now empowers the government to amend the Irish Constitution and the definition of citizenship, the government has handed the DUP on a plate the argument that the fundamentals of the Agreement can be amended.

This throws the Belfast Agreement into further disarray but shows how developments on one side of the border can shape and influence politics on the other, and is where Sinn Féin comes into its own as an all-Ireland movement representing not only the past, but the future.

The Real Slow Learners

Irish Examiner, 21 June 2004

It was Seamus Mallon who famously once described the Belfast Agreement as 'Sunningdale for Slow Learners', a soundbite which was immediately seized upon by opponents and critics of the Republican Movement. They were claiming, in varying degrees, that what was negotiated in 1998 was available in the power-sharing Sunningdale arrangements of 1974 and therefore republicans, by continuing the armed struggle, had to bear major responsibility for the continuation of the conflict and the loss of all subsequent life.

At first glance the statement appears fairly credible until one waits a moment and thinks. When one compares the true state of affairs in 1974 with 1998 (and 2004) the statement soon falls apart. It wasn't just the IRA which was fighting - but all sides were still at war and entrenched, including the British army and loyalist paramilitaries. The British, who were continuing their policy of internment in Long Kesh, viewed the Sunningdale deal and the cross-border security cooperation stemming from it as having the potential to undermine the IRA, both politically and militarily.

So why wouldn't the IRA be opposed to Sunningdale?

Anti-Sunningdale unionists were soon in the ascendancy and were quoting power-sharing with the SDLP (not Sinn Féin!) and the proposed Council of Ireland as the reasons for their opposition rather than the continued existence of the IRA. By combining with loyalist paramilitaries in the UWC strike they showed that, like the UVF of 1912, they were prepared to invoke civil war in order to maintain unionist privilege and the sectarian status quo. Are those the circumstances in which the IRA should have or could have ceasefired?

In 1974 the SDLP supported extradition (the Criminal Law Jurisdiction Act) and succeeded in making absolutely no changes to the RUC and Special Branch. Twenty five years later, they jumped enthusiastically into bed with the PSNI before the hard work of creating an acceptable police service was completed. If the SDLP had been so right one would have expected this to be reflected at the polls, whereas the verdict of the electorate clearly tells a different story.

So who are the real slow learners?

Evidence that the SDLP continues to be viewed as the soft underbelly of nationalism came last week in the victory speech of the DUP's Jim Allister who joked at the defeat of the SDLP in the European election but haughtily in the same breath called upon it to join with his party in 'voluntary coalition… while the offer still stands!' The DUP has marched up to the top of a hill and says it won't come down until the IRA surrenders. It thinks that through intransigence it can thwart the rights of nationalists established in principle in the Belfast Agreement. Last Saturday on Radio Ulster, Peter Robinson when asked what form of credible IRA decommissioning would satisfy him, suggested IRA weapons being destroyed and filmed by CNN whilst a flute band marched around the pyre.

There's a real slow learner.

It is no accident that Sinn Féin is viewed by its supporters and opponents alike as tough and tenacious. Those qualities distinguish it from the SDLP and those qualities emerged from republican ideology and aspiration, the experience of repression, struggle and resistance, long years of imprisonment, the reading of history.

To have got even just to this position (the unsatisfactory, current stalemate), both communities and many British people and troops, paid a heavy price. At what point after 1974 had the IRA surrendered would unionist politicians have accepted power-sharing, all-Ireland bodies, the introduction of a new police service, a Bill of Rights, given their continued rejection of equality and parity of esteem? At what point would loyalist paramilitaries have decommissioned?

Make no mistake about it, the very perception of the IRA having been defeated would have encouraged unionist intransigence and triumphalism, not magnanimity. Under such a scenario the negotiating muscle of the nationalist community would have been blunted, nationalists demoralised.

The conflict continued so long for many reasons, including the obvious fact that the IRA (apart from the ceasefire of 1975) refused to give up, wanted to win, believed it could win, said it would win and that the British could be forced to negotiate. When armed struggle (the 'long war') didn't supply the breakthrough, republicans supplemented the propaganda war with electoral politics. But when a clear military stalemate emerged, even after the re-arming of the IRA, republicans had to examine the option of ceasefiring and negotiating in a way that would optimise gains and might do justice, if that were ever possible, to the suffering and sacrifices of the past.

It was always going to be a dangerous exploration, one that required nerve and which deserved comradeship and loyalty, and it was one that the republican leadership never balked at undertaking.

The protracted nature of the conflict was not caused by the IRA but was principally caused by the British government which lied about the nature of the problem and with unlimited resources fought a dirty, repressive, relentless war (whilst futilely attempting to co-opt the SDLP into a poor settlement for nationalists). For four years the British tried to intern the problem. It wasted five years attempting to criminalise republicans and twenty-five years demonising them. 'Talking to Gerry Adams would turn my stomach,' said John Major, at a time when his officials were secretly talking to the Republican Movement.

Thatcher was calling the IRA a criminal conspiracy at a time she was being briefed by military officials (Brigadier Glover's report) that the IRA was politically motivated and was never likely to be defeated ('the cause of republicanism will remain as long as the island of Ireland is divided', Glover wrote).

British Ministers and their prison officials told the world the prisoners were common criminals whilst the governor really believed that criminalisation was a false aim and was 'always going to fail' (from Chris Ryder's *Inside The Maze*).

And now MI5's real thinking has been revealed in remarks made by an officer to a maritime security conference in Orkney. He said 'the IRA fought a just cause' and 'won a successful campaign' over thirty years.

Refreshing as it is to hear such truths belatedly admitted, the tragedy is that had such truths been acted on at the time this conflict would never have lasted the time it did and many people would still be alive.

So, who were the real slow learners?

Unionism Misunderstood –
Some Clarifications

The Beliefs of Mahatma Taylor

During the negotiations before the signing of the Belfast Agreement on Good Friday 1998, John Taylor, said he wouldn't touch Senator George Mitchell's proposals for a settlement with 'a forty foot barge pole', though he did stand by his party leader, David Trimble. Here are some of the things that John did touch on, during an illustrious political career.

Andersonstown News, 28 February 2000

John Taylor, former MP, European MP, and deputy leader of the Ulster Unionist Party, was Home Affairs Minister at Stormont at the time of Bloody Sunday and was later shot and seriously wounded by the Official IRA. A staunch Orangeman, and a former member of the extreme European Right Group (led by the French National Front's Jean Marie Le Pen), he has now retired from politics to concentrate on his business and property interests. [*In June 2001 John Taylor became Lord Kilclooney, and in the Assembly elections of November 2003 he became a member for Strangford.*]

A short selection of his quotes over the past thirty years usefully reveals something of his attitude to violence and democracy.

On the belief that 'one-man-one-vote' should be the sole basis of the franchise for local government elections in 1968 he said: 'Nothing could be further from the truth. Both in the Republic and Britain individual voters are given many additional votes on the basis of property ownership.'

In March 1970 after a UVF bomb attack on the home of Austin Currie he said that the attack would be to Mr Currie's 'political advantage'.

Responding to the arrest of a man carrying a hurley after coming out of the Falls Park with his wife and kids, in June 1971, he said: 'I am not surprised that the army should take such action when one recalls the provocative manner in which hurleys were used in connection with an IRA funeral in the city.'

In July 1971 he defended the British army killings of two innocent men, Seamus Cusack and Desmond Beattie: 'I would defend without hesitation the action taken by the army authorities in the city of Londonderry against subversives during the past two weeks where it was necessary to shoot to kill. It may be necessary to shoot even more in the coming months.'

On the issue of 'decommissioning' (as it was then not called), September 1972, he told a Vanguard rally: 'There is far too much talk about the handing in of guns... The time has come when the loyalists of Ulster must not give in to the campaign by Harold Wilson and the SDLP to disarm the law-abiding citizens of this province.'

On the use of violence, he told another Vanguard rally in Tobermore in October 1972: 'We should make it clear that force means death and fighting, and whoever gets in our way, whether republicans or those sent by the British government, there would be killings.'

In July 1974 he called for the formation of a Home Guard: 'I believe that it will be armed, that it will be some 20,000 strong, that it will defeat the IRA and that it will be a force born of the people and with the people. It will be a force which London will learn to respect, a force which loyalist politicians will support with or without London government legislation.'

On nurses from the south working in hospitals in the north he had this to say in December 1984: 'Too many jobs are being given to people from the Republic and many of them probably sympathise with the killing campaign of the IRA.'

In January 1989 he criticised the Dublin government after its decision to award £500,000 to the Society of St. Vincent de Paul (clearly mistaking it for the Society of St. Vincent de Paul, the dissident, breakaway IRA faction).

On the Catholics (Roman ones) you see in the street, he said in September 1991: 'One out of every three Roman Catholics one meets is either a supporter of murder or, worse still, a murderer.'

On the GAA: 'I can understand why loyalist paramilitaries would attack the GAA as it is perceived as a political and divisive force.'

In September 1993 he spoke out about the sectarian killings of Catholics: 'There is in particular amongst the Catholic community now increasing fear of paramilitary activities... And, in a perverse way, this is something which may be helpful because they are now beginning to appreciate more clearly the fear that has existed within the Protestant community for the past twenty years...'

It is quite obvious from the above that John Taylor has no problems with guns – provided they are in the hands of loyalists, provided they are used to maintain and protect the union. It is also obvious from his attitude to the negotiations leading up to the Good Friday Agreement and his stance since then that he has never favoured reform or compromise. Indeed, he was delighted when the Assembly and all-Ireland bodies were suspended by Peter Mandelson and boasted that unionists were happy to be back to direct rule with no Irish frills attached.

His views, unfortunately, probably represent those of more than one half of the unionist people – 'the British presence', as Billy Hutchinson prefers them to be called. The reluctance of a majority of unionists or their representatives to engage with nationalists on an equal footing is assumed as being acceptable and is glossed over by the British government and the media. British governments have also used it as a pretext for refusing to redress the injustices that were institutionalised as a result of partition.

To paraphrase Jim Molyneaux, the IRA ceasefire represents the greatest threat to the union in seventy years. Reactionary unionism understands that. It needs a scapegoat. It needs cover.

It would prefer the IRA back at war.

If I Were a Political Correspondent…

Questions I would ask Doctor Ian Richard Kyle Paisley, MLA, MP, Euro MP, if I were a political correspondent who had just won the lottery and no longer needed my job.

Andersonstown News, 20 March 2000

Q. In the penal days Popish clergy were banished from Ireland. Informers could get a bounty of £50 per Catholic bishop. Do you think this was a good going-rate?

Q. I know you are a strict Sabbatarian but have you ever had a wee swing on a Sunday or accidentally caught yourself whistling? Do you always wait until after midnight before you read the Sunday newspapers and, if so, who goes out and buys them at that hour? If must be handy having a corner shop open all the time.

Q. Have you never taken a drink – even a wee sniff?

Q. Have you ever cha-chaad, tangoed, jived or twisted? Ever sun-bathed in your bathing costume on the beach?

Q. Who's your favourite Beatle? Or are you a Stones man?

Q. Do you have an RTÉ aerial?

Interlude I

June 1959. A rally at the corner of Percy Street and the lower Shankill. Ian preaches Christ's message:

> You people of the Shankill Road, what's wrong with you? Number 425 Shankill Road – do you know who lives there? Pope's men, that's who! Fortes ice-cream shop, Italian Papists on the Shankill Road! How about 56 Aden Street? For 97 years a Protestant lived in that house and now there's a Papisher in it. Crimea Street, number 38! Twenty five years that house has been up, 24 years a Protestant lived there but there's a Papisher there now.

Q. You once claimed that Catholics worshipped gigantic phalluses. Do you still believe this?

Q. Did you ever get taking that oul Tricolour out of that window?

Q. Are the collections in the Martyrs Memorial Church silent?

Q. How much are you worth?

Interlude II

1966. UVF man Hugh McClean has just been charged with murdering 18-year-old Beechmount youth, Peter Ward, outside the Malvern Arms. He says: 'I am terribly sorry I ever heard of that man Paisley or decided to follow him. I am definitely ashamed of myself to be in such a position.'

Q. Were you a wee bit hurt by McClean's ingratitude?

Q. When you yourself were a jailbird did you wear the prison uniform?

Q. Were you a good cook in the prison kitchen?

Q. Was the exam for the Doctorate hard?

Q. Does the name Jimmy Dempsey ring a bell? In September 1969 you addressed your supporters in the Village area who later tried several times to march up Broadway and take down a barricade at Iveagh Street. Jimmy Dempsey dropped dead during one of these attempted invasions of his district.

Q. You take the Bible literally as the word of God and believe that we are all descended from Adam and Eve. Does that mean you are related to Gerry Adams – or, worse still, Pope John Paul II?

Q. Were you actually waving a shotgun licence on that Antrim hillside in the middle of the night all those years ago, or were you sneezing into a hankie?

Q. What ever happened to your wee Ulster Resistance red beret?

Q. Where'd you and Willie McCrea get the accents?

Q. During the loyalist strike of May 1977, organised by the UDA and yourself, Kenny McClinton shot dead Citybus driver Harry Bradshaw because he didn't join the stoppage. How are things these days between you and Pastor Kenny?

Interlude III

Ballycastle, 12 July 1997. Ian addressing the Independent Orange Order: 'I walked the Garvaghy Road and led a crowd of a thousand men without permission, up and down it, and they never fired a peanut at us. They came to their bedroom windows and they thought they were already in Purgatory by the look on their faces; they were so amazed that these men were up there, and there was enough of us to keep them in that order.'

Q. Was Peter's mistake in Clontibret to lead a crowd of just 500 men? Why did you help Peter-the-Punt pay his £15,000 fine? Did you not want him to go to jail and become a member of the Felons Club?

Q. Were you ever in a fight?

Q. Do you use Brylcream?

Q. When you are making a serious point you close your eyes for several seconds as you speak. What is it you are seeing?

Q. Why did you give your old trench coat to Gerry Kelly?

Q. Was David Irvine ever in your parlour?

Q. Have UVF men ever seen the colour of your wallpaper?

Q. Do you love me?

Q. Why doesn't Ian Jnr have a sense of humour?

Q. Is Rhonda still at the old crayons?

Q. Why do you think the IRA's never shot you?

Q. Do you think they think you're an oul eejit?

The Siege of Finaghy Road North

On the kid-gloves' approach from the RUC to loyalists rioting in Drumcree and blocking roads in Belfast, Down and Antrim, in protest against being banned from marching down their 'traditional route', Garvaghy Road.

Andersonstown News, 10 July 2000

A Tyrone labourer was driving home three nights ago when just outside the village of Clough in County Down he turned a corner and was stopped by up to ten masked people who had just emerged from a lane. As far as we know they weren't dispossessed kids-without-a-summer-school, frustrated by the bad weather and out for a bit of excitement. Nor did they belong to that feared band of international terrorists, otherwise known as Roden Street mothers-and-toddlers-group-on-steroids, who, at the drop of a nappy, can seal off the Western World.

These were serious guys.

They asked him where he was coming from and he had the presence of mind to say, Kilkeel, which in our circumscribed universe is, unfortunately, synonymous with Protestantism. They asked him where he was going, and, again, he had the presence of mind to say, Dunmurry village.

'Well then', one of them said, 'you should know *The Sash*. Sing us *The Sash!*' Somewhere, in the phantom fog of memory, most of us probably know a few bytes of lyrics that go, 'it was old and it was beautiful' and 'it was the Sash my father wore', but that's probably it. And that was as far as it went for our Tyrone traveller who, heart-pounding, quickly stuck his car into reverse and slammed down the accelerator, narrowly escaping under a hail of bricks and bottles, as he prayed to God that he wasn't going to run into another block just behind him.

He was lucky to escape with his life.

He didn't report the incident to the RUC. What was the point?, he said. What were they going to do about it? We know the answer. The answer lies in the disparity between the magnitude of the attacks on Catholic homes, on the RUC and British army personnel, and the number of arrests. In the disparity between the petrol and paint bombs thrown and the number of plastic bullets fired in response. In the velvet-glove approach to half a dozen people with prams blocking the M1 for five hours in comparison to the iron-fist approach to a half-hour Saoirse closure of another stretch of the West link at the Grosvenor Road just a few years ago. The poor RUC. The poor, Protestant RUC, who still don't get it.

Firstly, let it be clear that I don't believe that tanks should be used to run down demonstrators in the way that happened to Dermot McShane in Derry in July 1996, or that women and kids should be batoned or shot by plastic bullets. What I am saying is that there should be one law and if it proves to be excessive then people will unite in opposition to its repressiveness, and if it proves to be fair then people will support it. But the behaviour of the RUC this week is clearly understood by the world – it can't be easy for Trevor to arrest Cousin Billy or Norman, or spray them with cold water. And that is why the RUC has to go and a new start has to be made. But given the rejection by Peter Mandelson at Westminster of the SDLP's proposals to insert in the legislation a clear-break, things do not augur well.

While republicans have, thankfully, adopted a pragmatic approach the British, unfortunately, are still stuck in the past, still cannot get out of the old groove and a perverse loyalty to the ways of King Billy and the Orangemen. Produce a constabulary in this vein and nationalists will have nothing to do with it and, worse, some nationalists/republicans will shoot members of this constabulary. And if many support such a reaction it becomes an armed struggle and the situation is back in polarisation. This is the dice that the British toss and toy with.

Did you see Peter Mandelson interviewed on television after Harold Gracey refused to condemn the attacks on Catholic homes, the burning of cars and lorries, the setting up of illegal roadblocks, the building of barricades, the rioting and petrol-bombing of the RUC and British army, the refusal to talk with the Parades Commission and real people – those who live on the Garvaghy Road?

'I am sorry that Harold has not condemned it… He is a peaceable man,' said Peter Mandelson as if this were a tiff over a game of dominoes, and not a violent battle within unionism over the Good Friday Agreement and coming to terms with justice and equality.

If this were simply the case of people being robbed off their tradition or culture or rights then it is a battle that would have been fought before 1969. I have said this before and I repeat: the Orangemen marched up Broadway, onto the Falls Road, which was bedecked with red, white and blue bunting, and played *God Save The Queen* outside Broadway Presbyterian Church (now an Cultúrlann) up until 1965 when the demographics – not nationalist rioting or a residents' group – taught them the absurdity of their position. This was their traditional route. Why aren't they fighting over that? Better still, they marched to the Field at Finaghy Road North until the Sixties, as well. Of course, this was before the discovery of the wheel, before Neil Armstrong walked on the moon and the invention of CDs. Still, it begs the question: why aren't they fighting over the traditional route to the once-Orange capital of Ulster, Finaghy Road North?

I was dismayed when the Parades Commission, which is supposed to be objective, caved into the sectarian violence and intimidation, and proposed that the Orangemen could get marching down the Garvaghy Road within three-to-five months if they agreed to the Commission's 'road map', which includes engaging in direct dialogue. Whether Orange feet ever get on the Garvaghy Road is up to the nobility and graciousness of the people of that area, though it would be hard to stomach. Freedom is about having the choice. One resident of the Garvaghy Road said last Friday:

'I don't care if they want to walk through my living room. But if they do they have to have the manners to rap on my front door first. That is what we want. We want them to rap the door.'

In other words, we are human beings. And we are equal.

Giving a Dog a Bad Name

A profile of Johnny Adair after he was returned to jail having started a loyalist feud.

Andersonstown News, 28 August 2000

A load of old women,' is how UFF commander Johnny Adair described the leaders of his organisation's political wing, the Ulster Democratic Party (UDP) just before his arrest in 1994 on a charge of 'directing terrorism'. Recently, Adair physically threatened and belittled UDP leader Gary McMichael, describing him as 'toothless' because he was too moderate and had never fired a shot.

If this is how Adair treats one of his own colleagues you can imagine his attitude to nationalists or his adversaries in the Ulster Volunteer Force and its political wing, the Progressive Unionist Party with whom the Ulster Freedom Fighters are now at civil war. The feud has been described by the media and by Peter Mandelson as a 'turf war' over drugs and racketeering, a claim dismissed by Billy Hutchinson of the PUP who alleges that the real drug barons belong to the LVF and the UFF. Undoubtedly, drugs and racketeering are factors in this conflict, but the feud is also part of a major realignment of loyalist paramilitaries, growing numbers of whom are not happy with the Belfast Agreement, which they increasingly view as a victory for nationalists and republicans.

While the UVF has butchered Catholics in the past, and would have little hesitation doing so again, it appears to be genuinely dedicated to its cease-fire. Its political wing, the PUP, has at least a mandate, though small, with two representatives, Hutchinson and David Ervine, in the Assembly. The UFF, on the other hand, which is more corrupt, has little stake in politics and is divided over the Agreement. Its UDP candidate couldn't even save his deposit in a council by-election in the loyalist stronghold of Rathcoole.

Adair (36) cut his teeth in 'C' Battalion of the UFF on the Shankill Road, becoming an 'Area Commander'. In the late eighties he was increasingly critical of the old UFF leadership, which he saw as becoming too comfortable, cosy and corrupt. When some of its leaders were arrested and jailed as a result of the Stevens' Inquiry into missing RUC and British army files, Adair quickly rose to the top and reinvigorated the Shankill Brigade, which was behind some of the worse sectarian killings of the 1990s. It was around this time that he earned the sobriquet, 'Mad Dog'. It says something of his mentality that he is extremely proud of this term of abuse, usually used to demonise an individual. (Last Saturday he cheerily introduced his two-year-old son to a reporter as 'Mad Pup'.)

Such is his ego that he was forever boasting about his activities. Whilst driving a journalist from *The Guardian* around the Shankill in 1993 he discovered she was a Catholic and told her with grisly connotation that Catholics normally travelled in the boot of his car. He also boasted to RUC men in the street about his activities and that he was untouchable. He didn't know that he was being secretly recorded until he was arrested and charged in 1994 with 'directing terrorism'. He pleaded guilty – which means that we didn't get to hear the details of his activities – and was sentenced to sixteen years.

In the H-Blocks he was filmed by a BBC documentary team against a back-drop of wall murals, some of which read: 'Yabba, Yabba, Doo/Any Fenian Will Do'; 'Kill 'Em All,/ Let God Sort 'Em Out'. One of the murals he instigated on the Shankill Road was of a slogan, 'Wouldn't it be great if it was like this all the time!' underneath various banners bearing the names Greysteel, Sean Graham's bookmakers and the Devenish Arms – scenes of UFF slaughter of innocent Catholics.

Released last September under the early release scheme, he made no attempt to usurp the current Brigade Commander of the Shankill UFF simply because this man was an ally who shared Adair's opposition to the Belfast Agreement. And, anyway, Adair's authority and following, derived from his reputation for ruthlessness, stretches well beyond Belfast. Dismissive of the more reasonable Gary McMichael, he preferred the company of the UDP's John White, a double murderer, who in 1973 kidnapped and stabbed to death Senator Paddy Wilson and his Protestant friend, Irene Andrews. White, who enjoys a lavish lifestyle and lives in an expensive house on North Down's 'Gold Coast', has been repeatedly asked to explain the source of his vast wealth. He denied to the BBC being a drug baron and says that he has been lucky in property speculation and with his investments.

The Loyalist Volunteer Force was set up by the late Billy Wright who split from the UVF because he disagreed with its cease-fire. It is based mainly in Portadown and in parts of County Antrim. Three years ago the UVF unsuccessfully attempted to crush it. After Wright's assassination in Long Kesh by the INLA the LVF floundered for a time but last January in Portadown it killed Bobby Jameson, Mid-Ulster Commander of the UVF. The killings then spread to Belfast as the LVF appeared to become more assertive. However, the UVF strongly suspected that although the shootings were either claimed by or attributed to the LVF, the fingerprints of a certain UFF area commander were all over them.

This summer Adair attempted to emulate his hero, the late Billy Wright, by appearing alongside the Portadown Orangemen at Drumcree. His appearance a short time later, applauding an LVF show of strength beside an 'Eleventh night' bonfire, was meant to emphasise a continuity. When the Orange demand to get marching down Garvaghy Road was backed up by UFF and LVF violence, including the hijacking and burning of vehicles in Protestant areas by callow youths – Johnny's new recruits – mainstream unionists were dismayed and many Orangemen disgusted at the destruction. The presence of Johnny Adair, and the refusal of Harold Gracey, District Master of the Portadown Brethren, to condemn the violence, resulted in a debacle for the Orangemen at Drumcree.

Although publicly supporting the Belfast Agreement, Adair is privately opposed to it. All the evidence points to him trying to establish a new organisation (tentatively called the Loyalist Freedom Fighters) made up from the LVF, dissident UFF members, and religious fundamentalists in the Orange Volunteers and Red Hand Commandos. It was his 'C' Company that in July threatened to carry out reprisals against Catholics for 'a recent series of attacks on Protestant homes', only for the Housing Executive, supported by the RUC, to deny that Protestants had been attacked. Figures showed that the only people recently intimidated from their homes were eleven Catholic families. (In fact, over one hundred Catholic homes have been attacked in the past six weeks, receiving little media coverage.)

Days later a number of houses on the Shankill Road did have their windows smashed in an incident which is generally believed to have been contrived. This was quickly followed by gangs of UFF men driving into Catholic areas, shooting-up streets, paint-bombing houses and smashing up cars in a blatant attempt to provoke the IRA into breaking its cease-fire and having Sinn Féin removed from the power-sharing executive.

Adair was again in the news two weeks ago when a pipe bomb exploded near his car. He claimed it was an IRA assassination bid, a claim dismissed by the RUC. Other loyalists suggest that the pipe bomb exploded prematurely when it was in transit.

Months of planning had gone into last week's 'carnival', an exclusively-UFF event, complete with masked and uniformed men and a firing party on stage with Adair, the convicted murderer Michael Stone and the deputy Lord Mayor of Belfast, the UDP's Frank McCoubrey. (Ulster Unionists voted for McCoubrey back in June, despite his paramilitary connections, and opposed Sinn Féin's Alex Maskey for the mayorship on the grounds that Sinn Féin had links with the IRA!) The centrepiece of the day's events was the unveiling of sectarian and triumphalist murals along the length of the Shankill Road, effectively claiming all of it as UFF territory. The UVF, which is numerically smaller than the UFF and with a relatively more respectable image, believed they had an agreement through direct talks with the UFF that there would be no LVF presence. As we now know an LVF flag was flaunted outside a UVF-patronised pub and the long-simmering feud was sparked, with gunmen opening fire into the pub and laying siege to it.

Fifteen families with UVF connections were then driven from their Shankill Road homes, including veteran loyalist icon Gusty Spence. The UVF retaliated on Monday by killing Jackie Coulter and Bobby Mahood. These killings had the effect of uniting the UFF, some of whose Brigade Commanders despise the megalomaniac Adair who has on more than one occasion embarrassed them and undermined the loyalist cause.

A reporter from the pro-unionist *News Letter* happened to be on the Shankill Road just after the fatal shootings on Monday. She wrote: 'It was mob rule in broad daylight and convicted terror boss Johnny Adair was there at its heart, as the offices of the PUP were subjected to a frenzied attack…. I came across the feared former UFF leader at a crucial moment. At least 30 men launched a frenzied attack on the PUP office… The most extraordinary sight was Adair. Thrashing his arms about, tearing round in circles, his face full of creases and fury, he was like a man possessed.'

The significance of Peter Mandelson's decision to deploy British soldiers instead of drafting in extra RUC officers has not been lost on nationalists. Clearly, the Protestant RUC could not be totally trusted to police its own people on the Shankill Road. It was only after Adair repeatedly embarrassed the authorities that the RUC were ordered to arrest him.

Having experienced several republican feuds I know something of the sheer terror that the people of the Shankill Road are living under. The UFF and the UVF have rejected calls for mediation and have predicted further reprisals after a third man with UVF connections was shot dead on Wednesday night.

Meantime, the man primarily responsible for this latest outbreak of violence is sitting with his feet up in a cell in Maghaberry Prison – probably the safest place for him.

Willie Wonky

On the election of the DUP's Willie McCrea in a by-election in South Antrim in September 2000.

Andersonstown News, 25 September 2000

O ccasionally, documentaries on the history of the conflict re-run footage of the People's Democracy march from Belfast to Derry in January 1969. Before they are attacked at Burntollet, the marchers pass through south Derry. Along the road they are verbally abused by loyalists. If you scrutinise the footage closely you will see an apoplectic 20-year-old screaming at the students who are demanding 'one man, one vote' and an end to discrimination.

Two years later this same man is arrested and convicted for riotous behaviour in Dungiven. Closer to God than the rest of us, it wasn't until 1982 that I ran into him, in a street in Drumquin, County Tyrone, when we were electioneering. He completely ignored me when I wished him the top-of-the-morning and offered to share my bottle of buttermilk. No sense of humour whatsoever.

In June 1983 I was the Sinn Féin candidate in Mid-Ulster. On election day, loyalists repeatedly went into the polling station in the village of Coagh and threatened the Sinn Féin agent who had been challenging those impersonating. Thoroughly intimidated, the agent pulled out and considerable voting recommenced. At 9.30pm the DUP agent in the school in the nationalist village of Mountfield closed the station, alleging that there was personation. We arrived five minutes before the close of poll and got the station re-opened, but over a hundred people didn't get to vote.

The following day, my election agent Sean Begley and I parked our car in Campsie, Omagh, where the count was taking place. As we walked across the car park a tall, balding man suddenly pulled a gun on us and we thought we were going to be shot. For a few moments no one moved. Then the Reverend William McCrea emerged from a car and his bodyguard put his gun away.

At the count in Omagh McCrea's votes and mine climbed together. The unionist vote was split between McCrea and Willie Thompson of the Ulster Unionist Party.

The nationalist vote was split between Denis Haughey of the SDLP and myself. In the space of eight months Sinn Féin in Mid-Ulster was overturning an SDLP lead of four thousand votes.

As we got down to the last couple of hundred votes McCrea stopped talking, first, to his wife, then, to his bodyguards, then, to fellow DUP members. He paced the floor. Willie Thompson came over to me, jubilant. 'You're going to beat him!' he said. 'You're going to beat him!'

As the last vote was counted McCrea beat me by 78 votes. We asked for a re-count. One of my votes was discovered in his pile; one of his in mine. He was the winner by 78 votes. He got up and prayed to God in the ceiling for giving him victory and gave me some abuse. Then I wet myself as he sang a hymn. He was the MP for Mid-Ulster, a constituency with a nationalist majority, for the next fourteen years.

The constituency boundaries were later re-drawn and Martin McGuinness defeated him in the general election of 1997, despite the nationalist vote being split between McGuinness and Denis Haughey. That night there was a victory do in the Felons Club. I brought along one of Reverend Willie's albums, one with that same gospel song that he had personally performed for me fourteen years previously. Shockingly, the heathens in the Felons got up and jived to it. It was sweet. I am so shallow.

A BBC crew filmed McCrea's supporters waiting for their new MP to emerge from the count in Newtownabbey in the early hours of Thursday morning after the by-election in South Antrim. Why can I not take their Christianity seriously? Is it residual Catholic snobbishness? One of McCrea's supporters, not the best crooner in the world, sang, 'Simply The Best', the anthem of the Ulster Freedom Fighters. What's wrong with that? Willie shared a platform with Billy Wright who shot kids. Officiated at his funeral service. Twenty-five years ago Willie officiated at the funeral services for Harris Boyle and Wesley Somerville, two UVF members who were killed by their own bomb outside Banbridge as they slayed members of the Miami Showband.

So what are we to make of this vote? Okay, it was raining. Okay, David Burnside is a sleeping pill. But the soprano won, Trimble lost, and the Good Friday Agreement takes yet another big knock, with the usual cries for nationalists and republicans to turn their pockets inside out and give more.

Let's call the whole thing off, is a very tempting number.

The fact is that the DUP is absolutely right. The majority of unionists, unfortunately, do not want to share power. Some of them are afraid, many have been hurt, some of them are full of bitterness or hatred or both. Their attitudes are a mixed product of partition, complacency in never having to consider another viewpoint, triumphalism and intransigence, all coming to grief in a clash with reality and the nationalist demand for equality. The six-county state was not built with accommodation in mind.

And that is why the Good Friday Agreement, but more so the principles upon which it was founded, has such potential. Through treaty, through law, through public challenge and lobbying, the British government is held to account over equality, over justice, over policing, and, importantly, over unionism.

The Good Friday Agreement can be binned but those principles cannot be evaded. Back in the 1960s, which is were we came in, central government in the USA had a choice on how to deal with racism in the deep South. It could have caved in to those local 'democracies' which would not implement equality legislation. But it was firm, it implemented the law, it stood up to bigotry. It won the day – though there are still massive inequalities, and racism, in North America.

That is the test for this or any British government. It's their problem.

Unionism in a State

Andersonstown News, 2 July 2001

A s far as democracy is concerned, those folk ain't house trained yet… we do actually need to see the Assembly running so the checks and balances that are there eventually bring them to heel.'

So said David Trimble a year ago, comparing Sinn Féin elected representatives to dogs, only days after the IRA broke the political deadlock with an initiative described as 'a sensational development' by one national newspaper. After tortuous negotiations at Hillsborough in May 2000 – aimed at achieving nothing more than had already been agreed, that is, the full implementation of the Belfast Agreement – the British government promised to honour its commitments on the Patten Commission and on demilitarisation by June 2001.

The IRA, in a controversial decision which Gerry Adams later admitted dismayed and worried activists and grassroots republicans, announced: 'The contents of a number of our arms dumps will be inspected by agreed third parties who will report that they have done so to the IICD [Independent International Commission on Decommissioning]. The dumps will be re-inspected regularly to ensure that the weapons have remained secure.'

The IRA said that progress on the arms issue would be determined by all participants keeping their side of the bargain. 'The full implementation, on a progressive and irreversible basis by the two governments, especially the British government, of what they have agreed will provide a political context, in an enduring political process, with the potential to remove the causes of conflict, and in which Irish republicans, and unionists can, as equals, pursue our respective political objectives peacefully. In that context the IRA leadership will initiate a process that will completely and verifiably put IRA arms beyond use.'

And so the Executive and the Assembly were re-established and local politicians went back to work. However, problems soon emerged when Secretary of State Peter Mandelson on 17 May told the House of Commons that he intended incorporating the name of the RUC in the 'title deeds' of the new police service, and then began eviscerating the heart of the Patten proposals that were supposed to signal a new beginning. Republicans warned Tony Blair time and time again that this represented a reneging on the context in which the IRA made its pledges. The only message that came back was: Poor David, he needs our help and support.

Last October David Trimble banned the two Sinn Féin ministers, Martin McGuinness and Bairbre de Brun, from attending North/South ministerial meetings, a ban which continues despite being declared unlawful. In December and in March the IRA called upon the British to return to the Agreement but these warnings were never treated with the same seriousness as David Trimble's continual threats, repeated on the eve of the general election, to resign as First Minister if the IRA didn't begin decommissioning. And so Tarzan set himself a date, 1 July, and now off he's swung with Daphne by his side.

Unionists first used the demand for decommissioning in the wake of the IRA's cease-fire in 1994 and viewed it then as a way of keeping Sinn Féin out of negotiations, as they view it now as a way of keeping Sinn Féin out of the Executive. They made decommissioning synonymous with IRA defeat and surrender and as a form of atonement. Every IRA gesture in support of peace was rejected or called into question.

Unionists have actually made it difficult for the IRA, which also has a proud constituency, to put its guns beyond use. And, of course, unionist double standards are astonishing. Loyalists are assassinating Catholics, burning churches, bombing Catholic homes, invading Catholic districts, preventing children from going to school, manufacturing new pipe bombs and explosives, yet David Trimble has been concerned only with the silent guns of the IRA. When was the last time David Trimble met with the UDA and UVF to discuss decommissioning? When was the first time?

Irish people, North and South, overwhelmingly voted for the Belfast Agreement in the referenda, yet David Trimble delayed setting up the Executive for eighteen months and, supported by Peter Mandelson, pulled it down after seventy-odd days by threatening to resign. In the meantime, his procrastination fed the growth of republican dissidence. He had a perfect opportunity to move the peace and political processes forward when in the summer of 1998 both communities were united in revulsion against the burning to death of the Quinn children and the Omagh bombing, but instead his first major speech after those terrible events was to launch an attack on the IRA over decommissioning.

Under the Belfast Agreement 'all participants' pledged 'to use any influence they may have, to achieve the decommissioning of all paramilitary arms within two years following endorsement in referendums North and South of the Agreement and in the context of the implementation of the overall settlement.'

In the context of the implementation of the overall settlement.

That was the agreement that the British reneged on by indulging the unionists in their resistance to change and reform. IRA guns are not the real issue. The real issue is unionism's difficulty in sharing police, power and peace with republicans and nationalists because that begs the huge question: What was the state of Northern Ireland all about?

Shame on Them

Holy Cross schoolchildren attacked by loyalists at Glenbryn, North Belfast.

Andersonstown News, 10 September 2001

They called them slugs, scum, bastards, rats, whores, filth, shite. They spat upon them. Hurled stones, bottles, ball bearings, wooden fences, golf balls, a bucket of urine and a bomb. A chorus sang: 'Who let the Fenians out? Woof, woof!' One six-year-old girl was left in tears when a man, in his forties, labelled her 'Dumbo' and called her a 'big-eared bastard'.

Then, when all their intimidation failed and the parents continued walking their kids to school, they shouted, 'Shame on you!' when they should have been thinking, 'Shame on us.'

The people of Glenbryn are unionists, though middle-class unionists prefer the term 'loyalists' in attempting to distance themselves from this dark side of unionism. The people of Glenbryn say they have legitimate grievances but you couldn't hear what those were above their own din. Looking at their houses, they are not rich people. The local Protestant school is dilapidated. Whoever they elected over the years to look after their interests did not do a good job. Their MP, who won't sit in the same studio with certain elected representatives, sends out the apartheid message, 'the other side is inferior'.

Catholic parents faced a terrible personal dilemma in deciding whether to take their children to school along Ardoyne Road and risk serious injury or death or go in by the back door. Were they right to choose the former? Absolutely. They have done a service to the cause of civil rights. Before the end of the week, however, some people, including British journalists especially, whom I watched interviewing, were beginning to shift the pressure onto the parents of the Holy Cross schoolchildren. One journalist asked, what can be the mentality of parents who, after their children have been stoned and abused, still insist they would take the same route the following day? They were becoming part of the chorus shouting, 'Shame on you!' when they should have been thinking, 'Shame on us.'

They would not have asked Asian or Jewish parents if fascists in London were forcing their kids to run a gauntlet, 'Why don't you just take the long route and use the back door?' They would, in fact, have been calling upon the Prime Minister not to bow to naked racism. They would have been calling for arrests by the score for incitement.

To the people of Glenbryn and their kids the union, the state of Northern Ireland, has brought nothing but bunting and flags, UDA party packs of e-tabs and heroin, and, tragically for themselves and for us, a creaking superiority complex which is essentially racist and which is why what is happening to those Catholic schoolgirls bears comparison with what happened to blacks in the USA.

Rosa Parks, a seamstress and civil rights activist in Montgomery, Alabama, became a symbol of African Americans' determination to attain their civil rights. In 1955 she was arrested for disobeying a city law that required blacks to give up their seats when white people wished to sit in their seats or in the same row. She said she was no longer prepared to sit at the back of the bus, which is the same as saying, I'm not prepared to go in the back door.

Montgomery's blacks protested her arrest by refusing to ride the buses. Their protest lasted 382 days, which entailed a lot of suffering, a lot of walking. But it ended in victory when the city abolished the bus law. It would have been safer but wrong to shift seats. Rosa Parks was right.

On September 2, 1957, the night before school was to start, Arkansas Governor Orval Faubus, who opposed integration, called out the state's National Guard to surround Little Rock Central High School and prevent any black students from entering. A federal judge granted an injunction against the governor's use of National Guard troops and they were withdrawn on September 20.

When school resumed on September 23, about 1,000 protestors gathered in front of the school. The police escorted nine black students to a side door where they quietly entered the building, as classes were to begin. When the mob learned the blacks were inside, they began to challenge the police and surge toward the school with shouts and threats. Fearful the police would be unable to control the crowd, the school administration moved the black students out a side door before noon.

On September 25th President Eisenhower sent in 1,000 soldiers to ensure that the nine black students could go to school, through the front door. In the case of Ardoyne the kids aren't trying to force their way into a Protestant school, but their own school! It would have been safer but wrong for the black students to go to a different school. The nine students were right.

In 1962, James Meredith, a black who served in the US Air Force from 1951 to 1960, applied to the University of Mississippi. The public, including the governor of Mississippi, tried to prevent Meredith from registering for classes. Attorney

General Robert Kennedy sent federal marshals to protect him. A riot broke out on his first night on campus. Two bystanders were killed and 160 marshals were wounded. In the end, the university was integrated and Meredith graduated in 1964. It would have been safer but wrong for James Meredith to go to a different university. James Meredith was right.

In 2001 it would have been safer but wrong for eighty school kids and their parents to have gone the long way and used the back door, with the sign on it that reads '1968'. They were right. Absolutely right. And for fighting for their children, for raising our dignity, for taking risks, we owe them a great debt of gratitude.

Bending the Rules

Andersonstown News, 5 November 2001

Last month I was at the launch of the Linenhall Library's CD-ROM, 'Troubled Images' – a unique record of the posters, election literature and other images brought out by all sides to the conflict as part of the propaganda war. Many politicians, protagonists and journalists were present, including Cedric Wilson. After he split from Bob McCartney's UK Unionist Party Wilson founded the Northern Ireland Unionist Party, which is anti-Agreement.

He happened to be close to the sandwiches and as I went to satisfy my appetite we made eye-contact. I began to make small talk but suddenly he swirled around on his heels so that he was facing the opposite direction. The woman with him had to do the same. At first I found this funny and on my second date with a salmon sandwich I tried to talk to him again. But before I knew it I was staring at the back of his head, which was getting smaller as he disappeared down the history aisle. His action was pathetic.

Just twenty-four hours earlier I had been up at the Assembly watching the debate on the motion proposing the exclusion of Sinn Féin from the Executive, which ultimately fell because it didn't have the required cross-party consensus. Listening to the asinine comments of William McCrea and Sammy Wilson – though the snide remarks, particularly those aimed at women, were not exclusively from the DUP benches – it was obvious that there will never be a meeting of minds, agreement, reconciliation between these representatives of unreconstructed unionism and republicans/nationalists.

One has only to dip into Mairtin Ó Muilleoir's *Dome of Delight* detailing the antics of unionist councillors at Belfast City Hall to be reminded that the same politicians have learnt nothing and will never admit that fifty years of unionist misrule was the largest single contributing factor to the outbreak of violence in the North. Their arrogance and ignorance are breathtaking.

This week a coalition of fifty per cent plus one of Anti-Agreement Assembly members were able to block the re-election of David Trimble as First Minister by the rest of the Assembly: that is, thirty per cent blocked the will of seventy per cent. Those were the rules, which everyone went along with. Those rules were initially aimed at curbing unionist abuse vis-à-vis nationalist rights, but have now successfully been used against other (pro-Agreement) unionists.

It would be farcical for some members of the Alliance Party, mimicking the ineffectual tactic of the Women's Coalition, to now redesignate themselves as 'unionist' in order to create the right arithmetic for Trimble's election. (As I write this on Saturday, they have not done so.) Similarly, there is talk that the British government may bring in legislation that would have the effect of allowing David Trimble to be elected on a lesser unionist vote (though still an overall majority of Assembly members).

These machinations may well ensure that the Assembly limps along for another while but they would only be postponing confronting the fact that over half of the unionist representatives, presumably representing over half the unionist electorate, so despise equality and justice and reconciliation with the nationalist community that they are prepared to jeopardise the Assembly (because the Assembly isn't the Orange Hall which they have been demanding since 1972).

Their strategy has two objectives. Firstly, they want an election, particularly the DUP, which believes it can overtake the Ulster Unionist Party. Secondly, it hopes that after an election the outcome will lead to a renegotiation of the Belfast Agreement on terms more favourable to the interests of sectarian unionism and antipathetic to the rights of nationalists.

Neither the British government, the Ulster Unionist Party nor the SDLP favour an election, given that it is anticipated that the DUP and Sinn Féin would perform handsomely and gain primacy within each community.

Listening to the DUP spokespersons, the Ulster Unionist rebels, Bob McCartney and Cedric Wilson, et al, it is clear that there is no give, that the unprecedented gesture by the IRA of putting some guns beyond use has had no effect (though, elsewhere universally welcomed), that the amendment of Articles 2 & 3 was merely to be pocketed, that no compromise is to be brooked, no reciprocation made to the nationalist and republican offer of peace and friendship.

Do these people take nationalists for idiots? Do they think that nationalists will meekly go back into their ghettoes and accept a dilution of the principles behind the Belfast Agreement?

I know that the major concern of republicans is that a political vacuum is extremely dangerous. Events can take on a momentum of their own and uncontrollable violence could easily erupt. It was in the interests of stability and political progress that the republican leadership did what it did with the great gamble of two weeks ago, a gesture that will stand in its stead and which it should have no cause to regret.

Republicans cannot force the majority of unionists to support the Belfast Agreement, the Executive and Assembly, and if those cannot work and they collapse then that fact-of-life has to be faced, and the British government must be compelled to accept that unionist extremism is the problem today, just as it was in 1920.

Let's Not Talk

Why loyalists cannot be depicted as sympathetic characters on stage or in film.

Andersonstown News, 4 February 2002

A week ago I was phoned by a BBC television producer: would I take part in their monthly discussion programme, 'Let's Talk'? Now, I would prefer to take part on any of their arts programmes, but never receive invitations, and am bracketed solely as a political commentator. I asked who else was on the panel. At that stage the only confirmed guest was my old buddy, Kevin Myers, who writes A Confused Irishman's Diary in the *Irish Times*.

Oh good!, says I. Kevin and I bare wrestling live on TV! But I predicted to the producer that he would not appear. On two occasions he was invited to speak by Féile an Phobail at our annual prestigious event, 'West Belfast Talks Back'. And on each occasion, at short notice, he pulled out, citing one time that his wife had organised a garden barbecue and hadn't told him. Now whether it was because he heard that he would be breathing the same oxygen molecules as myself, or that last Thursday night he and his missus were having a winter barbecue, is anybody's guess, because on Monday, after he was told that I was to appear, he pulled out. I am not saying he is a cowardly custard but he might be a chocolate éclair which equally wilts in the heat. Someone should ask him.

Mark Carruthers chaired the discussion. On the programme was Arlene Foster, an anti-Agreement Ulster Unionist; Ivan Cooper, former Assembly Member of the SDLP, who is depicted by the actor James Nesbitt in one of the films about Bloody Sunday; and David Adams, former member of the now-defunct Ulster Democratic Party, which was considered to be the political wing of the UDA. David is now a commentator and has a weekly slot on BBC's 'Talkback'. (When the BBC decides that a republican like former Sinn Féin councillor Mairtin Ó Muilleior's period of 'quarantine' has expired, perhaps he will be given a regular slot. Or be invited to review the morning papers, like Andy Wood, former press officer at the Northern Ireland Office.)

The first question to the panel was a complaint about why it is that it is always the nationalist cause that is portrayed in films. This was in reference to the two recent films about Bloody Sunday (made by English men). It is incredible that unionists still do not realise how they are perceived across the world.

How could a filmmaker romanticise or portray as heroic the loyalist cause? How could the Ulster Workers' Council strike of 1974 be adopted as having been a revolutionary uprising with noble aims, given that it was against equality, justice and power-sharing and was all about bullying and intimidation for the sake of sectarian dominance? A film about the Orange Order – even a sympathetic one – would have Dennis Hopper, a Ku Klux Klan character camped out on Hill Drumcree throwing live toads into the pot as he recites the names Sean, Mary, Seamus, Dermot, Cathleen…

How could you make a presentable film, set in Glenbryn, about Billy who wakens to his alarm clock at five to nine, goes to the bathroom, sits on the toilet, collects his excrement in a plastic bag, goes up to the corner and tosses it at six-year-old schoolgirls? Incidentally, when I referred to that on 'Let's Talk', a unionist member of the audience replied, 'I don't know what Danny Morrison's complaining about; didn't republican prisoners smear excrement on the walls of their cells?'

The mentality.

It's true that republicans smeared excrement on the walls of their cells. They were protesting at being held in naked, solitary confinement, being beaten, being refused their own clothes, refused visits and letters and exercise. They didn't throw their excrement at innocent school children. And when objective film makers, writers or foreign journalists come to Ireland they show more interest in the nationalist cause, be it an important historical incident such as Bloody Sunday, or republican hunger strikers or IRA escapees or the electoral rise of Sinn Féin, not because Sinn Féin spokespersons are great, persuasive propagandists (as some unionist members of the audience claimed and believe) but because films about such causes and such people struggling against injustice are more relevant, interesting and engaging than stories about backward-thinking, toad-cooking, 'Yabba Dabba-Doo, Any Teague'll Do', sectarian supremacists.

Bobby Sands' story is more compelling than Billy Wright's. You cannot make a saint or martyr out of child-killer Billy Wright, no matter if you resurrected and employed the services in committee of Charles Dickens, Jane Austen, Thomas Hardy and Enid Blyton. Even Rudyard Kipling could not produce such a miracle.

Yet there could be moving portrayals of the suffering of the unionist people. For example, a film about Remembrance Sunday in Enniskillen when the IRA slaughtered members of that community. But if a film were made it probably would have to be made around Gordon Wilson who forgave the killers of his daughter Marie and called for no retaliation.

But it would also have to include how that man was snubbed and ridiculed by many in his own community because of his humility and Christianity and because he held out his hand in friendship and understanding.

But let's not talk about that.

Let There be a Referendum

What has unionism to offer the union?

Andersonstown News, 18 March 2002

The United Kingdom is 'a vibrant multi-ethnic, multi-national liberal democracy – the fourth largest economy in the world – the most reliable ally of the United States in the fight against international terrorism', David Trimble told his party conference in Belfast.

He called for John Reid, Secretary of State, to hold a referendum next year at the same time as the Assembly elections on whether the North should join a united Ireland, so that the issue could be put to rest for a generation and republicans stop daydreaming.

Sometimes people bite off more than they can chew.

I would like to ask David Trimble a question – not that I expect an answer. It is this. Do the people of the multi-national liberal democracy he believes he is part of also have a say and would he abide by the will of the majority?

There is an old slogan from the time of the US colonies, 'No taxation without representation', which, relative to the British public's massive subvention to the North, should allow their voice to be represented, to have a say. Indeed, if the costs to British taxpayers were more widely known (is it still £2 billion annually, or more?) taxpayers might even be more disenchanted with 'the union' than opinion polls consistently demonstrate.

Of the 18 surveys conducted by reputable organisations between 1971 and 1993, 16 showed more than 50 per cent of Britons supporting withdrawal. A *Guardian*/ICM opinion poll last August found that only 26 per cent of Britons believe that the North belongs to the United Kingdom.

And why wouldn't the British public vote to withdraw, if they were allowed a say?

What richness, what contribution, what culture, what liberalism, what philosophy does traditional unionism and its more fundamentalist derivatives add to this multi-national liberal democracy? Is there a sport it contributes? A language? A cuisine or even a type of pudding? A body of literature or poetry that hasn't been informed by contact with the indigenous population or isn't a synthesis of our shared history?

Unionism, as far as the British public is concerned, is a nuisance, its representatives always moaning, complaining of sell-outs here, there and everywhere. The House of Commons empties during Northern Ireland Question Time. Unionism is represented on the streets by loyalist paramilitaries who when they are not burning Catholic homes or shooting each other in turf wars are bombing the RUC in order to preserve the RUC. Unionism is represented by images of foul-mouthed adults wrapped in Union Jacks attacking school children, or, by people who dress up in bowler hats, wear sashes and gloves on the hottest day of the year, build arches, love marching through areas where they are not wanted and where they can cause the most offence.

People more British, more royal, blue and true, than the British themselves.

The main British parties feel the North is so British that they don't even organise branches.

Just a few days after Trimble's eulogy about being vibrant, multi and British, and his attack on the south (a 'pathetic, sectarian, mono-ethnic, mono-cultural state'), fundamentalist Protestants, who had threatened 'to take every action necessary, regardless of the consequences', prevented the 102-year-old Ballymena Agricultural Show being extended into the Sabbath for the first time. Paisley had warned: 'The turning of God's day of rest and worship into a day for worldly trade and gain can only bring a weeping of disaster'.

Even the spring lambs aren't allowed to gambol and frolic on a Sunday, the cows moo or the chickens cluck.

The Belfast Agreement allows for the holding of referendums on the union although it is not clear if a referendum can be called at the discretion of the Secretary of State or only in circumstances where it appears likely that a majority for unity has emerged. There is probably an overall majority in Britain for unity, in Ireland if taken as a whole, but not yet in the North. A *Belfast Telegraph* poll in February 2000 showed that in the North more than a third of Protestants – terminology one is forced, regrettably, to use – believe it likely the island of Ireland will be united over the next 20 years.

Three weeks ago the London *Independent* claimed that last year's census – to be published later this year – will show Protestants close to a bare majority, at 51 or 52 per cent, with only a five per cent buffer of 'others' between them and the growing Catholic population. No doubt there are pro-union Catholics who probably outnumber pro-unity Protestants but not the figure – 20-25 per cent – Trimble, in his speech, assumed there to be. He may have got that figure from a 1994 poll that claimed that 28 per cent of Catholics want the North 'to remain part of the UK'. But that was before the ceasefire and at a time when Sinn Féin's support across the North stood at only 12 per cent; in last year's Westminster election Sinn Féin took almost 22 per cent of the vote.

A referendum on the union is bound to galvanise party supporters across the political spectrum and not just those of Ulster Unionists.

Far from laying the issue to rest for a generation it can only remind unionists of a ticking clock and how outmoded and tenuous is their position. For some it may become an excuse for madcap terrorism; for others, the opportunity to look at how best we can progress towards agreement, and start building society and country together.

Enough Is Enough

Andersonstown News, 18 July 2002

They love some of the ministries, most of the ministries, want all of the ministries. They love their chauffeur-driven cars, want all of the cars. They love their offices and staff, and want more offices and staff; all of the offices, all their own staff. They love dispensing their taxes, your taxes, everyone's taxes. They love their Assembly seats, their salaries and expenses and would love more expenses, all of the expenses, more seats, all of the seats. They want to be governing their own, on their own, with their own – but ruling what you own. They want their own police force and third force and brute force. They want to beat their drums down their road, your road, someone else's road, everybody's road.

They want to have some guns, everyone's guns, all the guns, the only guns.

They want to have some votes, most of the votes, your votes, all of the votes.

They despise some of us, most of us, all of us. They despise some whom we elect, most of whom we elect, all of whom we elect.

They despise our representatives in the members' car park, in the Great Hall, in the restaurant, in the corridor, in the lift, in the rooms, in the Assembly, in the Executive – breathing their air.

They love the microphone, the camera, the limelight; most of the microphone, the camera, the limelight; all of the microphone, the camera, the limelight. They love having the floor, most of the floor, all of the floor.

They love one flag, their flag, the only flag. They hate the way I talk, you talk, we talk.

They said Articles Two and Three were the problem. They said IRA arms dumps were the problem. They said the lack of local power and decision-making was the problem. They said not recognising their Britishness was the problem.

I know who they are but I don't know, cannot be sure, how many of them there are. Are all in the DUP anti-Catholic, loyalist bigots? How many Ulster Unionists? A third? A half? More than half?

Do such MLAs and MPs represent more than half of the unionist people or are there a fair number of disillusioned, silenced unionists who see through the bullshit of their whingeing leadership and the threat they pose to peace and stability? If a majority really feel that way about republicans and nationalists then they represent the unionist orthodoxy – and the Assembly and the Executive are doomed.

I wasn't sure what to think of David Trimble. Was he a reformer, a bit of a leader, a flawed leader, but a leader nonetheless? He had been a member of the fascist Vanguard. He met with killer Billy Wright. He danced the Paisley jig on Garvaghy Road. He went into negotiations with representatives of paramilitaries by his side. But he went on to acknowledge in his Nobel Speech that the North had been 'a cold house for Catholics'. Does he forget those remarks? Were they for the cameras, the microphones, because he was in the limelight? Does he forget the compromises that republicans have made, the hoops they have jumped through, in order to help him, and show that they are serious?

All of us are products of our history and change takes time. The unionist god was Carson who in 1913 described their defiance of the British legislature and the illegal arming of the Ulster Volunteer Force in these terms: 'I am told it will be illegal and the government know they are illegal, and the government dare not interfere with them... Don't be afraid of illegalities.'

Ninety years later and I doubt if unionist leaders repudiate Carson's opinions, his example and his actions in regard to illegal activities.

I don't remember the Ulster Unionists having to change their constitution the way Sinn Féin did in order to make the institutions work – the Assembly side of which only unionists wanted. I can't remember Ulster Unionism having the same robust and consistent attitude to loyalist violence as it has towards the Republican Movement at a time in our history when republicanism, and supposedly, unionism, go through a transition together.

David Trimble has talked up a crisis and hopes that Tony Blair will come to his rescue by making more demands of republicans. But Trimble can't have it, and Blair – who has already reneged on promises he made a year ago – needn't think he can try that one again. Unionists have convinced themselves that republicans and nationalists are getting everything and they're getting nothing. The hard truth is that it is the challenge of equality that alienates unionists, not alleged IRA involvement in Colombia or Castlereagh. It is unionist leaders who have failed to convince the nationalist community of their sincerity. And they appear not to care about the political vacuum they shall create, or of the consequences of bringing down the Belfast Agreement.

If the majority of unionists do not want to share power with the majority of nationalists then let's say goodbye to the Assembly, the Executive, and everything that goes with it. But they cannot have all the power, all the offices, all the floor, all the streets, and they needn't think that nationalists are going to acquiesce in a dilution of the principles behind the Belfast Agreement.

Talk to people in West Belfast and they will tell you: Irish republicans cannot and should not give anymore. There is nothing more to give.

'I am what I am'

Interview with David Ervine, leader of the Progressive Unionist Party.

Andersonstown News, 7 October 2002

David Ervine MLA, the leader of the Progressive Unionist Party, who represents East Belfast in the Assembly, came to prominence after the UVF/UDA ceasefire in 1994, one of a new breed of articulate former loyalist prisoners. Twenty years earlier, at the age of nineteen, he was arrested with a bomb and sentenced to eleven years in jail where he was nicknamed Bamber (after Bamber Gasgoine who chaired *University Challenge* on television).

He is the subject of a new book, *David Ervine: Unchartered Waters* by Henry Sinnerton, a lecturer and Ervine's former French schoolteacher [published by Brandon]. Last week I interviewed Ervine in the PUP offices in the Assembly (which is actually next door to Sinn Féin's offices).

Ervine is friendly and affable and fairly honest. I have appeared opposite him on television and radio and watched his interviews, not really sure of what makes the man tick, if he is as genuine as he appears.

Was the book 'authorised' I asked?

'I never tried to stop it nor Henry from talking to my friends or Jeanette, my wife. She thinks it is very readable. It doesn't overcomplicate things. In some ways I am flattered by it. I also think that I must tell the truth but understandably there are bits that are missing.'

Why didn't he write the book himself?

'I've no time and I'm too young. Some of the things that I would have to write are so sensitive that I wouldn't be prepared to talk about them.'

Dark areas about his past or personal things?

'Both. It might take me some time to feel brave enough to write about these things, but I think that Henry gets the essence of it.'

One of the defining moments of his life was Bloody Friday, the day in July 1972 that IRA bombs in Belfast killed nine people. It was then he decided to join the UVF.

'I believed that the best means of defence was attack. I would refute that now. I would counsel no violence because it is counter-productive. The core issues in our society were flawed and violence upon violence never allowed us to deal with the core problems. We are trying to do that now, and so that diminishes anybody's remote right for violent action.'

Throughout the troubles the UVF was responsible for assassinating hundreds of uninvolved Catholics and for planting bombs in Dublin and Monaghan that killed thirty three people. When Peter Taylor in his book *Loyalists* asked Ervine how he felt about the bombings, he replied: 'I think certainly there were many within the unionist community who felt, and I may have felt it too, "Now you know how we feel".'

I asked him if he felt there was no qualitative or moral difference between the violence used by the British army, the UVF or the IRA.

'That's the case. However, there should have been, or should be, if war must be fought, rules that it needs to be fought under. Every one of those was broken here by all sides.'

He accepts that the outbreak of violence had its origins in the fact that the North was a one-party state and that there was discrimination. He is critical of the mainstream Ulster Unionist Party and says that the PUP is a forward-thinking socialist party. He says he will accept a united Ireland if a majority in the North votes for it.

'But we have to function on the basis of let's make life valuable for the people in this society.'

He concedes that the two Sinn Féin ministers are diligent, that progress has been made (the PUP and Sinn Féin recently put forward a joint motion on low pay), and states that the PUP will not be joining with the UUP to exclude Sinn Féin from the Executive in January. However, he argues that unionists see two processes at work, with the republicans working to their old agenda and deliberately creating difficulties for unionism.

'When I view the potential for January I'm saying to myself, "What is it Trimble wants? How many hoops have people to jump through?" What I am clear on is what the Republican Movement and loyalists need to do. Back off from the interfaces. Stop playing games and telling your own constituency lies.'

For example?

'That there'll be a united Ireland in sixteen years. It's not going to happen. I can understand that one needs to make a constituency feel comfortable. But you can't tell a constituency it is achieving victory when it is not. You've got to understand how unionism works. There is a huge insecurity within unionism. Unionism really hasn't had time to settle. They feel that the republican agitation is never going to stop. The one thing that unionists lust for is stability. It's the one thing they have never had.'

I told him that republicans are never going to stop agitating for a united Ireland and that they are going to continue to make demands for parity of esteem, for more accountable policing and open up the Good Friday Agreement to its full worth. Surely unionists will always feel insecure because they are in an overall minority in Ireland, they are threatened by demographic change and they are not really wanted by the people of Britain.

'How do you cope with the fact that people in Tallaght don't see you as quite as Irish as them?' he replies. (I had forgotten a great reply: 'Then why did they make Sinn Féin's Jack Crowe their TD?')

'I am what I am. I am both Irish and British but I'm a democrat too… There's nothing more fascist than someone telling you what you are, especially if you perceive yourself to be somewhat different.

'We are steeped in concepts of Britishness… but those who are the legal arbiters are the people of Northern Ireland. It is absolutely legitimate for republicans to argue the validity of a united Ireland but the new dispensation is worthy and there should be no Plan B. My mother and father were Irish, my grandparents, and very simplistically so. But there are arguments about the haunting mist of the 1937 Constitution that forced the unionist people to re-think their Irishness.

'The PUP is not afraid of change and we are also not afraid that the requirement during negotiations was that every institution that we had, changed… But, we have not made a fist of that at all and I can't blame Adams alone. When unionism began to play a la carte on day one of the Good Friday Agreement there was always going to be a destabilising process and a retaliatory strike process… Then those fools Bertie Ahern and Tony Blair opened their door and let single constituency benefit arguments to develop' [a reference to the unionist perception that Sinn Féin has been negotiating and making extra-curricular demands not necessarily defined within the Agreement].

The PUP, the Women's Coalition and the Alliance Party believe that, as smaller parties, they have been excluded by Sinn Féin, the SDLP and the Ulster Unionists from the real negotiations, and that only lip service is paid to the notion of working collectively.

'In 2002, after a lot of people dead, a lot of people wounded, a lot of people hurt, a lot of mistakes made, on all sides – shame on all sides! – I think there comes a time when you say: I think we can do better here. But it will only be believed if there's a collective; it will not be believed if we say it individually.'

Ervine is certainly an impressive advocate of 'modern' unionism, though how resonant his message is to the unionist community is another matter (he received just 10 per cent of the East Belfast vote in the last Westminster election). A little of his personal life is laid bare in this book and while he has the courage of his political convictions it might take him some time, as he admits himself, before he feels brave enough to write the full story.

Tell us the War is Over!

'Stormontgate': the third suspension of the Assembly follows PSNI raids on Sinn Féin offices in Stormont and the charging of republicans with possession of documents.

The Guardian, 14 October 2002

Perhaps now, the Ulster Unionists will realise the enormity of the situation they have brought about. Their objective was to force Tony Blair to move an exclusion notice in the Assembly against Sinn Féin and then during the subsequent debate hope that the SDLP would vote with them, bringing back something reminiscent of majority rule and turning the Northern Assembly into the old Stormont.

Blindness to political reality informed much of their thinking. Certainly, back in 1999 they might have had some cause for hope. David Trimble had been elected First Minister and Seamus Mallon Deputy First Minister a year earlier. For the next eighteen months Trimble refused to allow the other ministries to be filled until the IRA began decommissioning. Seamus Mallon guaranteed Trimble that he would move to exclude Sinn Féin if republicans did not fulfil their obligations. But that was then and this is now.

Did Tony Blair refuse this week to do David Trimble's bidding because he likes Gerry Adams and can't stand Trimble? Hardly. Had Sinn Féin been a weaker party, had the SDLP done better at the polls, the new SDLP leader Mark Durkan just might have been tempted to go down the road of exclusion. But last year's general election results changed that, and basic arithmetic stayed Blair's hand. Those thousands of people who opted for Sinn Féin over the SDLP, and made it the larger party, materially changed the political landscape and added real muscle to the negotiating position of the nationalist community. Where the SDLP has traditionally settled for less, Sinn Féin has robustly demanded nothing less than full rights.

Once Tony Blair decided not to introduce an exclusion motion against Sinn Féin it was obvious that he would move to suspend the Assembly. The one crumb of comfort the Ulster Unionist Party has is that it can face Assembly elections (should they be called) claiming that it has acted 'morally' and confronted the 'duplicitous' Republican Movement.

It is debatable if politics – or peace, for that matter – can work circumscribed by dubious, subjective notions of what is 'moral' or 'principled', rather than freed through a degree of pragmatism and flexibility. The taxes paid by pacifists support a government maintaining a nuclear weapons capability. The taxes of pro-life citizens support abortion in health services. Society is a complex machine, full of contradictions and double standards, its cogs oiled by hypocrisy and requiring compromises. Voters for a particular party endorse along with their preferred policies others that are anathema – even if they deceive themselves that is not the case. After being elected parties often deviate from their manifesto pledges and – depending on context and the legitimacy of the departure – their supporters will either forgive them or reject them.

Sinn Féin's vote went up after the first ceasefire. It increased even when the IRA ended that ceasefire with the explosion at Canary Wharf. It has grown after the Florida gunrunning trial, and after the Colombian and Castlereagh allegations. It will increase again because nationalists recognise that it is working for peace, not war.

Republicans are sitting in an Assembly they never wanted. The British government never gave a declaration of intent to withdraw. There is still a heavy British army presence in some nationalist areas. The police have not been reformed. The equality and justice issues have yet to be resolved. But do you throw the head up, become exasperated or disillusioned and walk out, the way unionists have over not getting all their own way? No, you get on with the business of making peace.

Unionists never wanted to share power. It must be extremely hard for people who established their own state (with the might of Britain), had their own paramilitary police and government, and who were raised in supremacist politics for so long to share power with even Castle Catholics never mind those 'who ain't house-trained'. True, the IRA, because it exists, does not make it any easier for unionists. But that is life.

Is the demand for IRA disbandment made by unionists because they have a legitimate fear that the IRA is preparing for a return to armed struggle or is keeping its options open? Or is the demand a mere ploy, because unionists know that it cannot be met and thus improves the chances of them achieving their objective of a unionist government, with a few Uncle Toms or Marks about the place?

The IRA re-emerged in 1969 and re-armed because the unionist institutions of the state threatened, abused and attacked nationalists. It obviously continues to exist because nationalists still feel vulnerable. But it can only return to armed struggle if the institutions and forces of the state attack nationalists or deny them their rights, which begs the question of unionists and the British: is the war over?

And if it is over, why do you want the Special Branch? Why do you not make the police service acceptable to nationalists? Why are the forces you support still bugging houses and cars, collecting files, gathering intelligence, targeting republicans, recruiting informers? Is it that old habits die hard?

Can you guarantee us that you will not go back to justifying and being cheer leaders for the proscribing of political parties, the internment of your political opponents, censorship, the ill-treatment of prisoners, shoot-to-kill operations, the use of supergrasses, excusing collusion? And can you assure us that you will cease your double standards which give political cover and thus encouragement to loyalist paramilitaries?

Can you give us one good reason why we should share power with you? Because you have a past does not mean that you cannot have a future. Here is the hand of friendship. Tell us that the war is over.

The Next 'D' Word

In response to Frank Millar, London Editor, Irish Times, *on the meaning of 'consent'.*

Andersonstown News, 28 October 2002

Don't forget, you read it here first! 'Dual Consent'. That's going to be the next buzz word in the unionist vocabulary as nationalists slowly but inevitably come into a majority in the North.

Following the 1994 IRA cessation unionists thought they could stymie or forestall political progress, and/or split the Republican Movement, by making potentially humiliating demands of republicans: that Sinn Féin go through a period of 'decontamination'; later, that the IRA must 'decommission'; and, more recently, that the IRA has to 'disband'.

Now it appears that many of them fear the IRA might actually disband, or – given Gerry Adams' futuristic scenario of a society without armed groups – make a gesture which gives unionists no excuse not to engage in politics under the terms of the Belfast Agreement.

Supporters of the Belfast Agreement commit themselves to 'recognise the legitimacy of whatever choice is freely exercised by a majority of the people of Northern Ireland with regard to its status, whether they prefer to continue to support the Union with Great Britain or a sovereign united Ireland.'

They are also pledged to recognise 'that it is for the people of the island of Ireland alone, by agreement between the two parts respectively and without external impediment, to exercise their right of self-determination on the basis of consent, freely and concurrently given, North and South, to bring about a united Ireland, if that is their wish, accepting that this right must be achieved and exercised with and subject to the agreement and consent of a *majority of the people of Northern Ireland*' (my italics).

This pledge is quite similar to others in the Downing Street Declaration and the Anglo-Irish Agreement. That is, a majority in the North, be it 65 per cent or 55 per cent, or 51 per cent, can determine the state's constitutional status. Republicans always challenged the basis of this 'majority', arguing, correctly, that 'Northern Ireland' was an artificial creation and that partition thwarted the will of another majority – the will of the Irish people.

However, since the Belfast Agreement republicans have been more pragmatic in their approach, their traditional theology muted.

Ironically, it is the unionists who are now about to rebel against this concept.

The London Editor of the *Irish Times* is Frank Millar, an excellent political commentator whose analyses are lucid and cogently argued. In the 1980s he was the Ulster Unionist Party's press officer and general secretary and remains a keen observer of unionism. He has an intuitive grasp of, if not an insight into, unionist thinking.

And that is what is so sulphurous about the comments he came off with in his paper last Thursday. Frank Millar said: 'In the matter of future constitutional change it seems clear that republicans and nationalists still adhere to the principle of consent by a simple majority – and not the principle of dual consent from which the Agreement derives its operational imperative... And if the consent of a majority of both communities is required to run a mere Stormont administration, it is plainly nonsense to suggest the emergence of a simple nationalist majority would be sufficient to effect a change in sovereignty and statehood.'

The only thing that is plainly nonsense is Frank Millar's disingenuousness. Plainly speaking, he is saying that a majority if it is unionist can maintain the union regardless of what nationalists think, but a majority if it is nationalist cannot have a united Ireland without regard to what unionists think!

The analogy he rests his case on is the conditions required for running 'a mere administration' – dual consent.

The compromise that is the Belfast Agreement was arrived at after a period of intense conflict, tragedy and suffering. Because of unionism's historic and sectarian abuse of power it was also a requirement of the Agreement that the political administration of the state, its institutions, its laws, which impact on the daily lives of everyone, require the support of a majority within the nationalist community and not just a majority within the unionist community.

But let's be clear about one thing. An emergent nationalist majority in the North would have the right to trigger the end of the union even though it might opt not to immediately exercise that right, especially if the devolved administrations were popular and effective.

David Trimble inherited his Westminster seat from the late Harold McCusker who was once asked what would happen if there was a nationalist majority in the North which voted for reunification. McCusker said unionists would simply repartition. Comments like that, and that mentality, which still pervades unionism, explain the traditional republican view that constitutional politics will not bring about civil and national rights but that armed struggle might.

It would be pathetic, but within character, for unionists to insist that the link with Britain is maintained by the notion of 'dual consent': effectively, a minority having primacy over the will of a majority. But it cannot be allowed to happen.

Of course a united Ireland has to make social, economic and political sense (and not only represent the fulfilment of a republican ideal, however just and overdue), especially if it is to be supported by people in the twenty-six counties, as well as a majority in the North. It is up to the people, all of the people, to decide whether a unitary state, a federal or confederal Ireland optimises peace, justice, equality, stability and prosperity. That is the debate unionists should be engaging in, instead of looking for ways of turning language on its head.

Targeting the Unionist Community

Multiple UVF breaches of its cease-fire ignored by PUP spokespersons.

Andersonstown News, 20 January 2003

So, the UVF has suspended contact with General de Chastelain's decommissioning body, and the Progressive Unionist Party has decided to end contact with Sinn Féin. Two reasons have been given: increasing disillusionment with the peace process and 'the wholesale targeting of the unionist community' by the IRA, a reference to the spy-ring allegations.

It is true that unionists will find offence in the continued existence of the IRA, or any republican activity from, on the one hand, political espionage, to, at the other extreme, arranging Easter lilies in a vase up in the Assembly. On deciding republican involvement in Colombia, Castlereagh and the alleged kleptomania for documents that don't belong to them, the non-jury is still out.

In truth, what unionists do not like is the full implementation of the Belfast Agreement simply because equality and parity of esteem threaten their ethos and hegemony and are synonymous with revolutionary gains for nationalists and republicans. They fear that the current talks might result in the British government moving towards the implementation of Patten and honouring the commitment not to prosecute republicans who are still on the run. That is why Ulster Unionist warnings are echoed in UVF threats.

When the IRA cease-fired in August 1994 unionist paramilitaries proclaimed it a victory for their campaign of sectarian assassination, and that they had brought the IRA to the point of surrender. When the Tory government didn't treat the republican offer of peace seriously the IRA did something even seasoned observers said it couldn't do – it ended its cease-fire with the bombing of Canary Wharf and only reinstated it when Labour came to power and opened up real negotiations.

Ulster Unionists and unionist paramilitaries who initially supported the Belfast Agreement understood the compromises within it but believed that the risks were worth it because in its outworking (one example being police reform) they could skin republicans. That is, that through their minimalist approach, their use of Westminster, their constant threats to walk out, through relying in part on the divisions between Sinn Féin and the SDLP and Dublin, and through exploiting the various moral commitments Sinn Féin and the IRA had made to peace, unionists could emerge in a handsome position in the Assembly and the Executive, the union secure in perpetuity.

But Ulster Unionists in their electoral battle with the DUP had to rely upon a big lie – that the Agreement (which was an accommodation, an historical compromise by them also) was a defeat for the Republican Movement and that 'the war had been for nothing', as if republicans had given up on the objective of Irish independence!

Even at a press conference on Friday, at which the Progressive Unionist Party announced it would no longer talk to Sinn Féin, this confusion was evident. On the one hand, David Ervine smugly states that republicans have accepted a partitionist settlement, then complains that the British government in the current talks, aimed at reaching agreement before a decision is taken about Assembly elections in May, better not make any concessions to the Republican Movement!

But let us look at the IRA's alleged 'wholesale targeting of the unionist community', given as the reason for the UVF and PUP's withdrawal from the process.

Who has threatened the unionist community in the last three years more than unionist paramilitaries? Who but the UVF stabbed to death 18-year-old David McIlwaine and 19-year-old Andrew Robb at the side of a Tandragee road in February 2000? Who but the UVF shot Jackie Coulter and Bobby Mahood in Belfast in August of the same year? Who but the UVF shot David Greer in North Belfast on 28th October 2000, and three days later Tommy English of the rival Ulster Democratic Party? Who but the UVF shot Adrian Porter in Bangor in March 2001? Who but the Progressive Unionist Party made excuses for these killings?

It makes no difference that these individuals were killed during a feud with the UDA/LVF that also saw UVF members and supporters killed. Who but loyalists rob their own community blind, holding up post offices, off-licences and petrol stations? Who but loyalists demand protection money from those building badly needed houses and shops in their areas? Who but loyalists terrorise and oppress the people of the Shankill Road? Who but loyalists are destroying the Protestant youth in areas like Ballymena, which they have turned into the heroin capital of the North?

Who has ignored the social and economic deprivation of the people of Glenbryn but their own unionist elected representatives?

There is no 'implicit threat to the peace process' from the IRA, whereas unionist paramilitary violence is explicit and real. When they are not fighting turf wars these groups are killing Catholics, attacking school kids, burning their classrooms and bombing churches.

Who burned to death Richard, Mark and Jason Quinn in Ballymoney two months after the Belfast Agreement was endorsed in referenda but the UVF? Whose bomb factory was discovered in the Mount Vernon area of Belfast two years ago but the UVF's? Who planted a car bomb at the Auld Lammas Fair in Ballycastle in August 2001 aimed at incinerating civilians but the UVF?

Who planted ten pipe bombs at a number of locations throughout County Derry last February but the UVF? Who were convicted three months ago of gun-running from Scotland but UVF members Donald Reid and Robert Baird? Whose weapons and uniforms were seized on Saturday night in Belfast but those belonging to the UVF?

Twice, the IRA has put arms beyond use, verified by General John de Chastelain. The UVF not only refuses to decommission but boasts that it will not and PUP leader David Ervine has confirmed that the organisation is rearming, which everyone knew anyway.

'The wholesale targeting of the unionist community?'

Think again, David and Billy.

Transparent Reminders

Andersonstown News, 27 October 2003

The two teenagers, Gavin and Michael, stood talking at the road junction on a late Sunday night in July, near the entrance to a GAA club. Gavin, a tall, handsome lad of eighteen, a Man United supporter, had just finished high school and was looking forward to his A-Level results. Michael noticed a blue Vauxhall Nova driving towards them. The rear window behind the driver's seat was rolled down and suddenly shots rang out. Gavin fell to the ground and Michael was shot in the foot as he tried to scale a fence.

The unionist gunmen laughed as they drove away, believing they had shot two Catholic kids. Gavin's father, Michael Brett, was called to the scene of the shooting, not far from his home, and tried desperately, but in vain, to save the life of his son whom he later described as 'my mate, my chum.' Catholics and Protestants attended the funeral of Gavin Brett at the Church of the Holy Evangelists. The Reverend Nigel Baylor addressing the congregation said:

'These men who murdered Gavin were Protestants, loyalists and they killed one of their own, thinking that he was a Roman Catholic... They have done nothing but bring shame on the name of Protestantism. They represent the evil wasteful past which is dead and useless to us all.'

This shooting happened just two years ago.

The Red Hand Defenders – that is the UDA/UFF – claimed responsibility. No one was ever charged. The guns were never seized. They have yet to be 'put beyond use'. The UDA/UFF and UVF are still active, are still engaged in violence and gunrunning and refuse to decommission. Those organisations sit on the Loyalist Commission, an umbrella group that includes Protestant church leaders and politicians, including leading Ulster Unionist David McNarry.

Last week the UDA threatened two of its former allies, David Adams and Gary McMichael, who are pro-Agreement. When the Commission tried to intervene the UDA told it to mind its own business – this was an internal matter. Did Mr McNarry resign from the Commission, or suspend his membership even temporarily, as some sort of leverage?

Sure didn't.

Last Tuesday General de Chastelain announced that the IRA had carried out a third act of decommissioning in significantly larger numbers than on the two previous occasions.

An hour later David Trimble reneged on a deal he had entered into with Gerry Adams. It didn't matter that the IRA had put beyond use a record large number of weapons. The unionist community, Trimble said, was not satisfied and had to see or hear for itself the exact details of all the weapons and explosives that the IRA had destroyed.

Frustrating though it is, we need to keep challenging unionist hypocrisy and double standards, though in the meantime we have to live with the unionist parties' equivocal attitudes to loyalist paramilitarism. One can expect nothing from the DUP, with its history of jointly organising the 1977 strike with the UDA, to marching up mountains in the dead of night waving gun licences and barking at the moon, or the not-so-Big Man in his wee red beret taking military salutes in the Ulster Hall.

Last Tuesday his answer – for the thousandth time – was to promise to smash Sinn Féin/IRA. How pathetic!

Without mature and responsible leadership the interests of the unionist people will suffer: without, of course, necessarily advancing the cause of republicanism. Unionism totally divided, and large numbers in despair, is dangerous. However, the leader of mainstream unionism, David Trimble, hadn't the courage to face down his dissidents and the DUP and recognise the magnitude of what the IRA did. Instead, he passed over the opportunity for the elections to be held in a positive and optimistic atmosphere, in favour of presenting himself as a hard man. And now he expects the IRA to bail him out, or, failing that, to provide him with a pretext for refusing to share power with Sinn Féin.

Of all the armed organisations in the North the IRA is the only group that has publicly committed itself to putting its arms and explosives 'completely and verifiably' beyond use. The now-abused General John de Chastelain, the British nominee to the decommissioning body most favoured by unionists, has witnessed its actions.

Finally, as David Trimble was reneging on his agreement with Gerry Adams last Tuesday, ten miles away in Belfast the inquest into the murder of young Gavin Brett on that summer's night in July 2001 was being held. Such inquests, along with the weekly statistics of sectarian attacks, transparently remind us that the chief ongoing source of violence is from within the unionist community.

145 Divis Street

Andersonstown News, 22 March 2004

It wasn't supposed to be like this, thought one of Ian Paisley's lieutenants as he looked out across the front lawn of the City Hall. Above him the Union Jack flew, but before his eyes were thousands of St Patrick's Day revellers; dancing and singing; children on their fathers' shoulders applauding Girls Aloud. A sea of green - but worse still were flags coloured green, white and orange: the hated Tricolour. What had gone wrong?

There was a time when 27,000 occupied houses in Belfast were unfit for human habitation. There was a time when in West Belfast male unemployment reached fifty per cent in places like Ballymurphy. In Enniskillen figures showed that Protestants were being allocated public housing at the rate of 11 to 1 over Catholics who made up half the population. There was a time when the IRA border campaign had fizzled out, when republicans were demoralised and were prepared to try new tactics, including participating in politics.

In Britain in September 1964 the Tory government called a Westminster general election for October 15. Sinn Féin was proscribed but for election purposes it stood as the Republican Party. On September 6, the republicans put a Tricolour in the front window of their election headquarters at 145 Divis Street.

The campaign got off to a slow start for all parties. Ulster Unionists were united and were standing in all twelve constituencies. The nationalist vote was badly divided – though in West Belfast Harry Diamond of Republican Labour was quietly confident that there was some unionist apathy and he could beat James Kilfedder for the seat, even though the intervention of former IRA prisoner Billy McMillan would split the vote.

The first scare came on Saturday, September 26, in a screaming front-page headline, when the *News Letter* announced: 'The Dollars Roll In – "Plenty" in Sinn Féin election coffers'. The main lead in its Monday edition was: 'Paisley to march against Tricolour'. Ian Paisley, Moderator of the Free Presbyterian Church, called upon Protestants to assemble in their thousands at the City Hall that evening to march on Divis Street. It was a call that sent a chill through the nationalist community, which had been subject to loyalist and police incursions in previous decades.

The RUC told the Minister of Home Affairs that it regarded the display of the Tricolour and Paisley's proposed protest as 'provocative acts'. (The flag had been in the window for three weeks without a complaint being made.) The Minister met Paisley and appealed to him. He agreed to call off the march but not the rally.

Later that day fifty RUC men, using pick axes and crowbars, smashed their way into the republican offices, seized the Tricolour, put it into a patrol car and drove off at high speed, whilst a sullen crowd of several hundred nationalists looked on. A notice was served on Billy McMillan, under the Flags and Emblems Act, which referred to the illegal 'display of the Tricolour flag or flags of the Irish Republic, or any other flag or anything purporting to represent the Irish Republic.'

From the street nationalists began shouting abuse at those in the republican office and demanded that a new Tricolour be displayed. The election directorate assuaged the crowd by issuing an ultimatum to the RUC that if the flag wasn't returned by Thursday it would be replaced.

That Monday night Paisley held a triumphant rally in the grounds of the City Hall where he welcomed unionist candidate, James Kilfedder. Kilfedder told the crowd: 'The republicans must not be allowed to fly the Tricolour, and when the last vote is counted on polling day we must show the world that there was no wavering in the determination of the people to keep the Union Jack flying over West Belfast.'

Unionist voters in the constituency were now galvanised.

In Ballynahinch, prime minister Terence O'Neill, surrounded by members of the Apprentice Boys, the Black Preceptory and six Orange bands, commenting on the seizure of the Tricolour, ridiculously declared that Sinn Féin was the main challenge and described the republicans as 'nothing more than modern anarchists who refuse even now to abjure the discredited policy of violence'. He ignored the fact that the threat of violence came from Paisley and the actual violence from the RUC under government instruction.

On Tuesday night Paisley held another rally at the City Hall and called upon the Minister to prosecute those responsible for displaying the flag. Over in Divis Street there was a standoff between a large nationalist crowd and riot police. On Wednesday night there were more scuffles, followed by RUC baton charges and stone throwing. On Thursday, after lodging their nomination papers, the republican candidates returned to the election headquarters and once again placed a Tricolour in the window to the cheers of supporters.

Shortly after 2pm a column of RUC men, backed up by a tender, arrived at the offices. They tried to break down the reinforced door and when that failed they simply smashed the pane-glass window, stepped in and seized the flag. Immediately, fighting broke out and by evening rioting was widespread throughout Divis Street and the Falls Road, and continued for the next two nights. Hundreds were injured and scores of people, including a mother of eight, were arrested and subsequently imprisoned for up to six months.

Calm was eventually restored but at the cost of nationalists biting their tongue: the Tricolour was never replaced in the window of 145 Divis Street - though the RUC didn't interfere either with the flag when it was carried in a parade from Beechmount to Hamill Street, which concluded in an election rally.

During the election campaign the British Labour leader (and subsequent prime minister) Harold Wilson issued a pledge to the Campaign for Social Justice that as PM he would outlaw racial and religious discrimination in the North. His remarks drew this page one headline from the *News Letter*:

'Interference in Ulster housing – Wilson bombshell'.

On October 15, James Kilfedder defeated Harry Diamond to become the Unionist MP for West Belfast. Billy McMillan lost his deposit. After the republican split in 1969 he became a leader in the 'Official' Republican Movement and was later assassinated by the INLA during a feud.

Kilfedder was carried shoulder-high at the City Hall amid cheers and the singing of 'The Sash'. He was greeted by an ebullient Ian Paisley who said: 'I am absolutely satisfied. Sandy Row and Shankill did their stuff. They are well able to answer the Falls any day.'

Last Wednesday, on St Patrick's Day, thousands of young people carrying Tricolours swarmed down Divis Street, past where 145 once stood, but oblivious to its history, through Castle Street and up Donegall Place to a concert outside the City Hall. It was the very route, in reverse, that 38-year-old Ian Paisley had threatened to take from the City Hall to Divis Street forty years earlier to remove from a window one Tricolour.

What, indeed, had gone wrong.

Collusion and the Dirty War

Nairac's Dirty War

Irish Examiner, 24 February 1999

During the day Captain Robert Nairac, a liaison officer with the SAS, would patrol Crossmaglen with fellow uniformed soldiers, and stop and question local people. Then, come night time, he would arrive into local pubs in his donkey jacket, often accompanied by his black Labrador, Bundle, would attempt to engage local IRA sympathisers in political conversations, would stand up and sing rebel songs, all the while thinking that he had fooled the Paddies into believing that he was really Danny McArevey, a Sticky from Ardoyne in Belfast.

Yes, British intelligence is very often a contradiction in terms.

One night in May 1977 after a sing-song in the Three Steps Inn in South Armagh, during which he insisted that himself 'Danny McArevey' be called to sing 'The Broad Black Bremmer', Nairac was pounced on by local men who beat him up and took him across the border to a small bridge over the River Flurry where an IRA man shot him dead. Later, people were arrested, charged and convicted despite the absence of a major piece of evidence – a body.

What happened to Nairac's body is a complete mystery. Presumably, another IRA unit took it away and buried it, given that Nairac put up a fierce and brave struggle (refusing to give information), and, from the IRA's view, was covered in potentially incriminating forensic evidence. The late informer, Eamon Collins, suggested that the body had been destroyed in a meat-processing factory, but given his unreliability that gruesome account can probably be dismissed. In its statement earlier this week (in relation to 'the disappeared', those victims of the organisation whom the IRA secretly buried) the IRA said complicating factors, which hindered their search for the remains, included the lapse in time, changes in leadership, and the deaths of both members and former members of the organisation. The campaign for the return of the disappeared has never included the Nairac family who appear to have remained aloof. Nor have they ever commented on the allegations that their son was not just a soldier but a ruthless assassin who knew no rule book.

Over the years the truth about Nairac's undercover activities has slowly emerged to reveal a picture of 'a thug' (according to one of his friends) who was perhaps working for a secret arm within the secret services. The story of his controversial life as an undercover soldier, or some of that story, is contained in the book, *Death of a Hero*, by John Parker. The picture Parker paints, through the testimony of British army officers and acquaintances, is, unwittingly, that of a sinister figure.

In London he drank around the pubs of Kilburn to 'improve' his accent and had even bought tapes to learn Irish. Shortly before he returned to South Armagh on his fatal undercover mission, Nairac confided in one friend, Martin Squires, in London, that he had infiltrated the IRA and was now one of its Brigade

Commanders! However, other soldiers felt 'uneasy' around him. Senior officers did not know what he was up to or whether he was working for some other arm of the intelligence services with a higher agenda. After his death his room in Bessbrook barracks was discovered to be 'awash' with top-secret files and he also possessed a perverse collection of photographs of scene-of-the-crime events.

One former intelligence officer, Fred Holroyd, who subsequently fell out with his superiors, has linked Nairac to the 'dirty war' and collusion with loyalist paramilitaries (a subject once again in the news following the recent killing of human rights lawyer, Rosemary Nelson). Holroyd says that Nairac showed him a photograph which he, Nairac, took at the scene of the assassination of Long Kesh escapee, John Francis Green, in County Monaghan, at the beginning of the 1975 IRA ceasefire. MI5 was opposed to the ceasefire and had hoped that the killing of Green would provoke the IRA. MI5 were also said to have been delighted when the power-sharing assembly collapsed in May 1974, after the Dublin-Monaghan bombings. (MI5 has also been linked to destabilising Harold Wilson's Labour government, in a book, *Spycatcher*, written by former MI5 officer Peter Wright.)

Holroyd, who objected to the illegal methods increasingly being used to fight the IRA, was removed from his post because of what the British army described as 'mental strain'. But English journalist Duncan Campbell, who specialises in intelligence matters, has discovered that the RUC completed a 900-page report on the Green incident and other claims Holroyd has made. It remains unpublished. Or, perhaps, unpublishable.

The Star pistol used to kill Green was later found at the scene of the massacre of the Miami Showband in July 1975, when UVF members (including two serving soldiers of the British army) accidentally detonated the bomb they were carrying.

Although Nairac was technically not a member of the Special Air Services (his regiment was the Grenadier Guards), he was allowed to wear the SAS badge, and his work included liasing between the different branches of intelligence, particularly in the South Armagh area, and running agents/informers. Commenting on the deployment of the SAS, veteran human rights campaigner Fr Raymond Murray said: 'What the real motive of the British authorities was can only be guessed at but the general idea seems to have been to terrorise the people by assassination, by highly unorthodox and criminal methods.'

One of the cases Fr Murray raised back in 1976 was the execution of Peter Cleary, an unarmed IRA man who was visiting his girlfriend's home at Tievecrum, close to the border in South Armagh. Uniformed SAS soldiers accompanied by a civilian, surrounded the house and fired a shot before putting the family under arrest. The civilian, dressed in a chequered coat and black trousers, then identified Peter Cleary. Cleary was kicked and dragged to a barn where he was beaten. The terse statement issued by the British army a few hours later said that Cleary was 'shot dead trying to escape' – the old cliché for shooting a prisoner. He had been shot three times in the chest. Nairac was 'the civilian'.

A few months earlier Nairac crossed the border and kidnapped Sean McKenna from the family home in Edentubber, County Louth. Sean McKenna's father was one of the hooded men who had undergone sensory deprivation at the hands of British intelligence at the start of internment in 1971. He never recovered from his mental breakdown and died prematurely at the age of 42. The British government refused to name or prosecute the people involved, even when indicted for torture by the European Commission on Human Rights. Young Sean was interned alongside his father and after his release moved to Edentubber. He was in bed asleep on the night of 12 March when two men climbed through a window and put a 9mm Browning to his head and ordered him to get dressed. 'If you put up a struggle or don't want to come with us, say now. I will have no hesitation in shooting you.'

He was taken across the border, handed over to the RUC, interrogated and forced to sign a statement that was used to sentence him to 25 years in jail. Ironically, the date of the trial – 14 May 1977 – was the date that Nairac was killed. McKenna spent 3^1/$_2$ years on the blanket and 53 days on the first hunger strike in 1980 before lapsing into a coma and receiving treatment

One of Nairac's old teachers at Ampleworth College (the Eton of well-off British Catholics) described him as being insecure, like his hero T.E. Lawrence. He was certainly one of Brigadier-General Frank Kitson's gung-ho offspring. Kitson, a so-called counter-insurgency expert, advocated a form of counter-insurgency that generated the dirty war of assassination, sectarian violence and black propaganda. Nairac – who had real and raw power at his disposal – fought that war. Yet he was so arrogant that even when the British army had been told that an IRA unit in Cullyhanna had said that it was 'going to get the curly-headed little SAS man called Danny', he got up after 'The Broad Black Bremmer' and insisted on singing another three songs.

Massacre on the New Lodge

Suspected collusion: the people organise their own inquiry.

Andersonstown News, 18 November 2002

It was early evening. Belfast was Belfast. A fella came into a café on York Road. February 3rd, 1973.

Where were you? Not even born?

This happened.

The café was owned by Alfred Fusco, an Italian Catholic. People thought the customer was drunk. He produced a sub-machine gun and sprayed the owner who was fifty years of age and married with four children. He was killed. Upon hearing the shots a Protestant pensioner, Samuel Reynolds, died from a heart attack.

At half ten that night, six nationalists from North Belfast were still alive. They might have heard the news. Who knows? They went about their short lives.

Two of them, Jim Sloan, aged 19, and Jim McCann, aged 18, were about to leave Lynch's Bar at the top of the New Lodge Road.

19 and 18.

A car drew up and a passenger opened fire and the two lost their lives.

Catholic passers-by heard the shooting, but could not place it, saw the getaway car, thought it was the IRA, had seen British military vehicles in a side street, parked in the way of the getaway car, and were convinced they were going to be caught. The car sailed through and was later found. It was found outside Tennent Street RUC/British army barracks.

Such a long runback. Such a risk they ran.

Policemen – thirty years older now, promoted to detectives and superintendents – back then said that the killings were 'inexplicable', another one of those – to be – one thousand, 'motiveless' killings. Nine millimetre bullet casings were found in the car. Some time later the UDA, in an interview with, I believe, Jack Holland, said that they were working hand-in-hand with the British army and that it was one of their specialities to carry out at an attack and provoke a republican response so that British soldiers could shoot active-service IRA Volunteers.

Jim Sloan and Jim McCann were in the IRA. They were not on active service; nor was another victim, Volunteer Tony Campbell. In fact, another fella was about to leave the bar in front of Sloan and McCann, only he realised that he had a phone call to make and let the lads go out the door.

A few days before the shootings the British army had been issued with the latest technology – night-sights. That night they shot most of their victims through the head. They said that they had shot six gunmen and wounded a seventh. They have never retracted that statement, though the inquests found that there was no forensic evidence to link the men with weapons. All the families were given compensation, though most were given derisory sums.

The men who died.

Jim Sloan, Jim McCann, Tony Campbell, John Loughran, Brendan Maguire, Ambrose Hardy.

The men who shot them?

Anonymous. Protected. The law. The government. The authorities. The newspapers. History. The real gunmen.

Now represented, defended and protected by Tony – the IRA must disband – Blair.

But now the people of the New Lodge Road are fighting back through their community representatives and groups, and next week, on Friday and Saturday, November 22nd and 23rd, the families of the dead are organising an inquiry and seeking answers into these murders which were never properly investigated by the authorities.

Back then, in 1973, the nationalist community was disorganised and besieged and had been deserted, more or less, by the Irish government. Even so, Sinn Féin, the Catholic church, then lawyers such as SDLP Councillor Pascal O'Hare, Paddy McGrory (who later represented the families of the Gibraltar Three), Ted Jones, and a priest, Father Blaney, attempted to carry out a number of fact-finding inquiries to nail the official lie. They were vindicated insofar as the inquests ruled that none of the accused was armed or involved in aggressive activity at the time they were shot dead.

The inquiry organisers, among them, Paul O'Neill, Tommy Quigley and Irene Sherry, on very limited resources, which involves most of the jurists paying their own air-fares, accommodation and expenses, have diligently researched that night in February 1973. They have knocked on doors throughout North Belfast; found the people extremely generous; have raised funds; coaxed frightened people into giving testimony and have been boosted by the firm of Madden and Finucane which, in the pioneering spirit of Pat Finucane, has sponsored a number of lawyers, including American, Colleen Kerr, to dedicate their time into researching what happened that night.

In contrast to the response they have received on the ground and from the victims' families the group have received no replies to the letters they have written to the Northern Ireland Office, the General Officer Commanding of the British Army, the Department of Public Prosecutions, the RUC/PSNI, or Nuala O'Loan of the Ombudsman's Office. When *North Belfast News* asked the British army to stand over its version of events it was told, 'Fuck off.'

'So far,' says Paul O'Neill, 'the whole history of this event has been told by the British, the British media and the British military. The people's history, the people's version of what happened that night hasn't been told or documented. We have fifty witnesses whom the RUC never sought. The relatives are not into vindictiveness, are not looking for revenge, for soldiers to be charged or to be jailed. They just want the truth and, from our point-of-view, the truth is revealing about the hand-in-glove nature of the relationship between loyalist paramilitaries and the British army.

'Like their strategy in Derry on Bloody Sunday it seems that they expected the IRA to spill onto the streets after the initial shooting outside Lynch's bar. The Brits had sand-bagged emplacements at Edlingham Street from early in the day, then, that night, opened fire on people on the New Lodge. It was only later that the IRA came out but no IRA people were wounded or killed on active service.

'However, the fact that the IRA was involved at all has been the pretext for much of the southern media in Ireland to ignore our press releases and calls for coverage.'

Tony Campbell was out for his nineteenth birthday.

John Loughran was in bed, getting ready to watch an Elvis Presley movie, 'Flaming Star', when he went out to help a neighbour.

Brendan Maguire had the 'flu but decided to go out and meet a friend. He drank a coke.

He drank a coke and was shot dead.

Suspicion Over Omagh

Andersonstown News, 17 December 2001

One interesting aspect of last week's clash between Nuala O'Loan (Ombudsman) and Ronnie Flanagan (Old RUC Chief Constable) was the performance of various radio and television journalists. Because the two did not debate each other publicly, journalists had to play the role of devil's advocate, dealing with two articulate and formidable professionals who were not disputing the constitutional question but the RUC's flawed investigation into and handling of the Omagh bomb. Thus, the familiar rules for ridiculing, for example, the criticisms of your average Sinn Féin representative – with the unionist presumption that he or she is actually Sinn Féin/IRA with devalued moral rights – could not be applied to O'Loan.

I cannot be sure if my own prejudices are distorting my judgement but I got the distinct impression, certainly from the aggressive interviewing tactics of Jeremy Paxman on 'Newsnight' and Noel Thompson on 'Hearts and Minds', that O'Loan (the reformer) was treated in a more hostile fashion than Flanagan (the arch-defender of the Special Branch) who played for sympathy by reference to his potential, albeit conditional, suicide (which was actually insulting to the clinically depressed who are struggling for help and support). Similarly, most of the establishment media, politically-oriented as ever, mounted a rescue mission for the embattled chief constable, even if it meant riding roughshod over the feelings of the relatives of the Omagh victims.

It is beyond dispute that the RUC Special Branch and British Intelligence for years have infiltrated, controlled and directed the loyalist assassination campaign. Many suspect that William Stobie, who threatened to incriminate his handlers if he was imprisoned, was eliminated because he knew much more than has been revealed so far. In 1987 Stobie had been involved in the UDA murder of Adam Lambert but instead of being charged the Branch conspired to pervert the course of public justice and recruited him as an informer, as part of their dirty war against republicans and nationalists.

In February 1989 Stobie told his handlers that a 'top republican' was going to be shot by the UDA and he told them who was involved and gave them details of the movement of the weapons. Prior to this, Special Branch detectives during interrogations in Castlereagh kept dropping Pat Finucane's name to loyalists as 'a top Provo'. Around the same time that Stobie was giving his information, another British agent, UDA man Brian Nelson, was scouting Pat Finucane's house for the assassins along with a British Intelligence agent, codenamed 'Mags'.

The simple truth is that the British government was responsible for the murder of Pat Finucane – even if a loyalist paramilitary pulled the trigger. That is why getting to the bottom of this quagmire is proving so difficult: powerful interests are involved, reputations are at stake and exposure will have massive repercussions for British rule in Ireland. That is why in the public row between O'Loan and Flanagan, British Prime Minister Tony Blair and secretary of state John Reid have played down the significance of her findings and will ultimately back Flanagan over O'Loan.

When former British army intelligence officer Fred Holroyd made allegations that SAS Captain Robert Nairac had been involved with loyalist assassins he was accused of being 'a Walter Mitty' character, the same description Ronnie Flanagan now applies to the informant 'Kevin Fulton' who warned of an attack three days before the Omagh bombing. (Fulton's information, up until recently, had been described by the CID as 'A1'.)

I have my own theory about Omagh. It is that the Special Branch and MI5 knew from their informers there was going to be a car bomb. Both they and the securocrats have never been happy with the fact that they could not defeat the IRA, nor with the peace process and the success of Sinn Féin. They are driven by their own pro-union, anti-Agreement agenda. The spate of car bombings in the wake of the 1998 referenda in support of the Belfast Agreement undermined Gerry Adams' peace strategy, gave the impression of a deep split in the republican movement, encouraged republican dissidents by giving them an inflated view of their own numbers, strengthened the hand of anti-Agreement unionists and was persistently used to undermine nationalist demands for demilitarisation, the disbandment of the RUC and a new policing service.

I believe that they expected the bomb to go off, but that the town would be cleared. They didn't expect that the explosion would cause the worst fatalities in any single incident of the entire Troubles. And that is why a critical internal police review of the investigation was sidelined, why the Branch had to hide their intelligence reports, why the contact sheets of Fulton's information have gone missing, and why the Branch are now repudiating their own intelligence reports which O'Loan's English detectives unearthed. English detectives, some of whom have over thirty years experience, and who are described now by the increasingly desperate Ronnie Flanagan as displaying 'astounding ignorance of how terrorist organisations operate.'

The Crime of Castlereagh

A look at the history of Castlereagh Interrogation Centre, one week after intelligence files were stolen in a raid.

The Examiner, 23 March 2002

This Citadel, this house of hell,
Is worshipped by the law.
It's built upon a rock of wrong
With hate and bloody straw.

(*The Crime of Castlereagh,* by Bobby Sands)

Paul Fox and I were on the dance floor trying to impress the girls when the doors of Clonard Hall burst open and British soldiers began firing rubber bullets. When the screams died down Paul (17) and myself (19) were arrested with seventy other males. By midnight the two of us were in Castlereagh Interrogation Centre in handcuffs, and dying of thirst. That was November 1972. Paul and I were subsequently interned in Long Kesh and after his release in 1975 Paul was killed in an explosion.

Palace Barracks had been shut as an interrogation centre shortly before our arrest because of bad international publicity and because the Irish government had taken Britain to the European Court of Human Rights on charges that Britain had tortured detainees there, following the introduction of internment in August 1971.

So 'business' was transferred to Castlereagh Barracks, in loyalist East Belfast. The name Castlereagh is derived from the 'Caislen Riabhach' or 'Grey Castle' of the O'Neill clan in the 13th century which once perched on the Castlereagh Hills. Of course, it was also the title taken by the Tory, Robert Stewart, who as the hated Lord Castlereagh and Chief Secretary to Ireland ruthlessly crushed the 1798 rebellion, crucially with the help of agents, which was quite apposite, given the later association of Castlereagh Barracks with informers.

The cells and interrogation rooms were separated from the main building by corrugated fencing, topped with razor wire. Access was through a gate with an armed guard, with more armed guards in charge of the cellular block.

I was to spend many other periods at Castlereagh over the years, but I was lucky. Because I had a public profile it was unlikely that I would be beaten as happened to so many other anonymous prisoners, eighty per cent of whom signed incriminating statements against themselves (the highest rate of confession 'evidence' made in police custody throughout Europe). This 'evidence' was then used in the Diplock Courts to fill the H-Blocks where, once again, the prisoners were beaten.

The RUC and the Northern Ireland Office denied that any one was beaten in Castlereagh and said prisoners were inflicting injuries on themselves as part of the propaganda war against the police. But in March 1979 Dr Robert Irwin, a police surgeon, went on television and said that in the previous three years he had seen over 150 cases in which he was not satisfied that the injuries were self-inflicted. A story, from official sources, was leaked to the press, aimed at discrediting Irwin. It claimed that Dr Irwin's wife had been raped in 1976 and that Dr Irwin had harboured a grudge against the RUC for failing to catch the assailant. A man with an English accent had raped his wife at home and at gunpoint whilst Dr Irwin was examining a prisoner in police custody. As it turned out, Irwin had nothing but respect for the officers investigating the crime. Nevertheless, for being a whistle-blower he lost many friends.

The Special Branch was a law unto itself and has remained a law unto itself, a force within a force, which is one of the reasons why Sinn Féin refuses to sit on the Police Board and is demanding further changes in line with the Patten Report.

In *Beating The Terrorists* the journalist Peter Taylor interviewed several detectives. One said, 'the book on Castlereagh could only be opened slowly, as what was inside was political dynamite. He [the detective] told me that several powder kegs were involved and that now was not the time to take the lid off. Some expressed the fear that one day someone would open the book on Castlereagh and they would all be called to account.'

That quote, from 1980, was solely a reference to the secrecy in relation to the beatings that were taking place, and not the 'dirty war' of the 1980s and 1990s when Special Branch and British intelligence were colluding with and often directing the loyalist death squads. That is a scandal of monumental proportions, which has only been revealed in part. Were the truth to come out it would show the involvement of 10 Downing Street in actual terrorism and not just a few loose cannons in MI5 or the Special Branch. Why otherwise does the British government stubbornly refuse to hold a public inquiry into the assassination of human rights lawyer Pat Finucane?

Castlereagh closed as an interrogation centre in 1999 but from within its bowels the intelligence services continue their dirty war. Last week's seizure of files by unmasked men who knew their way around had to have been carried out by British agents with the objective of destroying some of the records of their terrorist deeds in order to protect individuals or the establishment itself.

Activists who went through Castlereagh were offered huge bribes, the guarantee of immunity from prosecution no matter what actions they had previously carried out, were told they could still kill and bomb to maintain their cover provided they joined the British side. Republican sympathisers were threatened with blackmail or subject to bribery in attempts to recruit them as informers. Those who refused the emoluments were beaten, or framed, or held out and got out to tell the truth about what went on there. The truth to which the now 'startled' media commentators and politicians for years refused to listen because they were more concerned with protecting state interests.

Poor Souls Didn't Know What They Were Doing

The Examiner, 17 June 2002

In February 1989, six months after the assassination of Belfast solicitor Pat Finucane, two hooded loyalists, who were also serving members of the British army, smashed the front window in the home of a Catholic man, Loughlin Maginn in Rathfriland, and shot dead the 28-year-old father of four in front of his family.

The UFF claimed responsibility and boasted that Maginn was a member of the IRA, an allegation denied by his family who said the killing was sectarian. In order to bolster its claim the UFF, believing that it was engaging in a great propaganda stunt, showed a BBC reporter pictures of alleged IRA suspects acquired from security sources, including one taken of Loughlin Maginn in RUC custody.

But the move backfired on the UFF: the cat was out of the bag.

Incredibly, as the furore of allegations of state collusion with loyalist paramilitaries increased, the UFF, stupidly, even plastered RUC photomontages of republican suspects on walls on the Shankill Road. It turned out that the UFF had thousands of RUC and British army intelligence files in its possession, most of which had been handed over by RUC or UDR sympathisers, or British military intelligence, through agents it ran within the paramilitaries.

In September 1989, John Stevens, an English Deputy Chief Constable, was appointed to carry out an inquiry into these breaches of security. Stevens uncovered what nationalists and republicans knew for many years: that the RUC Special Branch and British intelligence were colluding with loyalists, and used loyalists to kill certain people the state wanted out of the way.

Stevens uncovered that the UFF's director of intelligence, Brian Nelson, was an agent for the Force Research Unit (FRU), an intelligence group within the British army. It later emerged that British intelligence also allowed loyalists to import weapons from South Africa – weapons which subsequently led to the deaths of hundreds of nationalist civilians, and responsibility for which must ultimately rest with the British government. One internal FRU file noted that since Nelson took up his position, 'the targeting has developed and is now more professional'.

Stevens was called in again, in April 1993, to investigate further matters relating to his previous inquiry and to 'tie up some loose ends'. At no time, in either inquiry, was he asked to investigate the murder of Pat Finucane, despite Brian Nelson's involvement in the planning of his death, and information about an impending attack from another informer, William Stobie (who was, himself, assassinated by the UFF last December).

Nelson had been involved in fifteen murders, fifteen attempted murders and sixty-two conspiracies to murder during the period he worked for FRU. Nelson struck a deal with the Director of Public Prosecution, cleared by the then Attorney General, Sir Patrick Mayhew, which meant that there was no hearing. He pleaded guilty to lesser charges, was described as a man of great courage by his handler, 'Colonel J' (Brigadier Gordon Kerr, who is now the British military attaché in Beijing), and was sentenced to eight years.

In 1999, after a UN report called for a public inquiry into collusion, Stevens, now the Metropolitan Police Commissioner, was called in to conduct a third inquiry, finally, into the murder of Pat Finucane.

Among the devastating leaks from his report, due to be completed in the next few weeks, are his findings that the relationship between loyalist paramilitaries and state forces bordered on 'institutionalised collusion'. He recommends that charges be brought against several police and army officers; and that there be a reform of procedures, possibly including a downgrading of the Special Branch. His report does not estimate the number of shootings that resulted from collaboration.

A BBC *Panorama* programme, to be broadcast next Wednesday, is expected to contain further details surrounding the Stevens Inquiry, including interviews with former members of the Force Research Unit.

'Devastating' though his report may be, nationalists are bound to remain cynical about his conclusion that the state itself did not officially sanction the assassinations. Downing Street, the British army and the former RUC hierarchy will be able to quote that Stevens found no official policy of collusion and that officers made mistakes because there was 'a culture of incompetence that left junior ranks effectively making up the rules as they went along.'

That is: the poor souls didn't know that supplying information to a proscribed organisation and covering up their involvement in murder was wrong. That destroying the tape evidence of a confession by Ken Barrett, the man who pulled the trigger in the Finucane case, was wrong. That confirming the number plate of (Lord Mayor) Alex Maskey's car to loyalist assassins was wrong. And a host of other wrongs expected to be made right by a wringing of hands and a promise that it will not happen again.

Few nationalists expect that any possible prosecutions will lead to prison sentences (the guilty know too much about and would threaten to implicate their superiors). Nationalists will continue to call for an independent public inquiry, despite the Finucane case, and other instances of collusion, being re-examined by Peter Cory, an international judge.

Nationalists have already seen the British government agreeing to an inquiry into Bloody Sunday, only for the Ministry of Defence to withhold full cooperation. Similarly, many people are wondering, if it has got nothing to hide, why does the British government continue to thwart the inquiry into the Dublin and Monaghan bombings?

The Perfect Form of Collusion

The British state's arrangement with Brian Nelson.

Andersonstown News, 24 June 2002

Michael Finucane, son of Pat Finucane, last week joined with his sister Katherine and brother John, in calling for a public inquiry into their father's killing, following the recent *Panorama* exposé, 'A Licence to Murder'.

However, a public inquiry is the last thing the British government wants, and John Stevens, currently putting the final touches to his report into official collusion between state forces and loyalist paramilitaries, knows it also. The strategy, it would appear from comments made by Stevens on the BBC programme (he is careful not to suggest that the British government, the police or army officially sanctioned these killings) and echoed by the programme maker John Ware, is to emphasise that collusion was down to some 'rogue elements' and that Brian Nelson was 'out of control'. We even had First Minister David Trimble attempt to set the parameters when he said: 'One thing there was not was collusion by the RUC organisation with the paramilitaries. There may be individuals who have behaved badly but it was not structural or systemic.'

This, of course, is a red herring. No one is claiming that the entire hierarchies of the RUC or British army were engaged in systematic collusion. In fact, had every loyalist murder gang been receiving instructions or help on a widespread basis then it would have been simple for investigative journalists to have unearthed evidence of collective collusion much earlier, given how leaky loyalist paramilitaries tend to be.

What the British army and the Special Branch had in their arrangement with Brian Nelson was the perfect form of official collusion. Nelson was the UDA's top intelligence officer and they controlled him and streamlined his target files, which he then went on to distribute to almost any murder gang that asked. If British Intelligence or the Special Branch wanted someone killed they just had to suggest the name or a different target if they wanted someone preserved. Either way the forces of law and order were murdering citizens through the use of proxies.

An example of what can go wrong when state forces engage in too generalised a form of collusion, and involve too many people, can be seen from the 'GAL scandal' in Spain which led to the fall of Felipe Gonzalez's socialist government in 1996. When Gonzalez came to power in 1982 he sanctioned the creation of special units called the Grupos Antiterroristas de Liberación (GAL), which essentially were paramilitary death squads made up of hired assassins and members of the security forces which hunted down Basque ETA members, mostly on French territory. They killed at least 28 ETA members, but also shot several civilians who had no political connections.

When allegations of state involvement in the death squads appeared in newspapers, relatives of the victims began a campaign for a judicial inquiry into GAL. The paper *El Pais* referred to kidnappings, the use of drug world figures as mercenaries and the purchase of guns in South Africa – all of which uncannily echo aspects of the terror scenario between the UFF, British Intelligence and the Special Branch. A higher court blocked the first inquiry in 1988 under Judge Baltasar Garzon.

Then Garzon – not unlike Stevens – took the case again in 1994 after two former chiefs of the Basque Civil Guard (paramilitary police) blew the whistle. In 1991 the two had been sentenced to 108 years in prison after confessing to acting alone in a series of attacks against Basque separatists. It transpired later that the State Security Department had paid the two defendants more than $1.5 million to keep quiet, and also provided monthly payments to their wives. When the money dried up the two decided to name names and tell their story to the newspapers.

The Supreme Court convicted two senior government ministers for ordering and financing the kidnapping of an alleged ETA activist (they had kidnapped the wrong man). A former interior minister and his security chief were jailed for ten years. GAL was established and organised by government officials (both from the central and regional governments), Secret Service officials and high-ranking police and military officers. The Defence Intelligence High Command masterminded it. In other words, the operation involved too many and was too loose.

Nevertheless, the trail got lost before it led to the cabinet room. Gonzalez and his colleagues, who denied all knowledge of Spain's dirty war against Basque separatists, were never prosecuted.

Michael Finucane is correct when he says that the truth about his father's murder would rock the foundations of the British state. We know that in 1989 the then RUC Chief Constable Sir Jack Hermon and two other senior officers gave a private briefing to the Home Office Minister Douglas Hogg in Belfast. Hermon had claimed that some solicitors were sympathetic to, and were helping, the IRA.

A few weeks later Hogg repeated the remarks in the House of Commons. According to Greg Harkin in last week's *Sunday People*, 'Within hours UDA's west Belfast commander Tommy "Tucker" Lyttle was meeting with his Special Branch handler... Lyttle would later claim that his handler had discussed Hogg's comments and said to him: "Why don't you whack Finucane?"'

'The UDA's intelligence officer Brian Nelson, an agent of the army undercover unit, the Force Research Unit, was summoned to Lyttle's home in Sydney Street West and told to prepare a file on the lawyer. When Nelson reported back to his handlers, rather than discourage him from taking on the operation FRU members actively encouraged him to go ahead and gave him every possible assistance.'

In places like Central and South America collusion between official government forces and right-wing death squads rightly dismays informed opinion in the West which views such countries as pariah states. However, the BBC, though it is to be praised for making the 'Panorama' programme, never broadcast any trailers in Britain, nor were there any immediate follow-ups on the 10pm news, *Newsnight* or *News 24*, which seems extraordinary. It certainly smacks of a certain ambivalence, indicating an attempt to cosset the British public from the truth about its government.

Or, as Michael Finucane put it: 'Here in its own backyard it is being charged with the most serious crime a government could be charged with – assassination of its own citizens... An inquiry is needed,' he said, 'to establish if those at the pyramid of power knew what was happening.'

A Shameful Story

On the publication of just 17 pages out of 3,000 in the Stevens' Inquiry into collusion. The British establishment comes to the rescue of its state assassins.

The Examiner, 23 April 2003

Newspapers around the world, after the publication of just part of the Stevens Inquiry, have indicted Britain with headlines such as, 'British Officers Helped Kill Ulster Catholics'. In any democracy this should have been the occasion for questions in the House of Commons, except that the report into the largest criminal investigation in British history – with its sensational findings of official collusion – was published the day after parliament went into the Easter recess!

Nevertheless, the reaction of some in the British media, coming to the rescue of their army, was to be expected. Max Hastings in the *Daily Telegraph* said that collusion was a 'dreadful policy' but glossed the immorality through a piece of sophistry. 'Most people find it hard to regret the deaths of those involved in any way with Irish terrorism… In the absence of a death penalty, many British people have rejoiced when the security forces killed IRA terrorists in firefights or hot pursuit. In the 1980s, the Army's Force Research Unit decided to give this benign process a helping hand.'

David Aaronvitch in *The Observer* wrote that, 'it was pretty much inevitable that some security force personnel would be tempted to use loyalist terror groups as a shadowy proxy… How can a man such as Michael Stone (or a Martin McGuinness, some might add) be walking free, and yet we are contemplating imprisoning the policemen who were trying – albeit illegally – to stop the terror?'

Benign process? Albeit illegally? The terror?

According to the book *Lost Lives* (1999) loyalist paramilitaries were responsible for close to 30 per cent of the deaths during the conflict, and British forces for 10 per cent. That latter statistic is regularly used as simplistic proof that the authorities acted in a controlled, disciplined and lawful manner compared to the IRA, which was responsible for almost half the lives lost.

During his inquiries John Stevens found the fingerprints of Brian Nelson on hundreds of leaked intelligence documents. When he was arrested he told Stevens that he was working for the authorities. It is reported that Nelson died of a brain haemorrhage two weeks ago.

Nelson was living in Germany when Colonel Gordon Kerr who ran the secret Force Research Unit recruited him. Nelson was groomed to become the UDA's chief of intelligence, liasing with his FRU handlers who passed on to him thousands of official documents on republican suspects, which were then used to assassinate people – and often the wrong people. Sometimes Nelson informed his handlers of impending murders but they chose not to act in order to protect his anonymity.

Stevens sent files on Gordon Kerr and other operatives, including a Special Branch officer in the RUC who is now a senior member of the PSNI, to the Director of Public Prosecutions. There were no prosecutions. The reason? 'It would not be in the public interest'.

In carrying out his inquiries Stevens met with resistance and obstruction. Even his headquarters was set on fire by the British army in an arson attack, which he accused the RUC of never fully investigating. It was reminiscent of other obstructions to inquiries into the RUC and military.

When Sir Arthur Young carried out an inquiry into the fatal assault on 42-year-old Sammy Devenney in Derry by the RUC in 1969 he could not identify those responsible because of 'a conspiracy of silence' among the police. When John Stalker came here in the 1980s to investigate a number of RUC shoot-to-kill incidents he found himself suspended over false allegations that he associated with Manchester criminals and was removed from the inquiry. He later stated that RUC Chief Constable, John Hermon, obstructed him.

Among the controversial deaths Stalker was inquiring into were those of three unarmed IRA men who were shot dead at a police checkpoint in Lurgan in 1982. Three policemen, who lied about the circumstances of the shooting, were charged with the murder of one of the men, Eugene Toman, but were later acquitted. Giving evidence, one of those charged said that he had been told by his superiors to lie to the investigating officers and that the Official Secrets Act would cover his actions. The three were acquitted and the judge, Lord Justice Gibson, perversely commended them, 'for their courage and determination in bringing the three deceased men to justice, in this case to the final court of justice.'

The judge's gung-ho support for killing unarmed republicans was not unusual and was part of a pattern between the judiciary, the British army and the RUC where law and order and notions of justice were distorted or often set aside in the interests of the war against the republicans.

In one honourable exception to this rule, the Armagh coroner, Gerry Curran, resigned, in 1984 just before the inquests into the deaths of the three unarmed Lurgan IRA men were to be held. He said: 'Within the past few days I have been engaged in the review of police files in these cases. Certain grave irregularities are documented and recorded on the file. Consequently, I am not prepared to preside at the inquest in these cases.'

Twenty-one years later, there have still been no inquests. Solicitor, Pat Finucane, became involved and represented the families in their attempts to have inquests until he was assassinated in 1989 in what we now know to be a joint UDA/British army operation.

FRU and MI5's operations were reported to the Joint Intelligence Committee on which sit members of the British cabinet. However, Stevens has been careful not to implicate those in senior positions within the military and political establishments. But a source within FRU is quoted in the *Financial Times* as saying that 'the activities of the unit had the support of officials higher up the political and military hierarchy although such support was given in a way that left few paper trails and could be "plausibly denied" if and when challenged.'

Another FRU whistle-blower, who uses the pseudonym Martin Ingram, has been gagged from talking about collusion, including acts of murder, by a court order taken by the Secretary of State for Defence, Geoff Hoon. Is it any wonder that many nationalists are sceptical that charges and/or convictions will follow?

As well as acting as an intelligence officer Brian Nelson was also involved in importing from South Africa a consignment of weapons, two-thirds of which the British military allowed to be distributed to loyalist paramilitary groups. In the 1990s these weapons were used to kill over two hundred and fifty people, in places like Greysteel, Loughinisland and Sean Graham's bookmakers shop on the Ormeau Road.

A number of these weapons have been seized but none has ever been decommissioned. David Trimble has never made a priority of the disposal of these weapons which are still being used, except as an afterthought or as a tag-on to his strident demand that the IRA must decommission its silenced guns and disband.

Clearly, once we factor in the figures for the collusion upheld by Stevens, the total number of people killed, directly or indirectly, by British forces suddenly soars. And yet not even those figures truly reveal the scale of British responsibility in stoking the conflict.

We know that British Intelligence has fought its war on many fronts. It was secretly involved in bombing the south of Ireland and now, despite promises of transparency, the British Ministry of Defence refuses to fully cooperate with Judge Henry Barron's current inquiry into the Dublin/Monaghan bombings. British intelligence infiltrated, influenced and directed loyalist paramilitary organisations over a thirty-year period with a policy aimed at sickening, demoralising and defeating the nationalist community, at thwarting it and its demand for justice and equality.

In 1972 Albert Baker, a former SAS soldier/UDA hit man wrote: 'Half the assassinations in the early 70s wouldn't have been committed if there hadn't been RUC backing. Half the people who died in those assassinations, or more, would have been living today if the RUC hadn't supported the assassination teams.'

The Stevens Report is only the tip of the iceberg – but it is still shocking and scandalous. Yet, watch as the British establishment rescues its assassins, covers its trail and declares that it is time to draw a line in the sand, to move on and forget the past.

The Stakeknife Affair

Newspapers name West Belfast man and former internee, Freddie Scappaticci, as a British agent.

The Examiner, 14 May 2003

Among some of the stories that have appeared in the newspapers in relation to 'Stakeknife', the alleged senior IRA informer, is that he was involved in setting up myself and others for arrest thirteen years ago.

On Sunday, 7 January, 1990, I was contacted by the IRA who said that one of their members whom they had arrested and interrogated had admitted being an informer. This man, Sandy Lynch, had also confessed that his Special Branch handlers had been forcing him to set up for assassination two well-known north Belfast republicans. They wanted these two men killed in revenge for an undercover operation that had gone wrong, resulting in the death of one of their colleagues.

In November 1989 Lynch had tipped off his handlers that a rifle was being moved to a house in Belfast's New Lodge Road area, in preparation for an ambush. Incredibly, two different groups of policemen, none aware of the presence of the other, raided the house from the front and the back, shot at each other, resulting in the death of RUC officer Ian Johnston. The Special Branch was furious, Lynch had claimed.

Lynch was abducted and questioned by the IRA after a number of IRA operations had gone wrong and suspicion fell on him. Lynch admitted being an informer. He agreed that he would go to a Sinn Féin press conference and would name his handlers and accuse them of forcing him to set the two men up for assassination.

It was a 'good' story, further proof of an RUC policy of shoot-to-kill. I was the Sinn Féin director of publicity and was sent for. But when I arrived at the house to meet Lynch, a raiding party of British army and police jeeps swept into the street behind me. I tried to escape but was arrested next door. Lynch, whom I never met, gave evidence in our trial and said that whilst he had agreed to go to a press conference he didn't believe it would happen and was convinced that he was going to be shot. We were variously sentenced to between eight and twelve years imprisonment.

At our trial Lynch – who was also found to be a liar by the judge – said that one of his interrogators was Freddie Scappaticci and that Scappaticci withdrew from the house on Saturday night. I had arrived on Sunday night. In the early seventies I had been interned in Long Kesh at the same time as 'Scap', as he was known, but I doubt if I have spoken to him more than once or twice since, and certainly not in the last fourteen years.

In October 2000 the British Ministry of Defence issued gagging notices against several newspapers prohibiting them from naming an IRA informer working for British Intelligence's Force Research Unit and whose codename was Stakeknife. On the back of collusion allegations and the Stevens Inquiry there was a claim that in order to protect Stakeknife from a UFF assassination bid in 1987 Brian Nelson, at the behest of FRU, diverted a UFF murder gang to the home of Ballymurphy man Francisco Notarantonio whom they shot dead.

I have always found something odd about this story. Surely, when this was revealed in October 2000 the UFF men involved in the 1987 killing would have remembered who was their thwarted target. After all, Nelson had been unmasked as a British agent in 1990 and loyalists are bound to have reflected and speculated on Nelson's decisions. There is only one conclusion: loyalists, who notoriously cannot keep secrets, did not know who Stakeknife was.

If Stakeknife was such a senior figure, sabotaging the IRA, then throughout the past ten years he or she did not do such a great job when one recalls the mortar attack on 10 Downing Street in 1991 and the bombings in Bishopsgate and Canary Wharf or on the British army's HQ in Lisburn in 1997 when a soldier lost his life. It is alleged that last year the IRA broke into the Special Branch HQ at Castlereagh and stole intelligence files and had a spy ring at the heart of government. If so, where was Stakeknife to stop them? Had he been retired or come under suspicion and been frozen out?

Stakeknife's usefulness as an informant might have expired, but rumours of his existence and claims about his seniority and influence, however preposterous, have been used in recent years by British intelligence in an attempt to sow confusion and fuel republican dissent. Republican dissidents enthusiastically latched on to these reports to support the contention that he or she was someone close to the Adams' leadership and that Stakeknife – through his or her dirty work – had enervated the IRA's capabilities and steered the movement towards compromise and the peace process – as if republicans weren't clever enough to work out for themselves the wisdom and justice of the peace strategy.

I think we can take with a pinch of salt some of the more lurid claims being made in so-called quality newspapers about the state of morale within the Republican Movement. One national newspaper wrote: 'Meanwhile in the North the IRA appealed last night for calm among members, but some spoke of "the heart being ripped out" of the organisation by the controversy, which had the potential to destroy it.'

I live in West Belfast where it is claimed that Stakeknife has been living for over twenty years. The above newspaper quote reflects nothing of the true stoic mood of the people in this area who examine closely all that has been said and who is saying what. And what they see is bizarre.

For years the British Ministry of Defence issued gagging orders against newspapers, which said they knew and would reveal the real identity of Stakeknife (whose name they originally received from a former FRU officer). When those newspapers did just that last weekend, the MoD was uncharacteristically talkative.

Firstly, it said that Stakeknife was safely out of Ireland and was in a British army base in the south of England. Security correspondents repeated that story until a journalist from the *Sunday People* found the West Belfast man who was being named, Freddie Scappaticci, at home. The MoD then stated that Stakeknife was not with them.

Secondly, MoD sources – who for years had been protecting Stakeknife – confirmed in off-the-record briefings that the man being named in the newspapers was their agent. Why did they confirm this when they knew that no one had fled Ireland or was in their custody? Why would they break one of the cardinal rules of intelligence (which is to remain silent) and place this man in danger? Freddie Scappaticci told the journalist on Saturday night, then again through his solicitor on Monday, that no one had warned him that he was going to be named as Stakeknife and he has denied all the allegations.

Stakeknife, if he exists, can do no more damage to the IRA. But if even half of what is attributed to him is true – that he was allowed to cull informers who were no longer of any use to British Intelligence – then he is a major liability to the British Ministry of Defence and the British government because he can reveal many truths about their dirty war in Ireland.

The Politics of Terror

Irish Examiner, 31 December 2003

In the current 'international war on terrorism' various civil rights and international human rights are being infringed. Such infringements happen in most conventional wars and national emergencies, and are tolerated in the short-term by populaces as long as the war is perceived as being just, or the curtailments as measured, and they believe their government when it says it had no other choice.

Just two weeks ago the Barron Report into the Dublin/Monaghan terrorist car bombings in 1974 was released. It was heavily critical of the inactivity and ineffectiveness of Liam Cosgrove's Fine Gael/Labour coalition government and of the Garda investigation. The report revealed that Liam Cosgrove had been given the names of the bombers, that those names had not been passed to the Garda, that the forensic material had been lost, that the investigation was wound down after just 12 weeks and that the files on the case have gone missing from the Department of Justice.

The conviction that British intelligence and not just a few of its operatives unofficially colluding with the UVF was heavily involved in the bombings has been strengthened by the refusal of the British authorities to fully cooperate with the inquiry and by the mystery of the missing case files and what they could reveal.

In the absence of an alternative explanation many commentators have concluded that the government of the day had a choice. It could have scrupulously pursued the case and had the suspicion confirmed that the British authorities were engaged in an act of terrorism against the Irish people. Such confirmation would have led to a total breakdown in Anglo-Irish relations, a radicalisation of Irish opinion and increased support for the IRA.

Long before May 1974 the coalition had already made up its mind which side it was on in relation to the North. Armed British soldiers caught in suspicious circumstances in border counties were returned to the North without prosecution. Special Courts were being used to convict republicans of IRA membership on the word of a superintendent and Section 31 of the Broadcasting Act was censoring republican views. It was only a matter of time before this corrupting atmosphere gave way to the 'heavy gangs' when detectives could assault prisoners in order to force confessions which sent innocent people to jail.

So, for the 'greater good' of Anglo-Irish relations there was no enthusiastic pursuit of the killers and no justice for the dead.

Logically, it should be that the truth and facts – knowledge – dictate one's decisions. But in politics it is often the choices that politicians make that decide how the narrative is to be put, and thus it is that the powerful have a monopoly on how the story is told. So, for thirty years the British government were the 'good guys', the poor unionists were the ones under siege, and Irish republicanism, in armed struggle or in peace process, was to be denied, suppressed, censored and demonised. The background to the outbreak of conflict in the North (fifty years of unionist misrule) was to be muted and, instead, the IRA was to be held responsible for provoking British state repression and the loyalist campaign of assassination.

Republicans were laughed at when they spoke about shoot-to-kill, and state collusion with loyalist death squads – until the (heavily censored) Stephens' Report this year finally confirmed it. At the time of writing, the British government still refuses to publish the Cory Report into collusion in the North.

Sinn Féin's vote was derided and explained in terms of mass impersonation – until November's election, held under the strictest electoral identification laws in the world, resulted in the party emerging as the voice of the nationalist community in the North.

The case of the 'Colombia Three' presents yet another example of how prejudice can blind. In a few weeks time in Bogota a Colombian judge will rule on the fate of Niall Connolly, Martin McCauley and Jim Monaghan who were arrested in August 2001 and charged with training left-wing FARC guerrillas.

Their arrest has had a profound effect on the peace process in Ireland and was used by unionists as one of the reasons for their withdrawal from and collapse of the power-sharing Executive in the North from which politics has yet to recover.

Before they were even formally indicted the then President of Colombia, Andres Pastrana, made prejudicial remarks and declared on television that the three were guilty. Earlier this year the current Colombian President Alvaro Uribe told *Newsweek* magazine, 'We have in jail three IRA men who trained FARC'.

All of this has undoubtedly placed the trial judge, Judge Acosta, under intense pressure to find the three guilty despite no evidence against them and strong evidence in their favour. Back in Ireland, anti-Agreement unionists, exploiting any issue to undermine the Belfast Agreement, also dismissed the Colombia Three as having any rights.

Coming from this quarter this was unsurprising. Of more concern were the remarks of Taoiseach Bertie Ahern, reported on April 29th. He said: 'What is required [of the IRA] is a commitment that paramilitary activity has ceased, will not occur again so that we can get on, so that we do not have another Colombia...'

Worse still were the remarks from Michael McDowell speaking to a Progressive Democrat party conference in 2002, prior to last year's general election. As the

Irish Attorney-General he should have known better and known that his remarks would be picked up and published in Bogota, as they were. He said: 'But I think I speak for the great majority when I say that a political party which sends fraternal delegates to Marxist-Narco terrorists in Colombia, which keeps closer ties with the government of Havana than with any other state... has little moral claim on the electoral support of the Irish people.'

More recently, on Today FM, McDowell, who is now the Minister for Justice, said that Sinn Féin was 'morally unclean' and alleged that it is in receipt of IRA proceeds from 'organised crime'. He refused to substantiate his remark, which was aimed at damaging Sinn Féin. Certainly, he is entitled to be concerned at the electoral rise of Sinn Féin, and the possibility that it could displace the PDs in a future coalition with Fianna Fáil. But had he no thought for the effects his cavalier comments would have on attempts to put together a power-sharing Executive in the North? Indeed, anti-Agreement unionists, to justify their refusal to share power with Sinn Féin, seized on his remarks. Anti-Agreement unionists have done far more to undermine the peace process than the Colombia Three inadvertently have.

To make the peace process work republicans compromised and the IRA engaged in major acts of decommissioning only for the British government to default on the full implementation of the Agreement.

The peace process in the North, though still bedevilled by difficulties, has provoked a reflection on the causes of the conflict, a desire for truth and a demand to know who was responsible for what.

The censorship of Sinn Féin was an insult to the Irish people. It meant that the government didn't consider the electorate mature enough to decide for itself. It deprived Irish people of one side of an argument, which thus exaggerated the moral case of another side to the conflict – those for partition and the union with Britain. It meant not pursuing those ultimately behind the Dublin and Monaghan bombings. It meant distorting the truth. The culture that was then created persists.

Speaking aloud about his ongoing pipedream, Conor Cruise O'Brien, the Labour Minister for Communications who introduced Section 31 in 1973, said the other day: 'I have some hope – though not much – that if there is ever again a Fine Gael-Labour coalition, it would reinstate the ban on broadcasts by Sinn Féin.'

Such an infringement might have been possible and tolerated back in 1973 but in 2003 people have been able to read beyond the restrictions in the Barron Report, imposed by those who withheld full cooperation, and have began to understand who the international terrorists really are.

The Media

The Nun's Car

On investigative journalism

Andersonstcwn News, 3 April 2000

I roll in the aisles with laughter every time I think of that poor wee nun's car being hijacked and her being trailed out by the wimple and forced to watch her only means of transport burn before her eyes. It was many Augusts ago – the weekend of August 9th, 1976 to be exact, the fifth anniversary of internment, long before Feile an Phobail supplied a festive alternative to being shot with plastic bullets whilst watching a bonfire at the corner of your own street.

There had been rioting that weekend and Máire Drumm was arrested after addressing a Sinn Féin rally in Dunville Park. The following day on the front page of the *Irish News* appeared the headline, 'Nun's Car Hijacked and Set on Fire', along with these details: 'One of the motorists to lose a car to the hijackers was a nun, stopped while she was driving along the Falls Road and ordered out of the vehicle. Like the others it was set on fire.'

Had you been there you could have cooked spuds in the chassis. Yum, yum, Sister. Have a roastie.

The German writer Erich Kastner wrote a novel, *Fabian*, about the life and death of an advertising copyrighter in Berlin in 1929, set at a time when civil and public life were breaking down. One of the scenes takes place in the offices of Fabian's newspaper. Munzer, a journalist, is stuck for a column filler as the paper's deadline approaches so he writes: 'Street fighting between Mohammedans and Hindus has broken out in Calcutta. Although the police soon had the situation in hand the casualties were fourteen dead and twenty-two injured. Order has now been fully restored.'

A colleague questions the ethics of inventing news but Munzer indignantly takes him to task: 'No fighting in Calcutta? Will you kindly prove that? There's always fighting in Calcutta… Besides, why all this sympathy for the fellows? They're still alive, all thirty-six of them, and sound as a bell.'

Try as I might I could find no trace of the nun. I telephoned all convents in Belfast. Yes, they had read the story but they were as baffled as I was. I phoned Bishop Philbin's residence. 'We're puzzled ourselves. If it were to be reported to any authority it would have been reported to us,' I was told. Then I did something I shouldn't have done. I phoned the RUC information office. I swear, I only collaborated for a minute. Plus, I used a false name. They had no reports of the incident either.

I telephoned the *Irish News* and was told that Tom Samways wrote the story. Eventually I got through to him. He said he stood over it. 'Where exactly did the hijacking take place?', I asked. At this stage Tom decided that he was no longer having this conversation with me. When I complained to the editor that the incident never happened he told me, just like Munzer, to prove that a nun's car hadn't been hijacked and burned!

Then somebody told me on the Falls Road that something had happened to a car belonging to a nun who was staying in the parochial house beside St John's Chapel. I telephoned and the nun in question agreed to meet me. She told me that one night over the weekend a youth was discovered trying to steal her car radio but was chased away. The following day a journalist telephoned, asked her had she been hijacked and her car set on fire and she said she hadn't, but explained about the break-in, and that was that.

Enough bad things happened during the Troubles without journalists embroidering details or inventing stories. Of course, the most inveterate liars were British journalists, as they sat drooling in the Whip and Saddle bar of the Europa, deadline approaching, desperately staring into the mirror, only to be struck by a brainwave. Republican Source would suddenly appear on their knee, or his grandfather, Senior Republican Source.

'It is believed,' whispers Senior Republican Source to Intrepid British Correspondent, 'that we are moving explosives through Stranraer this very Saturday on coaches carrying duped Celtic fans to the match. It is thought that we particularly hate the Royal Family and it is suspected that we are planning to bomb London on the Queen's birthday, though if this gets out, thanks to British Newspaper Exposes Cowardly IRA Plan, then Operation Pint of Guinness for Darby O'Gill and the Little People will be cancelled.

'The Security Forces,' continues Senior Republican Source, as he jealously spots his cousin, Source Close to the Army Council, on the knee of the man from the *Daily Mail*, 'have long believed that it is thought that tougher measures are feared by the IRA. I can confirm this fear, off the record.

'I can reveal that at least five members of the British Labour Party are if not almost in the IRA then they are almost sympathetic to some of our actions. It is thought we are no longer involved with the Angel Dust scam or pirate videos but have moved on to the more lucrative e-tab and counterfeit CDs market.

'Shergar's dead, my friend. An asthmatic attack.

'Senior Republican Source can confirm to you, and you alone, that this week's Chief of Staff is a Maguire from Fermanagh. Keep that under your hat. A former Benedictine monk and chess grandmaster, he owns five hotels in Bundoran, is a Marxist hardliner and speaks eight languages. As we sit here, fifteen Volunteers are on their way to Libya to be indoctrinated. It is understood that Nor-Aid has been kept deliberately in the dark.

'Senior Republican Source says get yourself another glass of Black Bush and put it down to expenses. Rendezvous, same time, same place, next deadline. You will recognise me. Senior Republican Source will be underneath your trousers, wearing your underpants, with his feet in your socks, Kemosabe.'

'Please wait!' calls out Intrepid British Correspondent. 'Before you go back to the labyrinthine alleyways of your bandit ghetto where your paramilitary womenfolk bare their breasts from their bedroom windows to enable your £1,000-a-hit Czech snipers to kill naive young British soldiers keeping two warring religious tribes apart, I must put it to you, Senior Republican Source, about the nun's car. What really happened?'

'That would be loose talk. I have no comment. I refuse to be drawn. Republicans are remaining silent. I am tight-lipped. No one was available. I have gone to ground. We have closed ranks. Prove it.'

A Right Paean in the Ass

Revisionism. Reading Kevin Myers – an Irishman's Diary, *Four Courts Press.*

The Examiner, 3 March 2001

Firstly, an interest to declare. Adrian Myers, aged 52½ doesn't like me. A few years ago he attacked the Arts Council for giving 'a grant to one of the most sinister IRA terrorists of all, Danny Morrison'. Last December he devoted his column to an attack on me because I had climbed out of steerage and complained about the service on the Enterprise train when we in second class had to wait for our breakfasts until those in first class were served. According to M, having a prison conviction pretty much disqualifies one from the human race.

'Danny, my boy, you're alive, and thousands are not. So shut up,' he wrote. Okay M, I'll listen to you instead.

M is a clever, provocative writer and often quite funny, if often pompous, pious and a paean in the ass. In the USA the President delivers a State of the Nation address once a year: our polymath in the *Irish Times* can give you up to four a week. M has doctorates on himself, guerrilla, trench and conventional warfare, art, motor cars, mobile phones, sport, nature and the environment, architecture, Dublin city, the weather, women drivers, summer schools, the modern family, single mothers, immigrants, travellers, and wine and food, wasps, spiders and bats.

Obviously, much of his writing is geared to creating controversy, and there may be some who buy the paper solely for their M fix. But he doesn't come cheap. Several out of court libel settlements have cost the paper a pretty penny, including £250,000 in costs and damages paid out to the relatives of those killed in Derry.

An ordinary mortal, M has his share of contradictions. A man totally opposed to violence (and boxing) he upholds the jolly blood sport of fox-hunting. 'Might not the swift hunger of a pack of dogs, whose individuals can dispose of a cat in seconds, collectively deliver to a fox a hastier and more merciful end... If they get a fox, it will be a lucky fox, one that this night or next will not now die of cold or famine or disease...'

Well, obviously not, since the poor thing has been eviscerated, drawn and quartered.

A psychologist might suggest that Squire M is suffering from secondary shell shock. For years he has championed the cause of the forgotten Irish who died in the ranks of the British army in the First World War. Their war was a 'courageous' one, was 'poignant', 'a true epic', full of sacrifice, even though, as it turned out, they weren't fighting for the cause that they thought. On the other hand, Irish republicans who fought in 1916 and in the Tan War, and who knew what they were fighting for, were stupid. The Easter Rising was 'an unmitigated evil for Ireland' which left 'a legacy of violence and murderous, clandestine covens.'

IRA Volunteers 'murdered', whereas RIC men and British soldiers were merely doing 'their duty'.

'I am not saying the security forces were not killing people at that time. But such killings were in spontaneous and occasional affrays.' During the current conflict British army killings did 'not compare with the atrociousness of the IRA campaign.' The security forces are 'amongst the true heroes of the Troubles.'

He despises Michael Collins, opposed the candidacy of Marys Robinson and McAleese for the presidency, opposed the peace process, supported the release of Paratrooper Lee Clegg (M was 'far from convinced that murder, in its full and premeditated sense, was what Clegg had in mind' when the two unarmed teenagers were shot in the back). Later, he admitted to being wrong in some of his opinions, but in subsequent diary entries he was stranded in no man's land, three battalions short of a regiment.

Adopting unionist-speak he refers to Sinn Féin/IRA. Republicans, he says, speak 'heathen gibberish', though I suppose I should be thankful that omitted from this book is that appalling piece he wrote describing dead IRA Volunteers as 'the progeny of a sow's litter'. M at his humanitarian best.

Five years ago in *The Spectator* magazine he wrote about an incident in the 1970s when he was working as a journalist in Belfast (and recalls it in this book). He said that he was in a pub in Andersonstown when a fight broke out between two men, one of who was badly beaten. The IRA arrived to sort out the situation and Myers says that he heard Gerry Adams say to the IRA about one of the men, 'Shoot him.'

What is extraordinary about this story is the Myers can't remember the name of the bar, the date, who was shot (if anyone was shot), and, strange for a journalist, didn't write about his 'exclusive' at the time. Surprise, surprise, he only remembered the story at the height of the cease-fire in 1995, and used it to denigrate Adams and call into question his commitment to peace.

If you are a fox, a feminist, a single parent, a supporter of neutrality, an opponent of imperialism or an ex-internee, on a country lane in the vicinity of County Wicklow, and you see a jaunty, liveried equestrian wearing a bowler hat, puffing up his cheeks to blow his horn, my advice to you is to run for your life, because Squire M takes no prisoners.

The Politics of Condemnation

Condemning violence: when it began and how the media adapted

Andersonstown News, 6 March 2000

A few days ago on BBC radio's 'Good Morning Ulster' two elected representatives were interviewed about the discovery of a new-type of rocket launcher abandoned near a British army base in Dungannon. Its discovery came hard on the heels of a military attack on a British army barracks in Derry and the bombing of a hotel in Irvinestown.

The first to be interviewed was Francie Molloy of Sinn Féin. As a nationalist/republican listener you had a fair idea of what he was trying to say: that the political vacuum and the undermining of politics caused by the suspension of the Agreement creates the conditions in which dissident organisations can thrive. However, the cogency of Molloy's reply and, in my opinion, the importance of his reply (alerting the unionist public to the really dangerous situation that is developing), was cut in mid-stream when the presenter turned the interview around and asked him did he condemn the attempted rocket attack. He didn't say that he did and he didn't say that he didn't and not for the first time an interview was squandered and the negative perception of unionist listeners reinforced.

The second representative questioned was Ken Maginnis, security spokesperson for the Ulster Unionist Party. As happens in such circumstances he had the advantage of commenting on the remarks of the Sinn Féin man whose interview was over and who was no longer on the air. Maginnis made hay of Molloy's ambivalence and reminded listeners that this was the man who a few years ago said that if the peace process failed, republicans 'would go back to what we do best.'

Maginnis interprets this statement solely as a threat of the IRA returning to armed struggle. While that may well be one valid reading, a study of what Molloy said in full at a commemoration in South Armagh, from where the quote is taken, indicates that he was talking in a much broader context, one of political mobilisation and street protest.

Maginnis then went on to say that the discovery of the rocket launcher proves the case for the demand for IRA decommissioning. In fact, it proves no such thing, but the interviewer never probed him on this point – that no amount of IRA decommissioning would ever remove the weaponry of dissident republicans from the equation, not least imported rocket launchers of this new type.

Between 1968 and 1970, the period before the IRA became active, most of the violence on the streets was either carried out by the state or loyalists in support of the state. I have searched through the pages of the *Belfast Telegraph* and the *News Letter* of that time and not once could I find an editorial condemning violence or a government minister being asked to condemn violence.

In fact, you cannot even find the word 'condemn'. Rather, both papers use the word 'deplore' when giving their opinions on the activities of the Civil Rights Association. In early August 1969, after at least three Catholic civilians (Francis McCloskey, Sammy Devenney and Patrick Corry) have been killed by the RUC, under an Ulster Unionist government, an editorial in the *Belfast Telegraph* says, 'There is little to be gained by apportioning blame'.

Suddenly, however, the story changes as the IRA arrives on the scene and starts its operations. The two unionist newspapers increasingly call upon the SDLP and Catholic clerics (Sinn Féin was a proscribed organisation and had few spokespersons) to dissociate themselves not just from IRA activity, but from barricade-builders, stone and bottle throwers, and the ongoing marches organised by the Civil Rights Association. IRA bombings and shootings were easy to condemn, though the latter demand was problematic for the SDLP whose members spoke at most of the banned rallies. But the net effect was that nationalists were placed on the defensive, and had to pass a test which wasn't asked of unionists and which, indeed, they couldn't have passed. The blame game had begun.

The British and the unionists simplistically divided violence into two: good violence, ours, associated with the activities of the 'Security Forces'; and bad violence, theirs, otherwise known as 'terrorism', see under The IRA. Media treatment and interview techniques followed suit. All of this gave unionists the psychological comfort of being able to engage in the fallacy that the IRA bore responsibility for the deaths of all those who were killed, a fallacy which informs and distorts their attitude to IRA decommissioning – the baddies must surrender.

The statisticians tell us that the British army killed only 200 innocent civilians but not once in 28 years of direct rule was a Secretary of State ever asked, in the aftermath of any of those 200 deaths, if he or she condemned 'last night's violence'. That would have been to query the rules of the propaganda war.

What galls me is that from the Ulster Unionists to the British government and from the SDLP to the Dublin government the demand that violence be condemned is hypocritical, given that they all support the use of violence – war, military intervention – in certain circumstances. The Catholic hierarchy in Britain, so much for independent moral thinking, condemned the hunger strikes of 1981 as acts of suicide but justified the Falklands War a few months later.

Bill Clinton and Tony Blair stood crying on the streets of Omagh and a few months later in Kosovo and Serbia killed children, women and men in greater numbers (over 500) than republican dissidents. By the way, many of these victims were its allies, killed in attacks on trains or by cluster bombs. The IRA around 1974 planted a hoax bomb outside the BBC, claiming that the BBC was broadcasting British propaganda. Journalists and leader writers widely condemned it as an attack on free speech. Compare that reaction to the silence when the British bombed a television station in Belgrade killing nine journalists and women cleaners because the station allegedly broadcast Serbian propaganda.

Francie Molloy was right to stand his ground. Better to be honest, even if it means being misrepresented, than to be a hypocrite.

We Now (Don't) Have a Party Political Broadcast on Behalf of …

Changes to the rules on election broadcasts

Andersonstown News, 21 May 2001

Imagine a Sinn Féin election broadcast making a point about double standards. It shows Ian Paisley in a trench-coat on top of a hillside with a hundred supporters, waving fire-arms certificates at the moon, subtitled 'Decommission ALL Guns!' Or Ian Paisley jigging with David Trimble at the end of Garvaghy Road with the message, 'No Walks Without Talks!' Or an election broadcast showing the Reverend William McCrea sharing a platform with the killer of Catholic kids, the late Billy Wright, or David Trimble going into the Assembly flagged by representatives of the PUP and UDP, and making the point about unionist hypocrisy.

Well, under broadcasting rules drawn up in 2001 by Ann Sloman, chief political advisor to the BBC, none of the above would be allowed. Up until about seven years ago, most party political broadcasts in the North boringly featured party leaders or spokespersons looking into the camera, reading from an autocue and addressing viewers. Then BBC and UTV announced that the parties could make their own election broadcasts, provided they met certain technical specifications, and that archive footage could be purchased from them.

Sinn Féin jumped at the opportunity and of all the parties was perhaps the most notable in its use of television archive, producing some highly visual and stirring election broadcasts. Often it had to fight with the local television controllers over the content. It was after several scrapes and a court case that – surprise, surprise – the BBC and UTV decided to cancel the sale of all but a strictly limited choice of archive material!

At the 1998 Assembly elections Sinn Féin got around this obstacle by purchasing the footage of, for example, RUC attacks on nationalists on the Ormeau Road and Garvaghy Road from other sources, including Sky News. But now, the effect of the new regulations has been to rule out even that, apart from the most bland of footage. The effect has been to emasculate party political broadcasts and make it impossible to effectively criticise one's opponents, their weaknesses and flaws or show them up in their own words and actions.

The regulations state that: 'The use of material featuring exchanges between the parties [in the Assembly] should not be included.' So, no banter between Martin McGuinness and Sammy Wilson, and no depiction of the virulent sexism of the DUP towards, for example, the Women's Coalition.

'Archive of news clips of members of any other political party should not be included.' In other words, one cannot use footage of that famous film clip showing David Trimble, Seamus Mallon, Martin McGuinness, Bairbre de Brun and Michael McGimpsey around the Executive table on their first day together. One cannot show McGimpsey and Adams together at the Mozart Requiem. One cannot show the political process working despite the fact that whether it continues working has been the single most important issue in all of the elections!

Now, one may think that this ban on including other parties is a good thing because it applies to everyone and perhaps robs Ian Paisley of supplementing his tired, old 'Smash Sinn Féin/IRA' message with footage of a long-haired, young Gerry Adams militantly addressing an Ard Fheis. But, in reality, it is the unionists who wish not to be seen doing business with Sinn Féin, not the other way around.

In May 2001 when Sinn Féin submitted its election broadcast to the BBC, the BBC (UTV allows the BBC to draft the rules) telephoned the SDLP and told them that in the broadcast there is footage of John Hume shaking hands with Gerry Adams. (This was in Dublin, along with Albert Reynolds, in September 1994, just after the first IRA cessation was announced.) And guess what? The SDLP successfully demanded that it be removed! So much for the hand of friendship and reconciliation.

It's hard to quantify what part, if any, a party political broadcast plays in influencing a voter's choice. One of the worst broadcasts several years ago – in fact, a Sinn Féin broadcast – could not be said to have had any measured effect since the two embarrassed individuals it featured were elected to the Assembly anyway. I think a good broadcast probably raises the morale of party workers and makes them feel good or proud and helps them work harder.

In the general election of 2001 the British Labour Party had originally planned to depict William Hague and Michael Portillo as the alien crew of a spacecraft threatening the City of London. They got the idea from 'Independence Day'. Another film showed Baby Hague – would you let this child run your country? – going down a waterslide wearing his wee bathing hat and chuckling with excitement.

With their Marquess of Queensbury Rules, what the BBC and UTV have now done is to narrow the creative possibilities and remove the opportunity for a bit of controversy and craic.

For the Cause of Liberty

On Kevin Barry and his IRA comrades on their re-interment in Glasnevin Cemetery

The Examiner, 8 October 2001

W hy could they not be exhumed and reburied in private? asked Chris Ryder of the *Sunday Times* about next week's state funerals in Dublin for the re-interment of ten IRA Volunteers who were executed by the British in 1920 and 1921. 'Like the Americans of today,' wrote Paddy Murray in the *Sunday Tribune*, equating 'the murderous deeds' of the Volunteers of the war of independence with the suicide bombers who flew into the World Trade Centre, 'they [the British] demanded retribution. Kevin Barry and nine others provided that retribution with their deaths.'

The funerals, wrote Fintan O'Toole in the *Irish Times*, will offer 'a great boost to those who want us to feel that the only difference between a terrorist and a patriot is the passage of time.' That is, Kevin Barry and, by implication, the rest of the IRA were terrorists. If that is the case what does that make their hangmen, the British? Well, I suppose they were just here reading us Jane Austen, teaching us cricket and helping our little nation to develop its natural resources.

Kevin Myers, also in the *Irish Times*, complains that next week's event is all about reaffirming 'a single narrative of suffering and sacrifice'. I don't know why. He seems to know the name of every British soldier killed by the IRA since 1916, or who died at the Somme and Passchendale. He has been writing their stories for years. He doesn't write about Germans. Is he not guilty of reaffirming 'a single narrative of suffering'? Calling for reprisals, after the recent bombing of New York and Washington, he wrote that he was all-the-way-with-the-USA, even though 'mistakes will be made'. So, it would appear that it is not the act of killing/terrorism, after all, that is objectionable, but the cause on behalf of which it is carried out.

These commentators, and opposition Labour leader Ruairi Quinn, have also alleged that the funerals are a cynical exploitation by Fianna Fáil, aimed at stealing what's assumed to be Sinn Féin's clothes and minimising that party's anticipated electoral advances. The oration, televised live, will be delivered by Taoiseach Bertie Ahern in Glasnevin Cemetery where Pearse spoke over the remains of O'Donovan Rossa. (However, don't be expecting 'Ireland unfree shall never be at peace', nor, hopefully, anything as gauche as 'Kevin Barry would have supported Fianna Fáil, NATO etc.')

The oration will be delivered on the eve of the Fianna Fáil ard fheis and it is suggested that this is no coincidence. After all, Fianna Fáil had ample opportunity to exhume the bodies during its many lengthy periods of government in the 1930s (before it brought in the English hangman, Pierpoint, in the 1940s to execute IRA men), in the 1950s and, for example, in 1966 during the golden jubilee of the 1916 Rising when pageantry was at its optimum. It chose to leave them lying in prison yards. At any stage, even during the recent conflict, it could have released the remains to the next-of-kin, but chose not to.

After the IRA ceasefire in 1994 spokespersons for the National Graves Association and Sinn Féin raised the issue of exhumation and re-interment with the government and in letters to the press (just as they did in regard to the remains of Tom Williams, whose remains the British released from Crumlin Road Jail for reburial two years ago). As far as I know, no request was made for a state funeral. However, even if the timing of the re-interments is suspect, for nationally-minded people, which includes most of Fianna Fáil and its supporters, these funerals represent due honour to patriots who sacrificed their lives in the struggle for independence.

What many of the opponents of the state funerals resent is the fact that the event is actually tapping into a buoyant public mood that they have strived for years to repress. These people would have Ireland feel guilty about its past, without begging the same moral question of Britain about its disastrous role in Irish affairs. Kevin and Fintan, and whoever, can choose not to like their grandparents, figuratively speaking, but they shouldn't get away with imposing that piece of Freud on the rest of us.

For phrases such as 'sending a dangerous signal to impressionable young people' and 'will be widely and dangerously misunderstood', read 'the people are stupid and we have to save them from themselves.' It is nonsense to suggest that for the country to pay its respects in this grand manner now makes its citizens retrospective conspirators to shootings and bombings, or that it legitimises the recent IRA campaign, or acts as a recruiting sergeant for the IRA. Ask any ex-republican prisoner or IRA Volunteer to name who or what influenced their decision the most to join the IRA. It will not be Kevin Barry. It will be, 'a British soldier.'

Anyone who has read the book *Curious Journey*, an oral history of the Tan War period, in which IRA veterans express their regret (and sometimes weep) for the suffering and death their actions caused, whilst not balking at the stance they took, will realise that these men and women are the first to acknowledge the ambiguities and complexities all conflicts throw up. These ten dead men were their comrades and for forfeiting their lives on our behalf they deserve the few hours of public honour they shall receive next Sunday.

'Ireland – Bobby Sands!'

Andersonstown News, 12 May 2003

If you type 'This Day in History, May 5th' into the search engines of the History Channel or most newspapers it will show up something along the lines of: 'In 1981, Irish Republican Army hunger-striker Bobby Sands died at the Maze Prison in Northern Ireland in his 66th day without food' (*Boston Globe*). In other words, Bobby Sands' name has been immortalised by his and his comrades' hunger strikes twenty-two years ago.

A news reporter on Fox News in the USA last week soon found out how much a legend is Bobby Sands when he attempted a crude joke on television. At the end of the news, Steve Shepherd, said: 'On this date Bobby Sands died after sixty-six days on a hunger strike in prison in Belfast, Northern Ireland. The moral of the story: eat more often.'

Irish-Americans were outraged and an online petition was soon organised which forced Fox News and Shepherd to apologise. Fox TV Network is, of course, owned by media mogul, Rupert Murdoch, an old friend of Mrs Thatcher and it was Murdoch's HarperCollins which advanced Mrs Thatcher $5.4 million for her almost unreadable memoirs.

Shortly after Bobby died in 1981 some idiot, in an attempt at irony, wrote on a gable wall in loyalist East Belfast, 'We'll never forget you, Jimmy Sands.'

Travel almost anywhere in the world, mention that you are from Ireland, and the response you are likely to get is, 'Ireland – Bobby Sands!' No one answers, 'England – Mrs Thatcher!' though nowadays they might answer, 'England – George Bush!' Bobby Sands' name lives on and the legacy of the hunger strikers continues to inspire not just Irish republicans but many nationalities that associate it with nobility, sacrifice and courage in the face of a bullying power.

Last year two small events showed how ordinary people if motivated and mobilised can make a political point and their voices heard. In November the BBC World Service, as part of its 70th anniversary celebrations, announced that it was holding a poll for the world's top tune.

The poll attracted submissions from all around the world. Nearly 150,000 votes were received from 153 countries, nominating over 6,500 songs. Even The Beatles failed to make the top ten. One of the strongest contenders was a patriotic Hindu song, 'Vande Mataram', which is considered by many as India's national song.

Someone, somewhere, came up with the bright idea of nominating 'A Nation Once Again' by The Wolfe Tones, and encouraging like-minded people to concentrate on that one song. Using the internet and the Irish diaspora, e-mails poured into the BBC. As a result, 'A Nation Once Again', written in the 1840s by Thomas Davis and first recorded in 1964, was voted the world's top song!

Of course, the reaction of the BBC World Service to this shock result was to announce that it was going to hold yet another poll to see if its listeners agreed with the result! Whether it went ahead I am not sure – but the psyche at play was quite revealing and not too far removed, for example, from that colonial practice of postponing native elections until one gets the results one likes.

Around the same time, BBC Radio Ulster carried out a poll for 'Ulsterman of the Century'. I hadn't even heard it was taking place and saw no reference to it in any internet bulletin boards, which suggests that there was little or no canvassing, yet, once again, Bobby Sands was up there in the Top Five (along with Ian Paisley, and the late Joey Dunlop who topped the poll).

The intransigence of the British government at the time of the hunger strikes was made possible because its behaviour was never checked by concerned, domestic pressure. The British public was left ignorant by the great British media who moulded the public's opinions of Ireland and of people like Bobby Sands. The conflict was presented as inexplicable or tribal or atavistic but never in an intelligent or, for that matter, in an honest or impartial way. We saw again in the recent Iraqi war how journalists identify and bond with their own troops.

Last year the veteran BBC correspondent, Kate Adie, published her autobiography, *The Kindness of Strangers*. Adie would be most familiar as that figure riding atop a British army tank, in her flak jacket and helmet, reporting from the Balkans or Afghanistan. But before that her job was often to explain the North to British viewers. And to her the hunger strike was 'bog-trotting stuff.'

I have written before, how on the morning that Bobby Sands died she interviewed me on the Falls Road. It remains the most hostile interview I ever did in twenty-five years. Still, I thought I acquitted myself well and got the better of her, but it was never broadcast. The BBC claimed that the film 'didn't come out.'

In her book she makes no mention of this interview but writes about sneaking into Bobby's wake 'in a headscarf and scruffy anorak'. She says: 'In his coffin, Mr Sands did not present a pale face of suffered humanity. He looked like a banana. Luminous yellow. I sniffled and coughed and looked hard. This was not the time and place to comment on the effects of hepatitis A and liver failure – nor the fact that the local embalmer had apparently used furniture varnish by the look of it. Thank God no one put a friendly arm round my shoulder at my supposed overcome state. I'd just learned what actors meant by corpsing.'

Earlier she compares the British army to the locals. 'The army was full of pink-cheeked lads, squat and muscley…'

Anti-H-Block marchers, on the other hand, were, 'pasty-faced, lank-haired young women, with pushchairs of mewling children. Skinny lads, with hunched bony shoulders and pipe-cleaner legs; middle-aged – or perhaps not, but older – women, in groups, all smoking during the six miles up the Falls, skin shiny with anti-depressants, and voices raucous…'

These weren't the people, the community I saw and was with during those dark, sad days: dignified people who were shot and pulverised on their own streets for daring to oppose British policy. Kate Adie claims that what came out of Belfast was, 'Efficient and carefully judged journalism', but in her own words she reveals something of the deep-seated prejudices which informed a style of reporting that kept the British public in ignorance and which did a disservice to the living and the dead.

After September 11

After September 11

Andersonstown News, 17 September 2001

Last May, driving through Scotland, I stopped at Lockerbie and went to the Garden of Remembrance that was established in memory of the 259 people killed in the explosion on board Pan Am Flight 103 and the eleven who perished on the ground in Lockerbie village on 21 December, 1988. The 270 victims came from 21 nations and their ages ranged from two months to eighty-two years. Thirteen years on, I am not sure whether any thing has been learnt from this tragedy.

There is a peaceful, almost serene aura about the Garden, which contains family plinths etched with simple tributes to loved ones. On a bronze plaque there is a poem, eerie in its premonition, written by twenty-year-old Karen Lee Hunt, a student from Syracuse:

> Something has happened to keep us apart,
> But always and forever you're in my heart,
> Some day soon, from now till forever,
> I'll meet you again and we'll be together,
> I'm not sure how, and I'm not sure when,
> Together, forever, somewhere my friend.

Immediately after the bombing the first suspects had been a pro-Syrian Palestinian group financed by Iran and known to have been active in Germany. Pan Am Flight 103 had taken off from Frankfurt. Six months earlier, an American warship, the USS Vincennes, fired a missile and killed 290 Iranian Muslims, pilgrims on their way to Mecca. Human beings with names, histories and families, just like those killed at Lockerbie. Iranian officials were quick to vow to avenge their deaths. So Iran had the motive and Syria, where the Palestinian group was based, had the means. The Americans, active in the Gulf in support of their ally, Saddam Hussein, who was then at war with Iran, apologised for the missile attack and said it was 'an accident'.

For many months after Lockerbie, Iran and Syria were the focuses of the investigators' attention. The following might be mere coincidence, but three years later, when Iraq was now 'the enemy' for invading Kuwait, and the USA needed Iran and Syria to join the anti-Iraq crusade in the Anglo-American war against Saddam Hussein, the spotlight shifted to Libya, and eventually two Libyans went on trial in Holland. Last January, Abdelbaset al-Megrahi, said to be a Libyan intelligence officer, was sentenced to life for the bombing. He is appealing the verdict.

In April 1990, when George Bush conferred the Legion of Merit award upon those responsible for the deaths of the 290 Iranians, the USS Vincenne's commander and the officer in charge of the ship's missiles, the media said little.

However, the media widely criticised Colonel Gadaffi for welcoming home Al Amin Khalifa Fhimah, the Libyan acquitted of the Lockerbie bombing. The West sends out a message of double standards.

In the Garden of Remembrance, an old, presumably married couple was arriving as I was leaving and I said, 'It's terrible sad, isn't it.' The elderly man, a North American, replied, 'Yeh, but what about the bastard who ordered it? We should've gone in and wiped out Gadaffi.'

I felt uneasy, given the IRA's past relationship with Libya. Even if Gadaffi had been responsible, was it that simple to punish the guilty? In Berlin in 1986 a bomb exploded in a disco, killing two US servicemen. Though suspicion subsequently fell on Syria, Libya was immediately blamed and Tripoli and Benghazi were bombed by US warplanes based in England. Many innocent civilians were killed, including Colonel Gadaffi's two-year-old adopted daughter.

It has to be obvious, even before Machiavelli wrote *The Prince*, that ruling a country and politics are inevitably dirty trades, which sit uncomfortably, if not impossibly, beside the concept of morality. The West calls itself the 'Free World' and the acknowledged leader of the Free World is the United States of America. It owes its pre-eminence and authority to many advantages and qualities, not least to its military prowess and its preparedness to use force which – if we are to be honest – is comparable, in the eyes of those who fall victim to it, to the very terrorism the US says it abhors.

Leaving Lockerbie, I was affected and disturbed and determined to write something to help me articulate not just my emotions but also my convictions, and strive for an opinion that was legitimate, defensible and independent.

On Wednesday, I heard the veteran BBC correspondent Charles Wheeler make some sense of the bombings in New York and Washington. He said that if there was an Islamic/Arab/Palestinian dimension to these attacks then it was not unrelated to the USA's foreign policy, the USA's perceived, blanket support for Israel, the resentment felt by oppressed Palestinians of Israel's continued illegal confiscation of their land, and their anger that the USA has conspired to frustrate them of the statehood they were promised through the peace process.

Supporters of the USA's dominant role in the world claim that without it the world would be defenceless against rising tyrannies and that it keeps rogue nations in check. I admit that there may be much validity to that claim, yet I don't see why it should compromise my right to criticise that nation's many excesses.

Right now one's thoughts have to be with the victims of Tuesday's bombings and the anguished relatives. The stories emerging are heart breaking. However, on Thursday I heard an Israeli government spokesperson on the radio say that there are now just two worlds: the Free World and the rest. The consensus sought by the USA around the world is part of this drive. In other words, disagree with 'us' and you are an enemy, are heartless and complicit in the bombings – which is ridiculous, as if one would support for a second such slaughter on behalf of any cause.

The longer that revenge or retaliation is delayed the better. That way, at least, the wrong people may not be targeted. In the longer term still it is to be hoped that American public opinion will shift towards a reappraisal of its government's foreign policy and will lobby for a more even-handed, just approach, which we can all support and be proud of, and which will minimise the possibilities of another Lockerbie or other mass killings of innocent civilians by suicide bombers.

In August 2003 Libya accepted responsibility for the Lockerbie bombing and agreed to pay $2.7bn in compensation to the families of those killed in the explosion, in an effort to get the international community to lift trade sanctions against Tripoli.

Terror Spotting

Andersonstown News, 10 December 2001

There has been a major breakthrough in the war against international terrorism thanks to a discovery made, yet again, by an Irishman, the famous author Colm Toibin, whose rise in popularity in British literary salons has been nothing short of meteoric.

Just two years after being short-listed for the Booker Prize in 1999, Toibin is now in line to clinch the 2001 Nobel Prize for Psychobabble after his findings were published in the respected journal *The London Review of Books* on 29 November.

The DUP, the CIA, retired militarists such as Margaret Thatcher, Henry Kissinger, General Pinochet and Brigadier Frank Kitson, the leader writers of the *Daily Telegraph* and *The Sunday Times* – and even more important tabloids! – have hailed Mr Toibin's work as 'ground-breaking', 'beautiful in its simplicity' and 'cost effective'.

Mr Toibin's remarks about his decades-long study – *Guevara's Children* – were published as part of an LRB debate on the bombings in the USA on September 11. This is what he had to say.

'Over the past twenty-five years in Ireland I have made a point of asking anyone who was at school with members of the IRA, the INLA, the UDA and the UVF what these people were like at the age of ten. All have agreed that each child displayed a nasty early sign of terrorism long before he had a "cause". One of them spoke for many others when he described his schoolmate, the embryonic terrorist, as "a resentful little cunt". Had a cause not come their way, these people would have beaten their dogs or their wives and children, attacked one another at hurling matches or taken out their resentment on a long back garden.'

Some experts have described Toibin's theory as sheer bunkum, comparing it to the now discredited theory of Phrenology (or Bumpology as it came to be known), which claimed that criminals could be spotted from the shape of their heads.

An angry Toibin has released some of the interviews on which he based his findings and asks people to make up their own minds. Below we publish a representative sample.

Eoghan Harris: 'Well Colm, as you said, the changes certainly started when she was ten. In primary seven she began calling herself The Markievicz, grew a beard, came to school wearing a beret and bought a tin whistle on which she played Christy Moore tunes. She might be the President now but we all know where she's coming from.'

Chris Patten: 'In our class, Colm, there was a big ten-year-old eejit called Myers who wore a steel helmet, marched up and down the corridor, left-right-left-right, blowing a whistle and shouting, 'Over the top! Over the top!' I wouldn't be a bit surprised to hear that he now runs the Provos.'

Having heard about the findings British Home Secretary David Blunkett has invited Toibin to a war-cabinet meeting with Mr Blair in 10 Downing Street. They are seeking his professional advice in drawing up lists to determine how many 10-year-old Muslim schoolchildren they would need to intern, given that every one of them have shown signs of 'resentment' at being racially demonised, are certainly 'little', and thus fulfil two of Toibin's scientific criteria in the psychological profile of your typical embryonic terrorist.

This great news for Colm – or should we say, in anticipation, Sir Colm! – has unfortunately been overshadowed by a hurtful accusation of plagiarism from Israel's Prime Minister Ariel Sharon. Sharon claims that he invented the theory first, and as proof cites Israeli government policy of shooting embryonic Palestinian terrorists before they reach the age of eleven. Toibin has stoutly rebutted this accusation, and has referred to the influence of Dean Jonathan Swift on his work.

'I do admit being influenced by Swift's *Modest Proposal* of 1729. It is true that the children of the Irish poor were a burden on their parents and the country. Swift's advocating that Irish children under six be roasted as meat for English tables was revolutionary and way ahead of its time. My theory simply represents a creative reworking of his brilliant idea in order to deal with underage terrorists, smokers and drinkers. We may have a difficulty with the United Nations Declaration on Human Rights, the NSPCC and Children in Need, but Tony and I are not prepared to let that get in the way. After all, it's not as if we're forcing the kids to go up chimneys.'

Heil, Adolf Sharon!

Andersonstown News, 8 April 2002

George Bush's best friend, the Prime Minister of Israel, Adolf Sharon, is a mass murderer, a killer of kids, a war criminal – every bit as guilty as Slobodan Milosevic – for his part in butchering thousands of refugees in the Sabra and Chatila camps twenty years ago. Every day in life he besmirches the memory of the six million Jews who were murdered in the Holocaust by invoking their sacrifice to justify his extermination policy against the Palestinian people.

Any country in the last ten years which has defied United Nations security resolutions, resolutions which the United States has also endorsed, has been bombed and invaded by the United States, usually supported by its lapdog, Britain, especially if the US can't get NATO or the UN to unequivocally go along with its war-mongering.

Any country, that is, except Israel.

Israel, which is armed, financed and protected by the USA, has defied over seventy UN resolutions since 1967, and can do whatever it likes under the flag of 'the right to self-defence', to quote George Bush.

Last Thursday George Bush, forced at last to respond to international pressure and outrage, asked Israel to pull back from its reoccupation of the West Bank. But the Israelis are so pompous and arrogant, and have the measure of the USA, that they feel no need to worry that any meaningful sanctions will follow.

In recent days Israeli soldiers stopped a pregnant Palestinian woman at a checkpoint, watched her give birth and watched her baby die rather than call an ambulance. They have occupied hospitals, destroyed operating theatres and vital medical equipment, and locked out doctors. They refuse Palestinians the right to bury their dead. They have cut off electricity and water, imposed curfews and looted shops, and their tanks have wantonly destroyed property. Captured Palestinian men were blindfolded, handcuffed, marched off, interrogated and then held in a sewer. They were the lucky ones. Other captured prisoners – including five from the National Security forces, including the manager of the Palestinian Authority orchestra – were summarily executed. Some weeks ago Israeli soldiers were stamping serial numbers on detained Palestinians.

What next? Force the Palestinians to sew little yellow crescents on their clothing? It would make sense. The Israeli forces already have them tied down in ghettoes and refugee camps. Forcing them to wear yellow crescents might ensure that Israeli soldiers will only shoot civilians instead of journalists, UN workers, international observers, priests, nuns, and anyone else who gets in Adolf's way.

The pretext for this latest invasion has been the emergence of the phenomenon of Palestinian suicide bombers, who have indeed slaughtered Israeli civilians out shopping, in cafés, at bus stops, in attacks that we consider unconscionable. But what drives someone to commit suicide and take the lives of others if not a sense of desperation and hopelessness, which Israel's policy towards the Palestinians actually engenders?

Three times as many Palestinians as Israelis have been killed in this conflict. Most of the Palestinians have been civilians; hundreds were children.

Adolf Sharon has exploited the suicide bombings in order to destabilize the Palestinian Authority, and destroy the Oslo Agreement, which he has always denounced. Yet, even though there is knee-jerk support within Israel for 'wide-scale war' there are signs of change [but not from the USA, which relies on Israel as a crucial bastion and garrison in the Middle East].

Going largely unreported is the fact that several hundred combat officers and soldiers of the Israeli Defence Forces have issued a proclamation declaring that they will not serve in the occupied territories. Some of these soldiers have been imprisoned and harshly treated because they said that all over the Occupied Territories they were 'issued commands and directives that had nothing to do with the security of our country, and that had the sole purpose of perpetuating our control over the Palestinian people...'

In a statement reminiscent of the anti-Vietnam war movement, they said that they now understood that the price of occupation 'is the loss of IDF's human character and the corruption of the entire Israeli society... We shall not continue to fight beyond the 1967 borders in order to dominate, expel, starve and humiliate an entire people.'

The media in Israel is gagged, reporting of the peace movement not only censored, but the movement itself physically intimidated, gassed and beaten off the streets. Even last Thursday a CNN camera crew, covering the protests, had their vehicle shot at by Israeli armed forces.

Perhaps the most heartbreaking aspect of the occupation is the effect it is having on Palestinian children. They have sent messages out to the world. One, fifteen-year-old Mizer Jibrin, wrote: 'The Israeli soldiers prevented us from going out to the kitchen or bathroom... One of them pushed me forcefully, and started questioning me: what are you doing, what's your name, how old are you. I answered them, and they were about to beat me, when my father cried, "Stop it, stop it; he is a child". Went to use the bathroom. They released me and broke into our home. They imprisoned my sisters, brothers and me in our small kitchen. And sabotaged our home. They arrested my father and beat him with the other men. They covered their heads with plastic bags, taking them to unknown destinations. I experienced the occupation and I will never ever forget it. I want to say stop your occupation, stop your tyranny and stop your killing, stop...'

Remembering All of the Dead

Andersonstown News, 9 September 2002

For much of the week there have been documentaries on all of the major television stations in the run-up to the first anniversary of the September 11 terrorist bombings in the USA. All of them were heart-rending, especially the interviews with relatives of the dead.

One of the most harrowing was that filmed by two French brothers, Jules and Gideon Naudet, who had been making a documentary about a rookie fireman. On September 11 they go out with his crew to investigate a reported gas leak not far from the World Trade Centre when a plane is heard overhead. Jules pans up and catches the shot of the first plane hitting the North Tower. The documentary is about what happens next.

However, also shown on Channel Four was a bizarre documentary based on a book published in France last May, *The Frightening Fraud* by French author Thierry Meyssan, and which was selling 100,000 copies a week. He claimed that American Airlines Flight 77, which killed 189 people when it crashed into the Pentagon, didn't exist because there had been no eyewitnesses. According to Meyssan, the damage was caused by a rocket fired by an ultra-right wing faction of the US government, aimed at justifying the creation of a police state. Once again, it was absolute rubbish.

After the bombings there were many conspiracy theories. A common one was that the attacks were carried out by the Israeli Mossad Secret Service to divert attention from the Israeli crackdown in the West Bank and Gaza, create a backlash against Arabs in general and the Palestinian cause in particular. It was also claimed that Jews who worked in the World Trade Centre had been warned not to go in that day. The theory was, of course, complete nonsense, and the enthusiasm with which it was greeted by people who consider themselves progressive (I received e-mails about it at least a half dozen times from comrades) is disturbing and should make radicals never forget or lose the distinction between anti-Zionism and anti-Semitism.

For the majority of US citizens, most of those in Europe, and probably most Arab leaders, there is little doubt – there has certainly been no denial – that the bombings were carried out by Al Qaeda, led by Osama bin Laden who was being hosted in Afghanistan by the Taliban fundamentalist government (made up of mainly ethnic Pashtuns). To contest that orthodoxy or to query the evidence is to certainly run the risk of being tarred 'a terrorist sympathiser and apologist', of being considered callous and anti-American. Yet, the only reason for arguing that the US should only respond in a measured way, with the consensus of nations in the region and within the context of international law, was to ensure that more innocent people – disenfranchised, powerless, poor people – did not die to satisfy a demand for revenge, in a war which had objectives far beyond the defensive, pre-emptive ones outlined.

And that is exactly what happened. The richest, most developed superpower bombed one of the poorest nations in the world and killed more civilians than died in the bombings on 9/11. What was accomplished? The Taliban government in Kabul has been replaced by the Northern Alliance (which is dominated by one tribe, the Tajiks), Al Qaeda has been scattered (probably, temporarily) and Osama bin Laden may have been killed or may not. Has it reduced the terrorist threat to the USA or its allies? It is doubtful.

Religious conviction, fanaticism, call it what you will, motivates Al Qaeda fighters. They – and other Islamic fundamentalists – despise the West, but particularly the USA because of its 'defiling' presence on the soil of Mecca. They despise the hypocrisy of the West. In Algeria, ten years ago, when it looked like the non-violent Islamic Salvation Front (FSI) was going to win the elections the government – supported by the USA and the EU – banned the elections. The FSI transformed into the Armed Islamic Group and Algeria has experienced a civil war since, with the loss of over 50,000 lives.

They view the West's boast of respecting democracy as hollow and hypocritical. They quote American support for Israeli repression, its murder of Palestinians, its expansionism, as one of the reasons for their jihad or holy war.

We have to listen to their arguments – if you can find them in a media largely dominated by one side – if only to reject or accept them in whole or part. I have no time for fundamentalism and would like to think that I would die to defend a pluralist society, or for many of the cultural values I share with the people of North America and Europe. But there is something seriously sick about our world.

Who will be remembering on 9/11 that other September 11 in 1973 when the USA inspired a coup in Chile against the democratically elected government of Salvador Allende, and replaced him with the military dictatorship of General Pinochet? Tens of thousands of Chileans were subsequently tortured, murdered, 'fell' out of windows, disappeared.

Who will remember this September that this is the twentieth anniversary of the massacre of defenceless Palestinian children, women and men in the Sabra and Chatila refugee camps in Beirut by right-wing Phalangists, coordinated by the war criminal Ariel Sharon, then Israeli Defence Minister, now its Prime Minister? How could you shake hands with, sip tea with, bear to be in the same room as the terrorist responsible for killing over 3,500 people in an act described by the United Nations as an act of genocide?

Yet George Bush does. He and Tony Blair want to go to war. The pathetic little generals. They want to go to war against Iraq, a war that will kill thousands more civilians. Have the two governments really no choice? Is there no other way? Are they telling us the truth? Has Saddam Hussein got weapons of mass destruction? If he has, on whom is he going to use them? Me and you? Israel? The USA? Britain? If he has these weapons why is he going to use them? Because he wants to? Because he's nuts? Because he has a death wish? Few dictators have.

In honouring the dead of 9/11 in the USA we have a responsibility to tell the truth. It isn't being anti-American. I would love the people of North America to elect a government which would present a beacon of hope to the world, and to defend freedom. Real freedom. Freedom from poverty, inequality, injustice and repression. Because that is the only way that fundamentalism and terrorism can be defeated.

Our Silence is Not for Sale

Andersonstown News, 3 January 2003

I have to keep saying to myself: George Bush does not represent the USA; George Bush does not represent the USA. Tony Blair is not the British people; Tony Blair is not the British people.

Yet both were chosen by their parties as leaders and both became leaders of their respective countries through the vagaries of their particular representational systems. I like to think – and I have many American friends who frustratingly make the same argument – that George Bush represents the state of politics rather than the state of the union and that not all North Americans share his warmongering.

Just look at what the high and mighty have managed to do! Certainly in the USA (and increasingly in Britain) they have made ordinary people apathetic and so disillusioned that the right to vote – what their forbears struggled and often died for – is considered a pointless exercise. In the last presidential elections only half the people who were registered to vote (which is significantly less than half the people entitled to vote) cast their ballot. In Britain it is estimated that 60 per cent of young people didn't bother to vote in the last general election which saw the lowest turn-out in eighty years.

For many in the working class and underclass across Europe – with the foremost exception being the nationalist community in the North – the political system is seen as an exclusive, impenetrable club.

US Congress, Senate and Presidential elections are contested by millionaires or wealthy candidates, bankrolled by millionaires, big business interests and multinationals, with one or other, or all candidates, supported by media monopolies out to secure their own interests. Imagine if the voting power of blacks (who make up 12 per cent of the population), ethnic minorities and the thirty three million people in the USA who live in poverty, was realised and impacted on the choice of representatives? Do you think the President could still go to war so easily? Or that he could allow Israel to continue with its slow genocide of the Palestinian people?

The world was supposed to be a dangerous place because of the division between capitalism and communism, epitomised, respectively, by the USA and its allies, and the former USSR and its comrades, and the proliferation on both sides of weapons of mass destruction. Yet the collapse of communism has only fed the arrogance of US imperialists who think they can do what they want across the globe without respect to other opinions.

The angry and dismissive attitude of the Bush administration to those members of the United Nations which advocate caution, giving UN weapon inspectors more time in Iraq and who refuse to roll over for Uncle Sam is a case in point.

No chemical, biological or nuclear weapons have been discovered in Iraq yet in a few weeks time US and British forces are going to invade that country and murder its citizens to get control of its oil. Afterwards, we will be told that Saddam Hussein was really overthrown because he was a cruel dictator (which is true) and that it was a war for 'democracy'.

Overthrowing cruel dictators and replacing them with 'our' social democracies sounds very noble if it weren't for the fact that US administrations have spent more time overthrowing democratic leaders and replacing them with dictators. It's a hard habit to break. Just last April the US fulsomely welcomed the overthrow by dissident army forces and big business of popularly elected Venezuelan President Hugo Chavez – only to discover that they had been a bit premature. Within days the coup was reversed and he was restored to power after the lower ranks of the army came to his rescue and crowds of supporters took to the streets.

US government spokespersons have also attacked the 'dangerous' policies of the most recently democratically elected President of Brazil, Lula da Silva, because he cancelled a large $700 million dollar fighter jet deal so he could plough the money into his fight against hunger and help put three meals a day on the table of his people.

Opposition to the forthcoming war against the Iraqi people is building – right across the world, including huge mobilisations in capital cities across the USA. Nelson Mandela has urged the American people to join protests against their president and has accused Tony Blair of being George Bush's foreign minister.

Here in Ireland there has been an ongoing protest at the use of Shannon airport by US forces on their way to the Middle East as part of the military build-up. Typically, one of the more crude and craven arguments given by detractors of the peace movement is that if we don't support the US war against Iraq we might alienate US investors in Ireland! This is the culture of greed and self-interest which actually creates the climate for war and perpetuates human misery.

But our silence is not for sale.

On Saturday week, February 15th, there will be anti-war protests in every major city around the world. Everyone – those with or without votes – will have the opportunity for their voices to be heard, to speak as one.

Then we shall see that George Bush does not represent the USA. And Tony Blair is not the British people. We shall see that ordinary people do not subscribe to their lies and double standards, and, that the USA, in the words of Nelson Mandela, 'has no moral authority to police the world.'

Lying Time Again

Millions of people across the world prepare to march against the impending US-British war against Iraq.

Andersonstown News, 10 February 2003

She gave her name as Nayirah and it was explained that she couldn't be fully identified as her family was still trapped in Kuwait. Nayirah was fifteen years old and was speaking before a Congressional Human Rights Caucus, just months after Iraq had invaded Kuwait in August 1990. She said she was a refugee who had been working as a volunteer in a Kuwaiti hospital throughout the first few weeks of the Iraqi occupation.

'I volunteered at the al-Addan hospital. While I was there I saw the Iraqi soldiers come into the hospital with guns, and go into the room where fifteen babies were in incubators. They took the babies out of the incubators,' she sobbed, 'took the incubators and left the babies on the cold floor to die.'

This horrific story became the lead item in newspapers, on radio and television, not just in the USA, but across the world. Amnesty International took out a full-page advertisement condemning Iraq. Six members of the US Senate said that this was good enough reason to go to war. President George Bush the First cited the incident in his speeches. It was repeated at the United Nations Security Council when Dr Ebrahim, a surgeon, stated that he had buried forty babies pulled from the incubators by the Iraqis.

On November 29, 1990, the UN authorised use of 'all means necessary' to eject Iraq from Kuwait. By January 12, 1991, when the US Congress authorised the use of force against Iraq, the number of premature babies removed and left on the cold floor to die had climbed to 312.

Nayirah, in fact, was a member of the Kuwaiti Royal Family and the daughter of Saud Nasir al-Sabah, the Kuwaiti ambassador to the United States. She hadn't worked in a Kuwaiti hospital and was in the USA when the Iraqis invaded. And, Dr Ebrahim was a dentist, not a surgeon, who, after the war, when the scam was exposed, and 100,000 Iraqis had been killed, admitted that he had never buried any babies or seen any.

Their stories were fabrications. Nayirah had been coached in her testimony by Lauri Fitz-Pegado of the Public Relations company, Hill & Knowton, hired by the Kuwaiti government to win American support for the war under the rubric 'Citizens for a Free Kuwait'. It didn't matter that the Emir of Kuwait, whom the USA was going to reinstate, had, four years earlier, disbanded the token national assembly and intimidated and censored the media. Free Kuwait sounded good.

Lauri Fitz-Pegado was a former Foreign Service Officer at the US Information Agency. She had previously been a lobbyist for the dictator, Jean Claude ('Baby Doc') Duvalier, President of Haiti.

Hill & Knowton's president, Craig Fuller, was one of George Bush the First's closest friends and political advisors when Bush was Vice-President under Reagan.

Last September, US television's ABC's 'Primetime Thursday' interviewed Parisoula Lampsos, a 54-year-old woman of Greek extraction who had lived in Baghdad most of her life. She is one of the sources used by Pentagon intelligence officials who claim that Saddam Hussein has links to Al Qaeda, links that are being used by Bush and Blair to justify the forthcoming war.

Parisoula claims that she was Saddam's mistress, that he was a Viagra enthusiast who enjoyed listening to Frank Sinatra singing 'Strangers in the Night', as well as torture victims crying for mercy. She says she watched him preen in front of a mirror declaring, 'I am Saddam. Heil Hitler!' She said that she had once seen Osama Bin Laden at Saddam's palace and that in the mid-1990s Saddam had given money to him.

Parisoula – the woman who launched a thousand Hawk missiles.

'The first casualty when war comes is truth,' said American Senator Hiram Johnson in 1917. When Britain was fighting the Boer War the British press carried hundreds of atrocity stories, including one about Boers attacking Red Cross tents while brave British doctors and nurses were treating the wounded. Documentary footage caused outrage when shown in British cinemas. But it was completely false and was shot on Hampstead Heath in London, using actors.

In September 2002 Tony Blair published a dossier on Iraq's chemical and biological programme, yet the CIA believes that the source of that report – an Iraqi defector – cannot be trusted and might be 'embroidering' his story.

Last Wednesday the BBC Radio 4's 'Today' programme quoted sources from British Intelligence taking issue with the way Tony Blair was distorting their reports in order to make a case for war. Sections of the CIA have made similar allegations that its reports are being 'cooked' by the Pentagon to sustain a case which may not exist.

On Wednesday, the US Secretary of State, Colin Powell, made his presentation to the UN about Iraq's alleged chemical, biological and nuclear weapons' programme and links to Al Qaeda. In the course of his speech he called attention to 'the fine paper that the United Kingdom distributed ... which describes in exquisite detail Iraqi deception activities'.

But within twenty four hours it emerged that large parts of the British 'intelligence' dossier were a 'cut-and-paste' job, taken from published academic articles, some of them ten years old, which indicates a real dearth of fresh and original intelligence conclusively showing that Iraq actually possesses weapons of mass destruction.

I watched Colin Powell interpret satellite photographs. He claimed they showed Iraqis cleaning up a chemical munitions bunker and their lorries taking away the contraband. Why didn't the satellites track the lorries and reveal their location to the UN weapons inspectors? If Saddam Hussein has chemical and biological weapons why didn't he use them against US and British forces when they drove him out of Kuwait? Why didn't he pass them on to Al Qaeda during the past twelve years of humiliation, when the no-fly zone was imposed on his air force, and when half a million Iraqi civilians were dying because of the embargo and through the spread of cancerous diseases from the depleted uranium shells fired by the US and Britain during the Gulf War?

We have been lied to repeatedly so we cannot now believe George Bush or Tony Blair. Support the anti-war movement and get out and march next Saturday!

Some Will be Innocent

People march against war

Andersonstown News, 17 February 2003

A million in London, one point three million in Barcelona. Half a million. A hundred thousand. Four hundred thousand. Staggering numbers of humanity across the world trying to prevent a war.

How long does it take to cast a vote? In the city – around half an hour at the most, maybe? But how long does it take to march through that same city? Or travel to that city for a march? Allow yourself plenty of time to travel if you are coming from outside. Allow yourself the whole day.

That was the commitment of ordinary people expressing their will against an unjust war. And for hundreds of thousands this was their first political demonstration, so strongly do they feel that a war against Iraq is immoral.

I marched in Dublin in one of the biggest demonstrations the capital has ever witnessed. And if I were Taoiseach Bertie Ahern I would take note of the angry mood of the people, including the results of a new opinion poll that show that the majority disapprove of the use of Shannon airport by US forces.

Were elections available, were the chief warmongers Bush and Blair to run on a manifesto of attacking Iraq, then millions – including in Tony Blair's case certainly, many of his erstwhile supporters – would reject them at the ballot box.

Six hundred cities! There were marches against Bush and Blair's proposed war on Iraq in six hundred cities across the world last Saturday, from Belfast to Berlin, from Dublin to Detroit. The last time there were numbers like that on the streets was at the height of the Vietnam War, yet these demonstrations were held even before the first shots of war have been fired.

The attitude of Tony Blair in his speech to a Labour Party conference in Scotland last Saturday was sickening and patronising. He said: 'I do not seek unpopularity as a badge of honour. But sometimes it is the price of leadership. And the cost of conviction.'

Who the hell does he think he is, that his convictions are more important than those of the next million persons? He went on to describe rogue states that have Weapons of Mass Destruction as 'answerable to no democratic mandate, so are unrestrained by the will of ordinary people'. Does he not appreciate the irony? Has he a democratic mandate for making war? He is so democratic that he won't even put the issue to a vote in the House of Commons and, despite the massive size of the march in London, he appears unrestrained by the will of ordinary people.

His speech included reminders that Saddam killed a million people in an eight-year war with Iran. He omitted that Saddam used mustard gas laced with nerve agents to kill many of those young Iranian conscripts and that in locating his victims he was guided by USA satellite intelligence, after relations with the USA had been restored. He omitted that the man who restored relations with Iraq back then was Donald Rumsfeld, the current US Secretary of State.

Blair reminded us that Moslem Kurds in northern Iraq had been butchered, and prisoners tortured, but omitted that throughout this period – including when Saddam used gas on thousands of civilians in 1988 – Saddam was a great trading ally of Britain, which maintained full diplomatic relations with his murderous regime.

Blair said that 135 out of every 1000 Iraqi children die before the age of five but omitted the numbers of children that had died through disease and malnutrition as a result of sanctions.

The one truth that Blair uttered was, 'If we remove Saddam by force, people will die and some will be innocent. And we must live with the consequences of our actions, even the unintended ones.'

Live he will: die they will.

What is the case against Iraq? Two Brownie photographs taken from outer space which even UN weapons inspector Hans Blix has politely ridiculed, and a plagiarised ten-year-old PhD? The USA and Britain said they had the proof and demanded that the weapons inspectors be allowed in – believing that Saddam would refuse them access and thus hand the USA a *causus belli*.

But the inspectors were allowed in and the USA and Britain haven't produced the proof, have relied instead on rhetoric and whipping up mass fear which has only raised suspicions that the war is about other issues, perhaps oil or as a deterrent to other rogue states. While Saddam is a cruel dictator he is no different from the normal cruel dictators the USA is routinely allied to.

Yes, the Iraqi people are entitled to freedom. Just as are the Palestinians who have asked for help, who are being killed and tortured and whose land has been invaded by a foreign power which has weapons of mass destruction and which has ignored US resolutions not for ten years but for thirty-six years.

If Saddam can be overthrown in conjunction with the Iraqi people, and not some exiled businessmen being groomed in Washington but people who are willingly prepared to sacrifice their lives and who wish to replace him with a democratic, secular republic, which will eliminate poverty and injustice, then the world would not balk at helping them.

It is just that we do not believe that this is what it is about and the track records of the USA and Britain are not reassuring. The people who will die in a US/Brit war on Iraq are the innocents, by the hundreds, by the thousands, whose opinions were never sought.

So, in Blair's case, a war for 'democracy and freedom' is to be waged on behalf of people who have not asked for help, against those people, by a government that has little support from its own people and is not prepared to consult its own parliament. Brilliant.

Yours Sincerely, Tony Blair

Andersonstown News, 24 March 2003

Some nice things can be said about Tony Blair. One, he has a nice wife who is cleverer than him, though she has been known to scare the life out of the paparazzi first thing in the morning, bringing in the Number Ten milk in her housecoat and with dishevelled hair.

Two, he is going to shaft Clare Short when the time is right. No International Development Secretary is going to get away with calling the Prime Minister 'reckless' three times on television and radio and keep the job.

What a fool she has turned out to be.

'Please stay on, Clare. We're going to need you to rebuild a shattered Iraq after we extend the desert and free the people.'

'Really?'

'Absolutely, you idiot.'

'Okay, I'll support the war to end all wars.'

Three, he has an interesting father-in-law, Cherie's father, the former actor Tony Booth, a bit of a philanderer, a great raconteur, who loved Elsie Tanner from 'Coronation Street', otherwise known as Pat Phoenix to us mouldy oldies, whom Booth married in September 1986, a week before she died of cancer.

Four, he has a son, a teenager, a harmless child, who has signed up to my Creative Drinking Course, Part II, 'It Cost a Fortune, Now Keep it Down.'

And that's about it. I have to admit, I was glad to see Blair elected prime minister in 1997 because out of self-interest I felt that a fresh government in Downing Street, particularly a Labour one after eighteen years of Conservative rule, might provide the opportunity for a resumption of the IRA ceasefire and new talks. It did, regardless of how unsatisfactorily Blair has subsequently handled his responsibilities and commitments relating to the Belfast Agreement.

When Blair appeared on television recently, before the vote in the House of Commons, he looked under pressure, gaunt and exhausted, and many people said that they felt a bit sorry for him because 'he sounded sincere.'

Even if Blair wasn't acting, even if he was sincere, it doesn't make what he is doing right.

Even if he and George Bush 'win', that doesn't make them right. Oliver Cromwell was very sincere, as psychiatrists will tell you are many serial killers.

Blair has contemplated, planned and is now executing the cold and calculated killing of innocent and – by his own definition – oppressed Iraqi people, as a consequence of the main event of removing Saddam Hussein and his regime from power.

Of course, as sincere and true Christians, Blair and Bush know that the fewer innocents that are killed the better for them in terms of public relations. But Blair isn't balking at indeterminate numbers of innocents being killed, be it a hundred or ten thousand. This is the man who stood on the streets of Omagh in August 1998, after the Real IRA bombing, and declared that no cause is worth shedding one drop of innocent blood.

No cause.

One drop.

He was sincere, wasn't he?

Yes, the man with the big bombs is sincere, okay. Tony Blair is the product of an imperialist tradition and culture that is alien to ours. Our oppressed nation gave birth to mere Irish freedom fighters. We're missing the gene for arrogance, the conviction that we were born to rule everybody else, beside ourselves.

The pretext for this war is that Iraq was under the grip of a dictator, the former friend and ally of Britain and the USA, who had or might have had, or might have in the future, weapons of mass destruction (not dissimilar to, but not as proficient or as prodigious in number as those possessed by Britain and the USA), and who might have used them against innocent people in the West to bring about regime/policy change if the West didn't act pre-emptively.

But that argument was thoroughly rejected by millions of people across the world –including, in the West, those Saddam Hussein would be allegedly targeting with his weapons of mass destruction.

I like nothing about Saddam Hussein but I have yet to be convinced that he has weapons of mass destruction or that he is a threat to Ireland or Europe. The only mad bombers I see are those taking off from Fairford in England, who then fly several thousand miles to drop tons of high explosives on the people of a city who have done them no harm. If Saddam has poison gas wouldn't he use it now when his back is against the wall and he has nothing to lose?

I am not sure about many things but I am pretty sure about this: one has no right to interfere in the affairs of another country. It causes trouble and the outcome stores up trouble.

In conventional terms the US and Britain will overthrow the Iraqi regime. Relieved citizens may well cheer the arrival of the troops, but it will be a false cheer. There will be resentment. A pro-western government will be installed and will be expected to behave in the interests of the West, beginning with paying for the war.

But out of anger, frustration and desperation some survivors of the bombing will be attracted to Islamic fundamentalism and its promise of avenging the death of innocent Iraqis. And who will have been the real recruiting sergeant for these future terrorists? Bin Laden? Fanatical mullahs?

Prisoners of War

Andersonstown News, 31 March 2003

The first pictures we saw of prisoners surrendering were on British television. Presumably, viewers in the USA watched the same images on CNN or Fox News.

We watched some of Saddam's bedraggled troops being marched down the road with hands on head, fear in their eyes, and other shots of some walking across a shimmering desert pathetically waving a flag made out of a white shirt at the end of a stick. Three hundred, we were told, had surrendered on Day One.

It was a great boost to morale for those supporters of the Anglo-American invasion of Iraq and early 'proof' that the Iraqis had no stomach for war, would roll over, and would greet the invading army with flowers and kisses at the prospect of being liberated from the despotic Saddam Hussein.

Then, a few days later, Iraqi television, facilitated by the Iraqi authorities, copied the exercise. But its broadcasting of captured US POWs provoked an immediate outcry. This was against the Geneva Convention, said Blair and Bush, who are waging war in breach of the United Nations Charter and international law and in defiance of the majority on the UN Security Council, and substantial numbers of their own citizens.

Two years ago in Afghanistan the USA launched its 'War Against Terrorism' and eventually drove out the Taliban regime, which had harboured Al Qaeda and Bin Laden, chief suspects for the 9/11 terrorist attacks in the USA. US forces captured Taliban and Al Qaeda fighters, which the Bush government then unilaterally declared were not POWs and transported them half-way round the world to a US-occupied part of Cuba, Guantánamo Bay. There, it allowed these prisoners to be televised dressed in orange suits, hooded and shackled, and wheeled out on hospital trolleys as they were taken between interrogation centres. Yes, the US government subscribes to the Geneva Convention, okay.

To this day, six hundred prisoners are kept in open-air, chain-link cages. Spotlights are kept on throughout the night. They have no access to their families or lawyers and they are only allowed two fifteen-minute exercise breaks every week.

Last Wednesday, Tony Blair condemned Iraqi TV, and the Qatar-based satellite channel al-Jazeera TV, for showing footage of two dead British soldiers.

I remember a British government having no qualms about the media broadcasting the images of two other dead British soldiers, the two army corporals who were beaten and shot by the IRA after they drove into the funeral of Kevin Brady in Andersonstown. The government correctly judged the images as extremely damaging for republicans. I also remember the RUC producing a leaflet after the La Mon Hotel bombing, when twelve people were killed by the IRA, which showed horrifically what the fire had done to a human being.

In these instances what guided the British government and the RUC was not ethics or concern for the dignity of the dead but the powerful propaganda value of the images. Similar images from Iraq, however, because of their potential damage to the morale of the troops, provoke demands for censorship (and in the case of Baghdad television and radio stations ongoing missile attacks for giving the Iraqi point of view).

Is it right to show captured prisoners and brutal and disturbing images of the effects of war on soldiers and civilians? The answer has to be, generally, yes. What both sides do to each other in war, or in the name of their society, should be shown to the population as part of the debate, which those who advocate, defend or apologise for war attempt to control and manipulate. Militarists want only selective pictures presented, ones of their heroism or popularity but not those that might lower morale or contribute to anti-war sentiment.

There is an old expression: sin has many tools but a lie is the handle that fits them all. Last Wednesday, fifteen people, including a mother and her three children who were incinerated as they sat in their car, were killed by a US cruise missile attack on a market in Baghdad. It was a sin, a war crime, and the big lie that had to be told by the warmongers was that it wasn't their missiles that did it. 'It may have been caused by a stray Iraqi surface-to-air missile or even sabotage,' said Brigadier-General Vincent Brooks.

Amidst all the bloodshed and suffering one small but important consolation is the daily, if not hourly exposure of Blair and Bush, their armed forces and their apologists as downright liars. Lies that are usually repeated and transmitted by many of the five hundred journalists 'embedded' with army units with whom they have patriotically bonded.

We were told that Saddam was dead, that Saddam was wounded. That Saddam was a stretcher-case who needed a blood transfusion. That it wasn't him on TV being interviewed the morning after the first raid – didn't you notice that a mole was missing beside his left ear – it was his double… or treble. That Umm Qasar was taken. That it wasn't taken. It's taken. It's not taken. It might be taken. It is taken. That there's an uprising against Saddam in Basra. There isn't. There is. There might be. There isn't. Oh well.

On and on and on come the lies, cover-ups, the deceit, the hypocrisy, the double standards. Fooling less and less people but, tragically, taking more and more lives.

WMD

Immunity from prosecution for US transgressors

Andersonstown News, 7 July 2000

I could pull out his toe-nails, break his ankles, smash his legs, castrate him, scalp him, puncture his ear-drums, gouge out his eyes, cut out his tongue, slit his throat, stab his heart, impale him, cut off his arms, amputate his hands and desecrate his body.

I could blow up a restaurant full of people to get him. I could massacre a bus of women and children. I could wipe out his family and their families as long as in the end I got Saddam.

Then I could collect my $25 million and appear on the cover of *Time* magazine. They'd wrap me in the Stars and Stripes flag. I would be a hero.

But I would still be a murderer.

What would I be if I hijacked a plane full of just ten or twenty Iraqi civilians – the number you would shoot in the average bazaar or after Friday prayers – and crashed it into Saddam's hideout? A freedom fighter?

Yes, under the hyperpower that is the USA, where foreign occupation is national liberation, where prisoners have no human rights and can be tried in secret by military tribunal and executed, the world is fast losing its moral compass, the world is a scary place where language has been hollowed of true meaning.

In the twentieth century 86 million people, the majority women and children, lost their lives in 250 conflicts. In recent memory, the Khmer Rouge in Cambodia killed over a million people. Indonesian forces in East Timor killed 200,000 people. Over 200,000 people were killed in the Bosnia war. Between April and June 1994, an estimated 800,000 Rwandans were killed in the space of 100 days. In the ongoing civil war in the Congo over 1,700,000 people have lost their lives.

It was against this background that a Coalition for the International Criminal Court, made up of over 1,000 nongovernmental organisations, conferred with governments in 1998 and eventually they drafted the Rome Treaty, which envisaged the establishment of an International Criminal Court (ICC) at the Hague. The jurisdiction of the ICC began in July 2002. Last February its 18 judges were elected.

The ICC has the power to investigate and prosecute individuals including heads of state (responsible for war crimes, crimes against humanity, genocide, rape, ethnic cleansing) both in countries that are party to the Treaty and, with the approval of the UN Security Council, those that are not. It has the power to impose large fines, prison terms of up to 30 years, and reparations that could include rehabilitation, repatriation, historical clarification and memorials.

However, from the very first day the court's most powerful opponent was the USA. It said it feared that its troops (which are stationed across the world) would be vulnerable to arbitrary, politically motivated and malicious charges. Negotiators took on board those fears and included a comprehensive list of due process protections, spelt out in greater detail, in the opinion of some, than those in the US Constitution. It was still not enough. The US threatened to walk away unless a provision – which became known as Article 98 – was added.

To keep the US onboard Article 98 was added. It said that the ICC may not proceed with a request for surrender of a citizen that would require the requested state to act inconsistently with its obligations under international agreements. This was perceived as providing an orderly and rational process for the handling of suspects among states cooperating with the court.

This was still not enough. The US then tried to introduce another provision that a state's consent would be required before the court could try its nationals. This would, in effect, have given a state overriding power to grant immunity to its nationals responsible for war crimes and would have neutered the court.

The US lost the motion and the Treaty of Rome was signed. Among the seven countries that voted against it were the USA – and Iraq! President Clinton reluctantly signed the Treaty but in May 2002 President Bush 'unsigned' it. Instead, he signed the American Service Members Protection Act, which authorises the use of military force to liberate any American or citizen of a US-allied country being held by the Hague court!

He also threatened – and carried out the threat this week – to withdraw military aid from any country that ratified the Rome Treaty and didn't sign a bilateral impunity agreement with the USA, exempting US military and civilian personnel from being charged with crimes against humanity under the jurisdiction of the ICC. Forty-three of the world's poorest nations caved in to the bullying tactics and financial might of the USA. Among thirty-five others, which are being penalised, are Caribbean governments, which have been told they will lose hurricane relief for refusing to sign Article 98.

Bush claims that these bilateral agreements are allowed under Article 98 but international lawyers argue that these impunity agreements violate the object and purpose of the Rome Statute.

George Bush's government doesn't give a damn. It overlooks human rights violations by its allies when it suits it. Its invasion and occupation of Iraq has no UN mandate. Its policy on sanctions prior to the war killed hundreds of thousands of Iraqi infants. It shoots down Iraqi civilians on their own streets with impunity. It drops clusters of 'freedom' bombs on playgrounds, fires 'freedom' missiles into busy markets and enslaves the people of Iraq and, with them, the terrified people of the USA with a language of lies and deceit. It is an evil administration.

Truly, George Bush is a weapon of mass destruction.

The Disappeared

On the prisoners being held illegally by the USA in Guantánamo Bay

Andersonstown News, 19 August 2002

How long does it take to question a man? A year? Two years? Ten years? A lifetime? Can the military do anything they want with him, without a tribunal?'

This was just one of the probing questions put this week by a frustrated federal judge in the USA who was hearing an appeal by a father of one of 'the disappeared' to find out what had become of his son since he was kidnapped in November 2001.

Amnesty International has reported that more than 1,200 people, mainly foreign nationals, have been detained by the US since September 11th. (How many are aware that there are also people interned without trial in Britain?) Many were held in prolonged solitary confinement, and suffered physical and verbal abuse.

Currently, there are several hundred prisoners being held in secret and the administration refuses to name them or grant them access to lawyers.

On September 11th last year over three thousand people, who had no involvement in US imperialism and were responsible for no oppression, were horrifically killed in terrorist suicide bombings in New York and Washington. There was widespread sympathy from around the world, including from many of its former enemies, for the pain the people of the USA were experiencing.

There was also some initial hope that the US administration would acknowledge that the bombings were not unrelated to US foreign policy, particularly its unqualified support in the Middle East for Israel and its maltreatment of the Palestinian people. There were intimations that US foreign policy would be more even-handed and that it would act on Israel to enter into meaningful dialogue with the representatives of the Palestinians. Indeed, on that assumption, many countries tacitly went along with the US/British bombing and invasion of Afghanistan to overthrow the fundamentalist Taliban government which hosted the principal suspect of the US bombings, Osama Bin Laden from Saudi Arabia.

But the administration of George Bush resiled from its promises and the Middle East, for one, is in a more precarious state than ever. And in Afghanistan it is not even safe to go to a wedding without being strafed by US fighter jets. (In early July US planes –including a B-52 bomber and an AC-130 helicopter gunship – dropped seven 2,000lb bombs on an Afghan village, killing forty people, mostly women and children.)

Yaser Esam Hamdi, aged 21, was captured in Afghanistan with Taliban forces, then flown half-way around the world to Guantánamo Bay in Cuba to a US naval base where he was held incommunicado. It was then discovered that he was born in Louisiana and was entitled to US citizenship. Earlier this year he was transferred to a Navy brig in Virginia. The US government has declared Hamdi an 'unlawful enemy combatant', entitled to neither constitutional protections nor international prisoner-of-war status.

Hamdi's father requested at two earlier hearings before US District Judge Robert Doumar that his son be allowed to see a lawyer. There is no evidence that he had anything to do with the September 11th bombings.

Doumar ruled Hamdi's right to see a lawyer but this was overturned by the Circuit Court of Appeals. Judge Doumar was then instructed to revisit the case with greater consideration to national security and the executive branch's constitutional right (that is, George Bush, the Commander-in-Chief's right) to wage war.

Michael Mobbs, a special adviser in the Defense Department, sent a two-page declaration of facts to the court to explain how they determined that Hamdi was an enemy combatant. Judge Doumar asked for additional information but prosecutors declined to supply it. The government was represented by Assistant

Solicitor General Gregory Garre.

The judge asked Garre, Who is Mobbs and what qualified him to be a 'special adviser'? Garre said Mobbs was an undersecretary of defense, substantially involved with detainee issues.

'My secretary's familiar with the Hamdi case,' the judge said. 'Should she decide? She's a special adviser.' The judge said that Mobbs' declaration of facts didn't say how long Hamdi would need to be detained and for what purpose.

'How long does it take to question a man? A year? Two years? Ten years? A lifetime?'

'The present detention is lawful,' Garre replied.

Doumar then asked: 'What restraints are there?'

Garre ignored the question and said Hamdi had asked to speak to diplomats from Saudi Arabia where he was brought up after leaving the USA.

'Can I beg you to answer my question? If the military sat him in boiling oil, would that be lawful?'

Garre said he didn't think that that was being proposed. He said that the courts had a limited role and that the executive was the branch that was in the best position to make the military determination.

Doumar said that he had no desire to have an enemy combatant get out of any status. 'However, I do think that due process requires something other than a basic assertion by someone named Mobbs that they have looked at some papers and therefore they have determined he should be held incommunicado. Just think of the impact of that. Is that what we're fighting for?'

Judge Doumar has reserved his judgment but made a damning comparison with what is happening to civil liberties since September 11th.

'I have tried valiantly to find a case of any kind, in any court, where a lawyer couldn't meet with a client,' he said. 'This case sets the most interesting precedent in relation to that which has ever existed in Anglo-American jurisprudence since the days of the Star Chamber.'

The Court of Star Chamber, 1487–1641, was named after the star pattern painted on the ceiling of the room at Westminster Palace where its meetings were held. It could order torture, imprisonment and fines and became a byword for misuse and abuse of power by the king and his circle. Court sessions were held in secret, with no right of appeal, and punishment was swift and severe.

In a brief the US government affirms, 'the military has the authority to capture and detain individuals whom it has determined are enemy combatants in connection with hostilities in which the Nation is engaged, including enemy combatants claiming American citizenship. Such combatants, moreover, have no right of access to counsel to challenge their detention.'

This means that the US has granted itself the power to go into any country in the world, seize any persons it wishes, bring these persons to anywhere it chooses, can ignore the Universal Declaration on Human Rights, can refuse to name its prisoners, does not have to charge them or put them on trial, allow them access to legal representation or access to family visits. These sweeping state and military powers are unprecedented, and they are all carried out in the name of 'the war effort', even though there has been no congressional declaration of war.

The right of the military to detain individuals indefinitely without charges or hearings were the hallmarks of fascist or communist regimes that had to be resisted and opposed.

At least that's what US administrations once told us.

In June 2004 the US Supreme Court ruled that prisoners held in Guantánamo Bay will be able to challenge their detention in American Courts.

A Proud Tradition

Andersonstown News, 10 May 2004

The *Daily Telegraph* wrote: 'The Royal Military Police are already investigating allegations of mistreatment of Iraqis by British soldiers in southern Iraq after the Mirror's publication of photographs said to show a member of The Queen's Lancashire Regiment urinating on an Iraqi lying in a military truck with a hood over his head.'

The Guardian wrote: 'The soldier at the centre of the new revelations in the Mirror, Soldier C, said he saw four beatings where PoWs were punched and kicked, the paper reported. In one, a corporal placed a sandbag over a suspect's face and poked his fingers in the victim's eyes until he screamed with pain.'

In the Commons, Tony Blair used prime minister's questions to say any 'human rights abuses, torture or degradation' of prisoners were 'wholly unacceptable'.

PRISONERS' STATEMENTS

'On the table was a small bottle of stuff, and two syringes with needles…Somebody came from behind and put on a blindfold. The soldier gave me an injection on the right arm, then he tied something round it, then he did something to my fingers… Then I felt this feeling in my arm, electric shocks, but two given to start off with, not painful, just uncomfortable. Then every time they asked a question, it only kept increasing.'

'He kicked my legs apart and stuck his heel into my privates. Others came in and said that half my district had been wiped out in the fighting. At about 4am I was told that I was to be taken for a ride in a helicopter and that I was to be thrown out.'

'After what seemed about one hour in the helicopter I was thrown from it and kicked and batoned into a lorry.'

'The next I knew was being put into a helicopter and taken away. I overheard voices talking about, 'Throw him out' Before I went into the helicopter I was asked if I could swim.'

'What was going to happen to me? Are they coming to kill me? I wished to God they would end it.'

'I was beaten again. I was taken out and made stand against the wall. The soldiers said, 'You are being taken out to be shot.''

'I was beaten and kicked in the stomach and privates for about half-an-hour. I was made lie on the floor. One put his foot on my throat and the other held my legs. The other one lit matches. He blew them out and then put them to my privates.'

'I was forced to stand against a wall with my hands supporting my body for a long time. I collapsed. My hands and legs were beaten whenever this happened and the insides of my feet were kicked until my ankles were swollen to almost twice their normal size. At the time that I was against this wall I got bread and water once and water alone on two other occasions. I was also punched in the ribs and in the stomach, as well as being nipped.'

'After being hooded I was led to the helicopter and I was thrown bodily into the helicopter. During this my hands and wrists were hurt due to the others handcuffed to me not being pushed equally. On being put into the helicopter, the handcuffs were removed and were applied to the back of the hood to tighten it around the head.'

'I would estimate that the helicopter journey lasted half an hour at the end of which I was put in a lorry. I was made to lie face downwards in the back with other men thrown on top of me.'

'A shot was fired. It went past my ear. They all had a good laugh at this.'

'I was not allowed to dress again but was told to put the hood back over my head. I was taken to another room, stood against the wall, the hood was removed and a flash picture was taken.'

PRINCIPAL METHODS OF INTERROGATION

Twenty-five principal methods of interrogation have been documented, which included: stretching a man over benches with two electric fires underneath and kicking him in the stomach; insertion of instruments in the anal passage; electric shocks given by use of a machine; urinating on prisoners; and psychological tortures such as firing shots close to their faces, playing Russian roulette or throwing them out of helicopters just above the ground (when the prisoners thought they were high in the air).

NEVER AGAIN

All of the above quotes are extracts from statements running to 4,500 pages, compiled by the European Commission on Human Rights over thirty years ago. They refer to the interrogations of Irish people in the North by the British military and Special Branch. The ECHR found Britain guilty of torture and inhuman and degrading treatment of prisoners. A British prime minister stood up in the House of Commons to state that 'ill-treating' (sic) prisoners was totally unacceptable and would never happen again.

It happened again and again and again. A proud tradition.

First in Ireland, now in Iraq.

People

The Life of Demitrios Tsafendas

On the assassin of Verwoerd, the architect of apartheid

Andersonstown News, 23 October 2000

When Demitrios Tsafendas was a youth in Mozambique it was discovered that he was infested with a giant tapeworm. A doctor gave Demitrios' Greek stepmother a powerful poison to help expel the worm and told her to keep its head for him to study. Demitrios passed the worm, which was two or three feet long, but panicked because his stepmother flushed it into the sewers – still alive, he believed.

Years later, in Cape Town, Demitrios went into a store and bought a large knife. A few hours later he went to the all-white House of Assembly where he worked as a uniformed parliamentary messenger. He was 48-years-of age, had an IQ of 125 and could speak eight languages.

That afternoon Prime Minister Dr Hendrik Verwoerd, the architect of apartheid, was exchanging greetings with those around him as he made his way towards the green leather benches. Demitrios briskly walked across the floor to where Verwoerd had sat down, drew his knife and stabbed Verwoerd four times in the chest. Verwoerd was dead on arrival at hospital. It was September 6th, 1966. Ironically, the Ministry of the Interior had just discovered that Tsafendas was actually banned from South Africa. It had written him a letter informing him that he was to be deported. The letter was still in an out-tray waiting to be posted.

Within days of Demitrios' arrest stories appeared in the media claiming that he told police that a giant tapeworm ordered him to assassinate Verwoerd. One psychiatrist quoted him as saying, 'I don't think I will be able to live in Cape Town after this, because of public opinion, you know… If I was ever offered a job in the House of Assembly again I do not think I would be able to face up to it.'

South African blacks who should have been dancing in the streets at the assassination did not know how to respond to this killing by a loner, who had no party political ties and who was described as just a crazy Greek. It is only when you probe further that you discover a life at the end of a name, in Tsafendas' case a sad life, a man who suffered racial abuse, and mental torment. In his successful blend of fiction and biography, *A Mouthful of Glass*, Henk Van Woerden tells the story of this unlikely assassin.

Tsafendas was born in Mozambique, the son of a marine engineer of Greek extraction and a mother, a 17-year-old maid of mixed European and African descent, whom his father disowned and he never knew. He was sent to live with his grandmother in Egypt but she died when he was six and he returned to Mozambique where his father had remarried a young Greek woman. At school

Demitrios was nicknamed, 'Blackie' because of his skin. It was only later that he found out that he was 'coloured' and illegitimate.

In 1936 he moved to South Africa, was a member of the Communist Party for a while, then joined the Merchant Navy and travelled the world. His mental instability was apparent and he ended up spending time in various psychiatric institutions, being imprisoned in several countries because his papers were not in order, and being deported. One report spoke of him hearing voices from hospital radiators.

In 1964 he returned to Africa, first to Mozambique to try to identify his mother and find her grave, before slipping into South Africa (where he was officially black-listed) and settling in the Cape where he was befriended by Patrick and Louise O'Ryan. No country wanted him. No country recognised him.

After his arrest in September 1966 he told police, 'I was so disgusted by the racial policy that I went through with my plan to kill the prime minister.' A judge found that he was unfit to stand trial and committed him. But instead of being sent to a mental hospital, the government exploited a loophole in the law and he was placed in death row for twenty-three years. There, warders spat in his food, urinated in his coffee and beat him while he was held in a strait-jacket. They destroyed the only photograph he had of himself as a child. His cell was next to the gallows where his fellow prisoners in batches of up to seven at a time were hanged. He heard their last screams and cries.

It was only in July 1994 that he was moved to a lower-security prison/hospital for infirm men. In recent years two people interviewed him: David Beresford (who wrote *Ten Men Dead*) and Henk Van Woerden. Van Woerden visited him several times for his book, though for his re-creations of Demitrios' past history he relies heavily on papers and reports that were never revealed because there was no trial. On one visit to the hospital there was such a racket that their exchanges had to be written on a pad. He says that Tsafendas wrote in untidy, block letters: 'I REGRET WHAT HAPPENED'.

'He began to cry. I took both his shoulders in my hands and shouted as loudly as I could: "Never mind. Other times. Not your fault". "A whole other time", he sobbed. "I am not that kind of person. It was something that happened. It was not in my nature. Besides, I was sick... It will not die. I'm helpless against this Dragon-Tapeworm."'

Demitrios also asked him who was the president of South Africa now. 'I wrote the name "Mandela" and showed it to him. "Nelson Mandela...? I would like to speak to him. He's a very strong man."'

Demitrios Tsafendas died aged 81, in October 1999, from pneumonia. About ten people, mostly members of the Greek community, spared him a pauper's funeral and gave him a proper burial, though his grave remains unmarked in the prison grounds. No one from the ANC attended, even though he had struck a significant blow against apartheid. The press, who were outnumbered by plain clothes and uniformed police officers, outnumbered mourners. One card on a wreath of white lilies on his grave read: 'Displaced Person, Sailor, Christian, Communist, Liberation Fighter, Political Prisoner, Hero. Remembered By His Friends.'

A sad, sick and stricken man but not half as sick as the architect of apartheid, Verwoerd, who introduced obscene political and immorality trials, outlawing sex and marriage between blacks and whites, and who was responsible for the deaths of thousands and the sufferings of millions.

Crucifying Jesus Christ

Capital punishment in the USA

Andersonstown News, 27 November 2000

Rickey Ray Rector's prison guards called him 'the Chickman' because he thought the guards were throwing alligators and chickens into his cell. Rickey, a forty-year-old black man had killed a black police officer during a shoot-out, then put his own gun to his head and fired, leaving him severely brain-damaged.

He was convicted of murder, and after ten years on death row was sentenced to die by lethal injection in February 1992, in the state of Arkansas. The state governor, Bill Clinton, the Democratic Party's presidential candidate, was canvassing in New Hampshire. According to opinion polls he had just lost twelve points as a result of the Gennifer Flowers' sex scandal. He flew back to Arkansas in the middle of his campaign to uphold Rector's execution and to show that he was tough on crime.

Just how much Rector understood about what was going on could be gleaned from the fact that after he had eaten his last meal he asked to save the pecan pie dessert for bedtime. Strapped to a stretcher he tried to help his executioners find a viable vein for the lethal injection, apparently believing they were trying to help him. They couldn't find a vein so they slashed the crook of his arm with a scalpel to insert a catheter. That took an hour.

Rickey Ray Rector told his attorney that he was going to vote for Bill Clinton in the following November's presidential election.

After the execution the chaplain resigned, saying: 'I hate murder and murderers. But to execute children? What was done to Rickey Ray Rector was in itself, absolutely, a crime. A horrible crime.'

John Paul Penry suffered cerebral damage at birth. He has a mental age of less than seven and suffered serious child abuse. He was sentenced to death in Texas for the rape and murder of a 22-year-old woman. He has spent twenty-one years on death row. He spends his day colouring with crayons and looking at comics he cannot read. He thinks there are six hours in a day and believes in Santa Claus.

When he was governor of Texas George Bush signed the consent form for Penry's execution but the US Supreme Court granted a stay just hours before he was due to be killed. He would have been the 150th person executed in Texas during the five years of Bush's tenure. Six mentally retarded people have been put to death in Texas since the state resumed executions.

In Florida, George Bush's brother Jeb, a so-called practising Catholic, is the governor. In 2000 he introduced a new electric chair, Sparky II. He has also limited the appeals of condemned inmates in a bid to speed up executions. One man, Thomas Provenzano, put to death last June, had been declared insane. Bush's colleague, Republican Senator Howard Futch said: 'Doesn't he think he's Jesus Christ or something? Why don't we just crucify him?'

When governor of Texas, George Bush devoted no more than fifteen minutes considering last-ditch appeals, and during the presidential election campaign on occasions took just four minutes to consign prisoners to eternity. Penry's lawyer, Kathy Puzoni, said: 'It's a disgrace. The only other country that executes the mentally retarded is Kazakhstan. What does that tell you about our supposedly great nation?'

Karla Faye Tucker, the first woman executed in Texas since the Civil War, had been asked on Larry King what she would say to George Bush if she could appeal to him personally. She replied, 'Please, don't kill me.' In 1999, after Tucker's execution by lethal injection, *Talk* magazine caught Bush making fun of the dead woman. Mocking her desperation, Bush pursed his lips and whimpered, 'Please, don't kill me.'

The USA has five methods of execution: lethal injection, lethal gas, hanging, firing squad, and electrocution. When Alpha Otis Stephens was being put to death in Georgia in 1984 the first jolt of two minutes of electricity failed to kill him. He struggled for six minutes, strapped to the chair, until his body cooled down sufficiently to allow doctors to declare that he needed a second jolt to finish the job.

During the 1992 presidential race, Bill Clinton (who once was an opponent of capital punishment) outmanoeuvred the republican candidate, George Bush Senior, and deprived him of accusing Clinton of being soft on crime by executing Rickey Ray Rector. Bush, playing to the capital punishment gallery, then called for 'stronger death penalties'! Commenting on this, one journalist, Barry Crimmins, speculated facetiously on what a stronger death penalty would entail. Inside a gas chamber the electric chair sits on a trapdoor of a gallows. Headphones are placed over the prisoner's ears playing, on a continuous loop, Clinton's anthem, 'Don't Stop Thinking About Tomorrow' by Fleetwood Mac. A noose is placed around the prisoner's neck and a bull's eye pinned to his heart. A lethal injection is inserted in the prisoner's arm, timed to take into account the drop from the gallows in the electric chair. At the strike of midnight the electric switch is thrown, the trapdoor is opened, the gas is released, the prisoner is injected and America's finest marksmen shoot the prisoner through the heart.

'If all goes as planned the condemned man will be simultaneously shot, hung, electrocuted, gassed and lethally injected. That'll teach him!... America did not become the great nation it is because it molly-coddles the doomed,' said Crimmins.

Under Bill Clinton's administration Congress in 1996 eliminated funding for the twenty Death Penalty Resource Centres that provided legal services for poor defendants. Currently, there are 3,600 people on death row, more than were killed in over thirty years of conflict in Ireland.

A very successful American business man, with whom I correspond, always points out to me when I rail against the US the good that country also does and the contribution it has made to peace in Ireland, which is a fair point. But good deeds can never be allowed to buy silence on bad deeds. And the reason I get angrier about the US than, say, China, Iran, Saudi Arabia and the Congo (which execute more than the United States) is because the US claims to be a bastion of human rights, and, as the most powerful nation on earth, has the potential to be such a bastion.

Capital punishment does not deter people from killing, as the statistics show an increase in the murder rate in states that use the death penalty. On the other hand, the murder rate in Canada dropped after its abolition there. A state that uses legal murder only encourages a culture of murder. In the USA the poor, the uneducated, the insane, and disproportionately more blacks, are being put to death largely to satisfy a lust for revenge.

As Doestoevsky, himself no stranger to jail, once wrote: 'A society should be judged not by how it treats its outstanding citizens, but by how it treats its criminals.'

The Man in Black

Andersonstown News, 22 September 2003

Johnny Cash, who died last week just four months after his wife and soul mate June Carter Cash, was a decent, honourable man as well as being a great singer and songwriter, a man who helped pioneer rock 'n' roll.

Many Irish people can be forgiven for thinking that the song 'Forty Shades of Green', which Cash sang, was a contemporary of 'Danny Boy', or 'Galway Bay' on the subject of the emigrant pining for home:

> I close my eyes and picture the emerald of the sea
> From the fishing boats at Dingle to the shores of Donaghadee
> I miss the River Shannon, the folks at Skibbereen
> The moorlands and the meadows and the forty shades of green.

It was, in fact, written by Johnny Cash in 1961, after he visited Ireland, and five or six years after he broke through the country music scene. He could entertain at several levels, not least in the light-hearted way he sang about the boy who in a saloon eventually meets the father ('the dirty, mangy dog that named me Sue') who deserted him when he was three and whom he pledged to kill. They fight it out with knives and guns and are close to murdering each other when the father explains that in naming him Sue he left him the means to get tough and survive! At the end they make up, but Sue swears that if he ever has a son he's going to name him, 'Bill or George... anything but Sue!'

In another funny song, 'The One on the Left is on the Right', Cash ribbed at the musical troupe that broke up in a free-for-all on stage because of political incompatibility!

> Well the one on the right was on the left
> And the one in the middle was on the right.
> And the one on the left was in the middle
> And the guy in the rear was a Methodist.

Cash was born in poverty at the height of the Depression in a shack in Arkansas. His father was a hobo labourer, picking cotton, doing various menial jobs until a New Deal resettlement programme allowed the family to take possession of a five-room house on twenty acres of fertile land. Cash worked in the fields along with his three brothers and two sisters.

He was influenced by the spirituality of his mother and by his older brother and best friend, Jack, who was tragically killed at the age of fourteen by a circular saw while cutting fence posts. He was deeply affected by that death and it explains why once he said, 'I taught the weeping willow how to cry.'

His recording career began in 1955. But unlike many other celebrity figures he refused to remain silent on social or political issues and recorded many protest songs, including 'The Ballad of Ira Hayes' about a Pima Indian from Gila River Reservation in Arizona. In the song, Cash's anger simmers as he sings:

> Down the ditches for a thousand years
> The water grew Ira's people's crops
> 'Til the white man stole the water rights
> And the sparkling water stopped.

Nevertheless, Ira Hayes went to fight for his country during World War II and was one of those who appear in the famous photograph of US marines raising the American flag over the Japanese stronghold of Iwo Jima. Three of the six men were killed while raising the flag. It was at a time when the War Department needed visible, tangible heroes to raise war bonds and the three survivors returned to the USA to be feted and appear at official engagements. Ira resented the public displays in which they were treated as pawns and repeatedly said that the real heroes were 'my good buddies' who died during the battles.

By the time he was released from duty he was an alcoholic and returned to the dried-up reservation where there was still no water or crops. On over fifty occasions he was arrested for being drunk and thrown into jail.

In 1954, at the age of 33, he fell drunk into an irrigation ditch and froze to death. The ditch where he died was the single source of water that was provided for his people by the US government that he had proudly served.

> Call him drunken Ira Hayes
> He won't answer anymore
> Not the whiskey drinkin' Indian
> Nor the marine that went to war.

Due to the rigours and lifestyle of touring Cash himself became a drug addict, dependent on amphetamines and barbiturates. It ruined his first marriage and when he was close to death June Carter, the singer-songwriter whom he later married, saved him by persuading him to undergo treatment.

Cash sang blues songs, American Indian ballads, hymns and love songs about the dangers of temptation ('I Walk The Line', 'Ring of Fire'). But for me he will always be the 'King of the underdog' for his stories about the hardship of life, the underprivileged and the marginalized in society, including prisoners in front of whom in Folsom Prison and San Quentin he played live concerts in 1968 and 1969. There is a part when he sings, 'San Quentin you've been livin' hell to me' and the prisoners erupt with passionate cheers.

Cash's anthem was 'The Man in Black':

> I wear the black for the poor and the beaten down.
> Livin' in the hopeless, hungry side of town,
> I wear it for the prisoner who has long paid for his crime.
> But is there because he's a victim of the times.

And he goes on to include the illiterate, those who never heard Christ's message about love and charity, the sick and lonely, drug-addicts, those in mourning and those killed in war. And he finishes:

> Ah, I'd love to wear a rainbow every day,
> And tell the world that everything's OK,
> But I'll try to carry off a little darkness on my back,
> 'Til things are brighter, I'm the Man In Black.

Rodolfo Walsh – The Writer as Freedom Fighter

Andersonstown News, 11 November 2002

Last month I had the honour of launching a book in Cultúrlann on the night that unfortunately clashed with a meeting in the Ulster Hall suddenly called by Sinn Féin in the aftermath of the British government's suspension of the Assembly. As a result, fewer people than might have been expected turned up to hear the author, Michael McCaughan, explain his fascination with Rodolfo Walsh, an Argentinian revolutionary, who was assassinated by state forces in March 1977.

The book, *True Crimes: the life and times of a radical intellectual*, published by Latin American Bureau, is the best I have read this year, for it is a biography, a love story, a literary study, a documentary, a history, an analysis, and, indeed, a breathtaking journalistic *tour de force*.

As his name suggests, Walsh was of Irish extraction, the great-grandson of Mary Kelly and Edward Walsh who fled famine and repression in Ireland in the nineteenth century and settled in rural southern Argentina. Rodolfo was born in 1927 and his first job was as a proof reader in a publishing house in Buenos Aires, before going on to become a translator and editor and finally a published writer of crime fiction (extracts from which are ingeniously juxtaposed in this book with real life events). Politically he first supported the emerging, charismatic leader Juan Peron, but turbulent events were to transform him.

One night in 1956 he was playing chess in a café where six months earlier there had been a shoot-out at the time of a failed Peronist rebellion which left twenty-seven people dead, eleven of whom were unarmed men, uninvolved in the uprising. They were taken away by the military to be summarily executed before martial law had been formally declared. A man approached Walsh in the café and whispered, 'One of the executed men is alive.' Walsh immediately investigated the events of that night and interviewed one of the seriously-wounded men who had escaped and gone into hiding. The resulting book, *Operación Masacre*, an indictment of the military authorities, became a best-seller and changed Walsh's life.

He went on to chronicle the forgotten people of his country, told the stories of those who were tortured, or 'disappeared', wrote about a leper community, and the lives of poor farmers. In one piece of investigative journalism, which he published as a story, he interviewed Moori Joenig, the army colonel and necrophiliac who kidnapped Eva Peron's body.

Walsh married in 1950 and had two daughters but he was a husband who strayed and stayed away a lot as he was smitten with the bug of revolution. He believed in the transformational possibilities of journalism, says Michael McCaughan. 'Events are what matter these days,' said Walsh, 'but rather than write about them, we must make them happen.'

In 1959 he moved to Cuba and helped launch Prensa Latina, an international press agency set up to counter the pro-US bias of international news agencies. It was Walsh, as an amateur cryptologist, who decoded intercepted CIA messages detailing plans for the Bay of Pigs invasion, thus giving Castro crucial warning of the impending aggression. He moved back to Argentina to pursue his writing career but after the death of Che Guevara in 1967 he decided to join the action and after a period in different organisations, he joined the Montoneros which were engaged in an armed struggle and he quickly rose through the ranks to become an intelligence officer in charge of infiltration of agents into the army and government.

In 1976 he was dealt a crushing blow when his daughter Vicki was killed whilst engaged in a gun battle with the army. Rather than suffer capture and torture she took the cyanide pill prescribed for all members of the Montoneros. Six months later government forces tracked down Rodolfo Walsh. Twelve agents were sent out to take him alive but he fought back and was shot dead. They took away the corpse, burnt it and dumped it on waste land. Earlier that day he had just posted a letter challenging the authorities.

Military rule ended in 1983, and in 2001 the government of Buenos Aires approved a city ordinance which directed all schools to read out Rodolfo's 'Open Letter from a Writer to the Military Junta' every year on March 24th, the anniversary of the 1976 coup.

Walsh had a bias towards what he called 'useful literature', by which he meant novels and stories which were politically instructive. When asked to pick a short story for an anthology he chose, 'The Wrath of an Individual' by an anonymous Chinese author because it offered a perfect demonstration of the relationship between power without limits and the individual. I'll finish on it.

> The king of T'sin sent word to the prince of Ngan-ling: 'In exchange for your lands I want to give you another property ten times bigger. I beg you to accede to my demand.' The prince replied: 'The King bestows on me a great honour and an advantageous offer. But I received my land from my princely ancestors and I wish to keep it until the end. I cannot agree to the exchange.'
>
> The king became furious, so the prince sent T'ang Tsu as an emissary. The king said to him: 'The prince is unwilling to swap his land for another one ten times greater. If your lord still has his little holding when I have conquered great countries, it is because up until now I have considered him a venerable fellow and I haven't taken any interest in him. But if he turns down what's good for him now, then he's making a mockery of me.'
>
> T'ang Tsu replied: 'That is not it. The prince wants to hold on to the legacy of his forbears. Even if you offered him lands that were twenty times bigger than his own he would still turn down the offer.'
>
> The king grew angry and said to T'ang Tsu: 'Do you know how the wrath of a king is?'

'No', said T'ang Tsu.

'It is millions of corpses and blood flowing like a river for a thousand leagues,' said the king.

T'ang Tsu then asked, 'Does your majesty know how the wrath of a mere individual is?'

The king replied, 'It is like losing the badge of dignity and walking barefoot while banging your head on the ground.'

'No,' said T'ang Tsu, 'that's the wrath of an ordinary man, not the wrath of a man of courage. When a man of courage finds himself forced to become angry, there will be no more than two dead bodies and the blood flows only a few feet. Yet all China will be in mourning. That day has arrived.' And he rose and unsheathed his sword.

The king's expression suddenly changed, he made a gesture of humility and said: 'Master, sit down. Why take things so far? I have understood.'

In the Simplicity of His Defiance

A tribute to the first blanket prisoner, Kieran Nugent, who died on 4 May 2000.

Andersonstown News, 8 May 2000

Kieran Nugent. A name that makes you proud to be from West Belfast. A name that was on our lips for years. So familiar. Yet, go back.

In truth, the Republican Movement in 1976 was very disorganised. One day a middle-aged man and woman, and their daughter, from Leeson Street, came into our offices at 170A Falls Road, the Republican Press Centre, and spoke to Tom Hartley. He took their details and called me down from the attic where I was editing the *Republican News*.

Their son had gone missing. They didn't know where he was. He had been sentenced to three years in jail a few weeks before. It's hard to believe but we hadn't followed the case. We knew about the Diplock courts. We knew that anyone convicted for an offence committed after March 1st would not get political status – but it hadn't really dawned on people outside the jails.

But it had dawned on the remand prisoners. I think it was Sean Morris who had used the defiant headline in Republican News from a Crumlin Road comm, 'They'll Have To Nail It To My Back'. 'It' being the prison uniform. I don't know if it was Kieran Nugent who said it but at the time of the 1981 hunger strike I interviewed him for a video and he said that if they had thrown him a towel after they stripped him of his clothes he would have started 'the towel protest'.

As it was, those cocky prison administrators tossed a blanket into this man's bare cell on September 14th 1976, expecting him to 'see sense' in a short period, or see their fists. And the rest is history. Bitter. Sore. Angry. Defiance. Our 1916. Giving rise to defiance and courage.

So here were Mr and Mrs Nugent and their daughter in our office trying to find out if we knew anything about their Kieran. A few weeks before, the British army had shot dead IRA Volunteer Danny Lennon at the wheel of a car, which had then careered across Finaghy Road North and crashed into Mrs Anne Maguire and her kids. Joanne (8) and Andrew (six weeks old) died instantly and John (2) died the following day. Out of this incident the controversial Peace People were formed and the confusion and low morale within working-class nationalist areas meant that the blanket protest and, indeed, the first two years of the H-Block and Armagh protest movements on the streets were seriously retarded.

Yet, from the jails names emerged. We began to hear that a Ned Flynn was on the blanket, and, later, that Fra McCann, Gerard Murray, Jimmy Duffy and Joe Maguire were on the blanket in the Crum. Those were lean days. Uphill battles. Poor publicity.

There is a great description in Peter Taylor's book, *Beating The Terrorists*, of the gung-ho atmosphere in the Monday morning briefings in Stormont Castle involving direct-ruler Roy Mason, RUC Chief Constable Kenneth Newman and the GOC of the British Army. Each of them became orgasmic as the statistics of the previous week's arrests, interrogations and chargings were outlined. But in our Falls Road office we were receiving smuggled statements from the jails about the beatings in Castlereagh and Gough, about how this one had his ear perforated or a finger broken or an eye blackened or a rib cracked. Could we get the media to carry these statements? Could we get the SDLP to protest? Four years. No letters. No books. Batons. Beatings. Forced scrubbings. It would make you, even now, want to murder.

Kieran Nugent. The first blanket man.

Tom Hartley gave a fine oration and talked about the simplicity of his defiance. Just before that, Fra McCann had described Kieran, who died suddenly and shockingly last week, as 'larger-than-life'. And wasn't it poignant that he should leave this earth on the nineteenth anniversary of the death of his comrade, Bobby Sands?

I have a few memories of Kieran. There is film of him on the day he got out of jail. Pale white face – not having seen the sun in three years. Later, he stood on a platform opposite Dunville Park and clenched hands with that other hero of prison protest, Billy McKee, whose 1972 hunger strike won political status recognition.

One night in 1983 Kieran, Fra McCann and myself were on the Dublin-to-Belfast train, returning from a Sinn Féin meeting. I was recognisable from my public appearances. A rugby club from Portadown was also on the train and some of them spotted me and started giving us abuse at the bar (well, where did you think we would be?). One of them said, 'Get Big Stevie. He'll sort the bastards out!' So the word went down the train, 'Get Big Stevie!'

Big Stevie had to bend down four feet to get through the door and began salivating when he spotted me and started growling now that we were passed Kilnasaggart and were in the North.

Kieran set his bottle of beer on the table and said, for everyone to hear, 'First one to touch you, Dan, loses an eye with this.' Big Stevie grunted and groaned, huffed and puffed, bent down four feet to retreat, and to this day can see his kids.

So, we buried Kieran Nugent last Saturday. Friends and family. Comrades. A guy who didn't have a lot. Who life messed about. The first H-Block blanket man.

Kieran Nugent.

Terence 'Cleaky' Clarke

A tribute to a former republican prisoner who died on 13 June 2000

Ireland on Sunday, 18 June 2000

Ten days after the SAS killings in Gibraltar, I stood with Richard Behal, a republican from Kerry, and the journalist Mary Holland, beside the hearses that had borne the coffins of Mairead Farrell, Dan McCann and Sean Savage to the republican plot in Milltown cemetery.

Gerry Adams had just began his oration when, suddenly, grenades began exploding around us and there was gunfire. Pandemonium broke out as people fell bleeding and screaming. Among those killed by the loyalist Michael Stone was my friend, IRA Volunteer Kevin Brady. Three days later, we were burying Kevin. I was carrying his coffin on the Andersonstown Road when, once again, there were screams and panic among mourners as a car sped towards us at high speed. It careered into a cul de sac, reversed quickly but found itself blocked by a taxi. Once again we were being attacked by loyalists and the people were terrified. The driver of the car produced a gun and began firing as a crowd surged around the vehicle, caring little for their own lives.

One of those who disarmed the driver was Terence 'Cleaky' Clarke. The two men were dragged from the car and the passenger was found to be armed as well. The IRA intervened and took the two gunmen away. As we continued with the funeral we heard more shooting. Of course, it later turned out that the men were not loyalist paramilitaries but plain-clothes soldiers. To this day, their presence at Kevin's funeral has never been explained. They were very badly beaten by some of the crowd before the IRA shot them dead.

Most television viewers saw the brutal deaths of these two soldiers as akin to a lynching. Cleaky Clarke and those others involved in disarming the two men were crucified by the media. Peter Brooke, the secretary of state, daubed the people of West Belfast, 'the terrorist community'.

Actually, Cleaky Clarke was a hero who courageously risked his life tackling the unknown – two gunmen, just three days after another gunman at another republican funeral had killed three mourners and wounded sixty men, women and children. For this, Cleaky was sentenced to seven years in jail. And it was while in jail in 1990 that he was diagnosed as having cancer. I myself was on remand in Crumlin Road Jail when we heard the bad news.

Republican humour can be very black and Cleaky, who specialised in gallows humour, knew not to expect any exceptional treatment. Comrades would come up to him and say, 'Cleaky, leave us you denim jacket,' or, 'Leave me your shoes; we take the same size.'

After I was sentenced I was often on the same H-Block as him. Sometimes at night, before we were locked up, he gave me soup that he was on as part of his diet. One night I had no appetite so he offered it to another prisoner who had only recently arrived. This young fellow hesitated taking the bowl of soup and quick as a shot Cleaky said, 'It's only cancer I have, not leprosy!' The young fella was embarrassed until Cleaky and I burst out laughing. On the day that he left H-5 another prisoner came up to him and solemnly shook his hand in case he never saw him again and Cleaky, in that droll manner of his, said, 'Christ, thanks!'

I imagine it is very difficult for readers unacquainted with the republican experience in the North to appreciate what makes republicans tick. There is a media version of the conflict, and then there is the truth – the actual story of our lives, so surreal, passionate, serious, tragic, and so incredible in drama that sometimes its wonder even amazes us.

In 1971 Cleaky was arrested in possession of a gun and was on remand in the dirtiest jail in Europe, 'The Crum'. Cleaky said, 'The Crum's so bad it would put you off going to jail.' He was there a short time. A rope ladder came over the wall while remand prisoners were playing football and a whole team, Cleaky included, escaped. He was on IRA active service on the South Armagh border for several months and in Derry after Bloody Sunday, but was caught in August 1972.

He was sentenced to five years by Lord Justice McGonagle. Cleaky shouted to him, 'There'll come a day when I'll be sitting where you are and you'll be down here charged with war crimes.' McGonagle, a former SAS soldier, doubled his sentence. In Long Kesh Cleaky unsuccessfully attempted to escape, along with several other prisoners dressed as British soldiers. His escape trial was held in Newry courthouse from where – yes – he escaped, before being caught on the border.

He was returned to Cage 11 where he was the life and soul of the camp. Here, he met Bobby Sands, during Bobby's first round in jail, and Gerry Adams, who had been interned but was now convicted for attempting to escape. In 1978 a prisoner returning from a visit was involved in a fight with prison warders. Cleaky and several others scaled the fence to go to the stricken man's aid. Over this incident he and IRA leader Brendan Hughes had their political status withdrawn and were sent to the H-Blocks where they joined the blanket protest. Cleaky's two brothers, Gerard and Seamus (who was to escape in the mass break-out in 1983), were now on the blanket – which meant that all of Maggie Clarke's sons were in prison.

In 1984, after Gerry Adams was shot by loyalists, body-guard teams, drawn from ex-prisoners, were assigned to protect republican leaders. Upon his release from jail in 1993 Cleaky became the co-ordinator of these teams and was himself in charge of Adams' personal security. It was in this capacity that he came to be well known and well regarded by journalists. It was an indication of his determination that for ten years he fought the cancer that racked his body until his death last Tuesday. His comrade, Martin Meehan, who had been on active service with Cleaky after their escape from 'The Crum', said, 'He fought many battles with courage and commitment but his last battle was fought with dignity.'

Cleaky married Mary Doyle, herself an ex-prisoner and former hunger striker, whose own mother Marie was killed in a loyalist bomb attack on a North Belfast bar in 1975. They have two children, Marie and Seamus.

There is a grainy photograph of a group of prisoners in Cage 11, taken with a smuggled camera, on a summer's day in 1975. The prisoners are wearing jeans, vests, some are bare-chested, and they are strikingly happy and smiling. Among them are Tom Cahill (brother of Joe); Tommy Tolan (who had escaped from the prison ship Maidstone and who would be killed by the Official IRA within two years); Brendan Hughes (who had escaped from internment and who would be the leader of the 1980 hunger strike), his arm resting on the shoulder of a long-haired Gerry Adams; and Cleaky Clarke, with his left arm around Bobby Sands who was due for release a few months later – none of them seemingly aware of the freight of history they carried in life, and in death.

A Story of Revenge

On the genocide of the Armenians

Andersonstown News, 19 March 2001

They took everyone away… They struck and cracked my brother's skull with an axe. They took my sister and raped her. As soon as the soldiers and the gendarmes began the massacres, the mob was upon us too and my brother's head was cracked open. Then my mother fell from a bullet or something else. I was struck on the head and fell to the ground...

'I do not know how long I stayed there. Maybe it was two days. When I opened my eyes I saw myself surrounded by corpses... I saw my mother's body; she had fallen face down. My brother's body had fallen on top of me. When I stood up I realised that my leg was injured and my arm was bleeding...'

That's how Soghomon Tehlirian began describing the Turkish massacre of 20,000 of his fellow Armenians from Erzinga in 1915 when he was a teenager. Turkey, at the centre of the Ottoman Empire, had earlier become a constitutional monarchy after a coup by the Committee of Union and Progress (popularly known as 'the Young Turks'). They initially promised their multi-racial subjects reform and equality and were thus supported by the Armenians, who even joined the Turkish army in large numbers at the beginning of the 1914 war.

However, the C.U.P. became increasingly nationalistic and xenophobic, began 'Turkifying' the empire and demonising the Christian Armenians who had occupied their homeland for several millennia. The Armenians – like the Jews – had often been subjected to massacres; Turks and Kurds killed 300,000 in 1895 alone.

Talaat Pasha, Minister of the Interior, was the principal architect of the 1915 massacre which Soghomon Tehlirian had survived. The genocide of the Armenians was well planned, and, just as the Nazis were to do two decades later, was carried out in a systematic manner under the cover of war. In 1914 Armenian army recruits between the ages of 16 and 60 were mobilised and transported in the back of covered trucks – believing they were going on a training exercise. Instead, they were publicly executed in town squares or taken to torture camps were they were murdered. Armenian intellectuals, MPs, teachers and doctors were next rounded up in Constantinople (Istanbul) and executed, leaving the Armenians leaderless.

Talaat signed the deportation orders for civilians in Armenian towns and villages. Whole populations were rounded up and removed to distant locations before being liquidated, 24,000 being killed in one three-day period of mass shootings. Others were placed on ships that were scuttled in the Black Sea or were forced on death marches to the Syrian Desert. At least one million were killed and two million displaced. Thousands were also rescued and sheltered by compassionate individual Turks, Kurds and Arabs, but these were a minority of cases.

Soghomon Tehlirian escaped into the mountains and was protected by a Kurdish family until his wounds healed. When war ended with the defeat of Germany and the break-up of the Ottoman Empire the Allies said that the Turks responsible for the massacres would be punished but they were never seriously pursued. Talaat Pasha and his cohorts escaped, Talaat being given shelter in Germany where he lived under a false name. In his absence he had been tried, found guilty and sentenced to death for ordering the massacres.

After the war Tehlirian returned home but only two families were left in Erzinga

– and they had 'converted' to Islam. He wandered from place to place, suffered several nervous breakdowns, and whilst in Constantinople learnt from newspapers about Talaat Pasha's central role in the exterminations. In 1920 he went to the USA where he joined the Diasporan Responsible Body, received special training, then went to Berlin where he and his comrades began the job of tracking down Talaat. Within three months they discovered his residence. One morning as Talaat came out of his home Soghomon Tehlirian killed him with a single revolver shot. Over the next year other members of the Armenian DRB executed the top six former leaders of the Young Turks in what later came to be called 'The Armenian Nuremburg'.

Today Armenia is an independent republic with close ties to the former USSR. Some of its territory still remains under Turkish rule. To this day Turkey still denies the Armenian genocide – which is one of the main obstacles to it being accepted into the European Union.

Tehlirian was arrested in Berlin and charged with the murder of Talaat but a German jury – listening spellbound to his account of the Erzinga massacre and the killing of his entire family – acquitted him and described the shooting as justified homicide. He lived out the remainder of his days in California – an Armenian hero.

Simple Song of Freedom

Andersonstown News, 28 January 2002

In 1967 the bodies of ten prisoners, who had been shot dead, were discovered secretly buried on a farm in Arkansas, in a scene that could have come straight out of the Paul Newman film, *Cool Hand Luke*. Back then, prison farms were expected to be self-supporting. Thus, trusties took the place of salaried guards, and the law sanctioned the whipping of prisoners with four-foot long straps. Furthermore, torturing prisoners by electricity or old-fashioned pliers was sanctioned by custom.

In 1968 an anti-government song, *Long Line Rider*, in memory of the slain prisoners was written, part of which went:

> Someone screams investigate
> 'scuse me sir it's a little late..
> This kinda thing can't happen here
> 'specially not in an election year...
> And the ground coughs up some roots
> Wearin' denim shirts and boots...

The man who wrote that song was booed off the stage when he tried to perform it. He was also prevented from singing it on the Jackie Gleason television show in the USA and walked off the set.

That man was fifties' teenage idol Bobby Darin.

We were listening to the radio a few Sundays ago and by accident came across a documentary about his life. Darin was born Walden Robert Cassotto into poverty in a Harlem ghetto in 1936, a sickly, fatherless child, who suffered from several bouts of rheumatic fever which damaged his heart. He wasn't expected to make his sixteenth birthday.

I had liked his hits, *Splish Splash*, *Dream Lover* and *Beyond The Sea*. But he was among a haze of singers from my childhood who just preceded my generation's Beatles and Stones. I had also liked his version of the Kurt Weill/Bertolt Brecht song *Mack The Knife* which sold two million copies and made his name.

(Incidentally, the song comes from *The Thrupenny Opera* (1928) and tells the story of Mack, a prison escapee. Polly, daughter of Peacham, king of the London beggars, is in love with and marries her father's younger rival, Mack, who protects beggars through his friendship with the chief of police. Disapproving of his daughter's match, Peacham persuades the chief to arrest Mack. Mack escapes from prison, is recaptured and is about to be hanged when the King intervenes, pardons him and makes him a Lord – in a parody of operatic convention. I know, I know, it sounds ridiculous, but I remember dancing to Richard Harris singing 'Someone's left the cake out in the rain…')

Darin was a gifted composer, wrote over one hundred songs and starred in thirteen movies. But from the start he was resented as a pompous brat. 'Little Singer with a Big Ego' was the headline on one magazine. He refused to do encores or sign autographs, was critical of the prying press, and boasted: 'I hope to pass Frank [Sinatra] in everything he's done.' This provoked Sinatra and Dean Martin to pin his picture to the wall and use it as a dartboard.

In the early 1960s he said: 'Every time I hear some little singer being congratulated for being "such a good example to your teenage followers", I feel like throwing up.' Yet, he was to change as a result of the civil rights movement, the race riots, the campus revolts, the Vietnam War and after meeting Robert Kennedy. He became an activist and a natural ally of the oppressed. During this time his sister approached him and said that if he was going to be involved in politics there was something he should know. 'I'm not your sister; I'm your mother.' He was shattered and said, 'My whole life has been a lie.' She refused to tell him who his father was (his alleged father died in Sing Sing prison before he was born).

Nevertheless, he continued to canvass for radical change. The assassination of Robert Kennedy in 1968 during his presidential bid brought about another profound effect in his life. At his graveside he experienced an intense mystical revelation. 'I emerged a better person, at peace with myself and strived to help the world change towards goodness.' He sold all his possessions, moved into a trailer for a year and spent his time reading. It was during this period that he wrote his anti-war song, *Simple Song of Freedom*, though it was Tim Hardin's version that made the charts in 1969, just as our own conflict was beginning. He was a loyal friend, a supporter of many charities and an ambassador for the American Heart Association.

In 1972 he went to the dentist to have his teeth cleaned and because he had a heart condition was supposed to take a course of antibiotics as a preventative against blood poisoning. He didn't complete the course and contracted septicaemia, which contributed to the cause of death during a heart operation in December 1973. There was no funeral service as he had donated his body for medical research. He was only thirty-seven years of age.

> Come and sing a simple song of freedom
> Sing it like you've never sung before.
> Let it fill the air
> Tell the people everywhere
> We, the people here, don't want a war...
> Seven hundred million are you listening?
> Most of what you read is made of lies
> But speaking one to one, ain't it everybody's sun
> To wake to in the morning when we rise?...
> No doubt some folks enjoy doing battle
> Like presidents, prime ministers and kings.
> So let's all build them shelves where they can fight among themselves,
> and leave the people be who love to sing...
> Let it fill the air, tell the people everywhere
> We, the people, here don't want a war...

Spike Milligan

On the death of the comedian, 27 February 2002

An Phoblacht/Republican News on 7 March 2002

One of the books most passed around during internment was Spike Milligan's *Puckoon* which, I was assured when it was given to me, was about Crossmaglen and the Brits. Only later did I discover that it was published in 1960, was about a 'partitioned' village (set in Sligo, I think) and was written before Milligan even set foot in Ireland.

Nevertheless, it brought some light relief back in those days with scenes that certainly anticipated Father Ted. In one, Father Rudden is trying to raise funds to restore the chapel and in desperation tells his congregation that he will perform a miracle and ask God to make fire fall from heaven. The pews are packed with expectant parishioners as the priest says: 'I command fire to fall from heaven!' Then a voice comes from an altar boy in the loft: 'Just a minute, Father, the cat's peed on the matches!'

Our love of Milligan was simplistic: he was an iconoclast of the British establishment and boasted of his Irish heritage at a time when many other Irish-born comics were anxious for promotional reasons to emphasise how Brit-friendly they were, and weren't a bit behind the doors at performing as 'Paddies' for their British audiences, regardless that such buffoonery reinforced the 'thick Irish' stereotype. Or else, they presented themselves as well-behaved Man Fridays, with avuncular Irish accents, won over to the cultural might of England.

Terence Allan Milligan was born in 1918 to Irish parents in India. His father, who was from Sligo, was a serving British soldier. Young Milligan was educated at convent schools, before moving to London at the age of sixteen when his father retired from the army.

He was a promising jazz trumpeter and got his nickname from British jazz composer and critic Spike Hughes. He told a story that when he was called up during the Second World War he had to be dragged from the house by eight military policemen. Nevertheless, he was proud of his service with the Royal Artillery Regiment. 'We beat the [German] bastard, we really give it to them,' he said. It was whilst serving that he was blown up and seriously injured by a German mortar. His manic depressiveness dates from that time. After the war he went into entertainment, playing to the troops before making his reputation with the Goon Show on BBC radio, where he pioneered the joke without a punch line. He appropriated the word 'Goon' from a Popeye cartoon, a word he deployed for a lovable, interesting idiot.

He wrote most of the Goon shows and it was the pressure of writing and recording that caused him to suffer four nervous breakdowns, and also the break-up of his first of three marriages. He described that period as one of the unhappiest in his life.

One day he went to renew his passport and was told that he wasn't British.

'Some creep there said, "Do you know you're not supposed to have this passport?" There was a law passed that said that an Irish man whose father was born in Ireland before 1908 was no longer entitled to a British passport.'

'So, I went to the Irish embassy and said, "Can I get an Irish one?" He said, "Oh Jesus, yes, we're awful short of people."'

Milligan wrote six volumes of memoirs, including, *Hitler: My Part In His Downfall, Monty: My Part In His Victory*; books for children; poetry (very sad and very mad ones) and even songs. He also wrote a serious book with his psychiatrist, Anthony Clare, *Depression and How to Survive It*.

On accepting a lifetime achievement honour at the British Comedy Awards in 1994, Milligan, on live television, called Prince Charles 'a little grovelling bastard' after the royal had sent his congratulations in a letter. Afterwards, he faxed him saying: 'I suppose a knighthood is out of the question now?' He explained his behaviour by saying that he had drunk two bottles of wine, was 'pissed' and didn't know that he was being presented with an award.

Six years later he was given an honorary knighthood, although technically his Irish citizenship forbade him from using the title. At the ceremony Prince Charles tried to convince him to take the oath of loyalty and become a British subject again, pointing out that even he had to do it as Prince of Wales. Spike replied that it was different for Charles because he had to pledge allegiance to his mother as she provided him with bed and board.

Subject to mood swings and on daily doses of lithium, in between stays in psychiatric homes, he could turn abrasive and often preferred the company of animals to humans. He was an environmentalist and animal rights campaigner but I read somewhere that in his dotage he also spoke out against interracial dating, marriage and breeding and advocated compulsory contraception in developing countries. We'll put that down to the shrapnel, rather than allow it blot the entire life of a man who broke the barriers in comedy and entertained many millions of people with his zany comments on the absurdity of existence.

He was at his best when he interviewed the laconic Van Morrison for *Q* magazine in 1989. Spike, at the age of seventy-one, wearing a large, pink, penis-shaped false nose, set down Mr Morrison.

'Van, I must ask you something. Dutch descent? You must be.'

Van replied, No.

'No? You're an Irishman?'

'Ivan is my name.'

'I see. A Russian! I'm baffled now.'

He asked Van was he 'a Proddy'. Van said that theoretically he was Church of Ireland. Van was emphasising that he kept his private and public lives very separate but Spike wanted to know if he had a wife, a girlfriend 'or a bloke?'

Elsewhere, Spike had said that all he wanted out of life was 'a long-lasting friendship. Just like I wanted a long-lasting marriage. Just like I wanted to live in one house all my life, the house I was born in. I am a nostalgia freak. I don't know what this yearning for anchorage in my life is.'

The best part of the interview is where Spike begins talking about his own past. 'My father was born in Sligo, Van. Very Irish working-class family, very poor. He used to live in a romantic world. He loved a drink; he was full of stories… He used to tell the kids all these stories about shooting elephants, strangling giraffes by hand. I said, "What's all this, Dad? It's all lies, isn't it?"'

'He said, "Oh yes, all lies. But what would you rather have: a boring truth or an exciting lie?"'

So, when we read him back in Long Kesh we suspended our disbelief and pretended he was railing against the partition of Crossmaglen, that he was anti-Brit and anti-royalist, whilst all along he perhaps didn't know who he really was, except that he was himself best when he was making people laugh and not locked away in a dark room, terrified of the world.

Mayor Alex Maskey Pays Tribute

Honouring the service men and women of two world wars

Andersonstown News, 1 July 2002

Belfast Mayor Alex Maskey's decision to pay tribute to the courage and sacrifice of those Irish men and women, who for diverse and contradictory reasons, fought in the First and Second World Wars, was a difficult and controversial one, and unprecedented for Sinn Féin. Yet, it is the correct decision and reflects on the maturity of Sinn Féin and the party's attempts not just to be inclusive and sensitive to the unionist tradition at a time when Sinn Féin is in the chair, but also, ironically, to acknowledge another side of the nationalist experience which for historical and political reasons has been largely suppressed.

Returnees to the unionist community, from the 36th Division (the old Ulster Volunteer Force which had been set up in 1912 to resist Home Rule) were given a heroes' welcome, whereas returnees from the 10th & 16th (Irish) Divisions, amongst others, to the nationalist community across Ireland met with hostility. Some, like Dan Breen and Tom Barry, brought the skills they had learnt in the British army into the fledgling IRA and emerged as leading guerrilla fighters.

When my great Uncle Paddy returned from the First World War and called in to see his brother, my Granda White, in Ward Street, my granda refused to let him cross the threshold and told him to come back when he took off the uniform. My Granda Morrison also fought in that war, attached to the Royal Flying Corps. He returned to his Massarene Street home in the Falls, but was later arrested and charged for being at an IRA meeting in Currie Street Hall.

Prior to 1914 the regular British army had many Irish regiments. Service, like emigration, was a means of escape from hunger and unemployment. However, after September 1914 there was a huge influx from the Irish Volunteers when the leader of the Irish Parliamentary Party, John Redmond, made a recruiting speech in favour of the British army. The Act promising Ireland Home Rule had been passed at Westminster but its implementation was suspended until after the war.

The Irish Volunteers had been established to support Home Rule, but were divided over Redmond's call. The minority of the Volunteers, especially those under the influence of the Irish Republican Brotherhood, saw England's difficulty as Ireland's opportunity and planned a rising. But most of the men marched off to war, naively believing that by fighting, Ireland would get a better post-war deal. The loyalists believed the same for Ulster and, as it turned out, the loyalists were correct.

In total, up to a quarter of a million Irishmen fought in the First World War, 50,000 of whom gave their lives.

While the Irish were away fighting the Germans, Irish republicans at home organised the 1916 Easter Rising. The response of the British government in executing the leaders of the Rising and the actions of British army regiments caused an upheaval in public opinion in favour of republicans and Sinn Féin quickly supplanted Redmond's Irish Parliamentary Party.

When soldiers from a nationalist background were demobilised they returned to a different Ireland, one at war with Britain and facing the threat of partition. They experienced public antipathy and animosity (though in the North ex-servicemen were to defend nationalist enclaves in 1921 and 1922). In the south, a World War One 'veteran' became associated with the other 'veterans' who made up the Tans and the Auxiliaries and who carried out atrocities. Commemoration and memory of the war became associated with support for the British administration in Ireland.

In the North, unionists appropriated the war dead but, selectively, laid emphasis on the 36th (Ulster) Division's sacrifices at the Somme (as if no Irish nationalists had also died in that battle). Unionists also turned the Poppy into a unionist emblem, the wearing of it a sign of loyalty to their Northern Ireland state.

On Easter Sunday republicans remember and honour the patriot dead. But the issue of how they can formally acknowledge the courage and sacrifice of their other forebears, and those from the unionist community, who took part in the two world wars, without giving assent to militarism and imperialism, is truly a difficult one that Alex Maskey is honestly attempting to breach.

I want to remember and pay tribute without distinction to all the war dead – just as I do not distinguish between the sufferings of families who lost loved ones whether in the IRA or in the British forces (though I certainly distinguish between the nobility of their causes). It is not a hollow aspiration, though I can understand unionists scoffing at the sentiment because of what the IRA did in Enniskillen on Remembrance Sunday.

In the twenty-six counties in recent years efforts – some genuine, others perverse – have been made to revise this part of our history and, justifiably, recall and commemorate the courage of these soldiers. But some revisionist journalists employ an argument, and invective, aimed at making it difficult for those who do not share their political analysis to embrace the war dead. They have sought to create a sense of public guilt about the way returnees were mistreated. By making disparaging comparisons between the warfare and sacrifices of those Irish who fought against the British and those who fought with the British abroad, they seek to return to the days when Pearse and Connolly were spat on as they were marched through the streets of Dublin.

In their view the IRA's War of Independence should be rejected, its heroes tarnished (and in the process the cause of Irish reunification). We should not allow them to shape our response.

Finally, just as it is possible to admire the fortitude and heroism of the Protestant defenders during the siege of Derry in 1689, and yet regret the political legacy of their victory, so too should nationalists and republicans throughout Ireland feel able to acknowledge the selflessness and patriotism of those thousands of Irish men and women who participated in the two World Wars.

'A Spiritual Act, A Holy Deed'

A tribute to Native American Leonard Peltier
as he enters his twenty-eighth year of imprisonment

Andersonstown News, 19 May 2003

In Cultúrlann restaurant on Friday a Cork woman stopped and asked me if I was Danny Morrison. She said she wrote often to Leonard Peltier and had sent him my books, and he liked my writings. I felt very humbled to be appreciated by such a great person as Leonard Peltier who has been in jail for twenty-seven years, falsely imprisoned for killing two FBI agents.

In 1998 he wrote: 'This is the twenty-third year of my imprisonment for a crime I didn't commit. I'm now fifty-four years old. I've been in here since I was thirty-one. I've been told I have to live out two lifetime sentences plus seven years before I get out of prison in the year 2041. By then I'll be ninety-seven. I don't think I'll make it.' (From *Prison Writings: My Life is My Sun Dance*)

What is happening today to the Palestinian people – a nation being destroyed before our eyes by a militarily superior force which supports seizure of territory and colonised settlements, and which limits the Palestinians to 'reservations' – is exactly what happened to the native peoples of North America as a result of European colonisation beginning with Columbus. Throughout the nineteenth century treaties, which the US Congress signed with the Native American Indians, were each in turn repudiated as the greed and demand of the colonisers became insatiable.

In 1968 the American Indian Movement (AIM) was formed to combat police brutality, high unemployment and federal government policies.

Leonard Peltier was born into poverty in a reservation in North Dakota. He had thirteen brothers and sisters. At the age of eight he was taken from his family and sent to a boarding school run by the US government. Students were forbidden to speak their native languages and suffered physical and psychological abuse. His reservation had been chosen as a testing ground for the government's new termination policy of forcing Indians off their reservations and into the cities, by withdrawing, for example, benefits, including food assistance, to those who remained on the land.

He became an organiser and fought Native Land Claim issues, then joined the AIM. In 1972 he occupied the Bureau of Indian Affairs building in Washington in the 'Trail of Broken Treaties' protest.

In December 1890 the great leader Sitting Bull, who had defeated General Custer at the Battle of Little Bighorn, was shot dead, allegedly resisting arrest. Fearing further reprisals his followers fled but a few days later, three hundred and fifty Sioux, consisting of 120 men and 230 women and children, were rounded up and placed in a camp on Wounded Knee Creek. An order was given to disarm them. During a fracas a shot was fired and the federal troops killed 153 and wounded 44 people, half of whom were unarmed women and children. Survivors were pursued and butchered by US troops. Twenty-three soldiers from the Seventh Calvary were later awarded the Congressional Medal of Honor for slaughtering these defenceless Indians.

In February 1973 a group of armed members of the Sioux nation, the Oglala Sioux Civil Rights Organisation and the AIM reclaimed Wounded Knee and for the first time in decades ruled themselves and celebrated death, marriage and birth in their traditional manner. Supporters arrived daily from all over the country, slipping past federal marshals and the National Guard. They demanded an investigation into the Bureau of Indian Affairs, corruption and the misuse of tribal funds. Food supplies and electricity were cut off and there was daily, heavy gunfire. Twelve Indians were captured by the FBI and were 'disappeared' and never seen again. After the 71-day occupation there were 1200 arrests.

Following the siege there was a three-year 'Reign of Terror' on the reservations, instigated by the FBI in collusion with vigilantes of the pro-government tribal council, and which resulted in over sixty members or sympathisers of the AIM being assassinated.

These were the preceding circumstances in June 1975 when Leonard Peltier was asked to help protect the people of Pine Ridge Reservation against attack. Two FBI undercover agents chased a pickup truck onto the reservation and there was a shoot-out during which they and a young Native American were killed. Three people were brought to trial. Two, Bob Robideau and Darrell Butler, were eventually acquitted on grounds of self-defence. Leonard Peltier was arrested in Canada on the strength of an extradition warrant, which contained an affadavit from Myrtle Poor Bear. She said she was his girlfriend and saw him shoot the agents at close range.

After he was extradited the prosecution withdrew Myrtle Poor Bear's evidence. It turned out that she wasn't his girlfriend, had never met Peltier and wasn't present at the scene of the shooting. Furthermore, the judge barred her from testifying for the defence on the grounds of mental incompetence. Three teenage Native witnesses testified against Peltier, all admitting later that the FBI had threatened and forced them. Still, they did not identify him as the gunman. During the trial the FBI withheld important documents from the judge, jury and the defence, which showed that the casings from the bullets used to kill the two agents did not come from the gun tied to Peltier.

Leonard Peltier was sentenced to two terms of life imprisonment to run consecutively and has been imprisoned for the past twenty-seven years. All of his appeals have been denied and because he will not admit to the murders the parole board refuses to consider him for temporary release and says that it will review his case in 2008. His appeals attorney is former US Attorney General Ramsay Clark, a man who walked on the Falls Road in Belfast in 1981 in support of the H-Block hunger strikers.

Amnesty International, Nelson Mandela, Archbishop Tutu and the European Parliament, amongst others, have all called for his release but the US authorities are merciless. Hopes were high that Bill Clinton would issue him a presidential pardon when he left office in 2001. But instead he pardoned fugitive billionaire Marc Rich, who had been living in Switzerland avoiding indictments on charges of racketeering, tax evasion and trading with Iran in violation of a US embargo.

Peltier responded: 'We can see who was granted clemency and why. The big donors to the President's campaign [a reference to Rich's wife, Denise] were able to buy justice, something we just couldn't afford.'

In prison he has established himself as a poet and prose writer and author of a moving biography, and as a talented artist, portraying the culture and history of his people. Despite suffering from diabetes, a heart condition and a stroke, which has left him partially blind in one eye, he remains unrepentant and unbroken.

'My people's struggle to survive inspires my own struggle to survive. Each of us must be a survivor.'

His role has been as a symbol of his suffering people.

'In the Indian Way, the political and the spiritual are one and the same. You can't believe one thing and do another. What you believe and what you do are the same thing. In the Indian Way, if you see your people suffering, helping them is an absolute necessity. It's not a social act of charity or welfare assistance: it's a spiritual act, a holy deed.'

Mary Robinson – 'An awkward voice'

A tribute to the former Irish President for her work on human rights

Irish Examiner, 20 March 2002

As Mary Robinson and her three-vehicle convoy drove through the Palestinian town of Hebron two years ago someone opened fire and a bullet struck one of the cars. She had been touring the West Bank and Gaza to investigate complaints by the Palestinian Authority that Israeli soldiers had been using excessive force against their people, especially young stone throwers. The Israeli army blamed Palestinians but Palestinian police said militant Jewish settlers fired at the convoy in an Israeli-controlled part of the town.

Given that the UN High Commissioner for human rights was there to investigate Israeli behaviour, it's not too hard to guess to which side the gunmen belonged. Though upset, she refused to allow the incident to intimidate her or deter her active commitment to international human rights. In the end it wasn't bullets that persuaded her not to seek a fresh mandate when her term runs out in September, but the machinations of the US government and the fact that her department was starved of proper funding.

Washington was angry at Robinson's outspokenness and the fact that she took her responsibilities quite literally and was not a mere stooge of western foreign policy interests, though she was initially supported by Tony Blair and President Bill Clinton in 1997 as she was completing her term as the first woman Irish President. From 1969 to 1989 Robinson had been a member of Seanad Éireann. In a highly conservative Ireland she campaigned on women's rights, contraception, divorce, homosexuality and abortion.

In 1990 she shook the establishment and broke the cartel of the major parties when she was inaugurated as the seventh president of Ireland. Her presidency was characterized by inclusiveness and a concerted effort to use the office not only to improve the situations of marginalized groups within Ireland but also to draw attention to global crises.

In 1993 she was invited to attend 'A Celebration of Culture and Creativity' in Ballymurphy. Despite an intense lobbying campaign by a coalition which would have withered the steeliest of souls, and which included John Major, Sir Patrick Mayhew, all the Unionist parties, the SDLP, the nationalist *Irish News*, Cardinal Cahal Daly, Irish Foreign Minister Dick Spring and opposition leader John Bruton, President Mary Robinson set all their protests to one side, went into West Belfast, met the local community and shook hands with their elected representative Sinn Féin President Gerry Adams.

By this gesture – courageous in political terms – she was following her own principles that you do not demonise, marginalise or alienate the dispossessed. For setting an example of the merits of communication she was pilloried by politicians and the media. She was right, of course, and they were wrong – as subsequent developments were to show. Her politics on the North, incidentally, were by no means pro-republican. She resigned from the Labour Party in 1985 in protest at the Anglo-Irish Agreement which she felt had been imposed on unionists without consulting them.

As a UN representative she travelled extensively from her Geneva base, often causing controversy with her interventions. In May 1999 she warned NATO against inflicting civilian casualties in Belgrade during the Kosovo conflict, but also persisted in the case for prosecuting Slobodan Milosevic for war crimes.

At the United Nations conference on racism in Durban, South Africa, last September, which she spearheaded, the United States and Israel walked out because of criticism of Israel. The US had also opposed apologising to former African colonies for the slave trade in case this led to demands for reparations.

She called for international observers to be allowed into the occupied territories but also condemned Palestinian suicide bombers. She described the September 11th bombings in the US as 'a crime against humanity' but also said that US military actions in Afghanistan had led to excessive civilian casualties.

'I cannot accept that one causes "collateral" damage in villages and doesn't even ask about the number and names of the dead.' (More Afghan civilians have died in these bombings, than in the September 11th attacks.)

She also criticised the US for its treatment of prisoners from the war in Afghanistan now being held at Guantánamo Bay, Cuba. She said that the US is wrong not to recognise the men at Guantánamo as prisoners of war and afford them the rights set down by the Geneva Convention.

Though enjoying much support in Western Europe and many Arab and developing countries it was the fact that she was a thorn in the side of the world's largest superpower that ensured she would not be re-nominated for a full second term. *The New York Times* quoted a senior Bush administration official as saying: 'We made clear, quietly, our views that she shouldn't be renewed.'

'Annan will have to pick some person that is more agreeable,' a Western ambassador told the United Press International.

What has happened to Mary Robinson is nothing short of a disgrace and it leaves the world a much more dangerous place. Praising her, Swedish Foreign Minister Anna Lindh said: 'It is easy to criticise small countries, but she has dared criticise also the big countries.

'She has paid the price for her willingness to confront publicly big governments like the United States and Russia when they violate human rights,' said Reed Brody of Human Rights Watch.

Mary Robinson once said: 'I've always recognised the importance of standing up to bullies, addressing shortcomings and being outspoken – an awkward voice.'

Those who have allowed her to be sidelined are the very authorities that claim to believe in democracy, freedom of information, free speech and, above all, human rights. In getting rid of Mary Robinson they have weakened the voice of human rights and, through seeking a compliant replacement, have shown that that is their exact intention.

Said and Frankl – Race and Belonging

Andersonstown News, 7 August, 2000

Edward Said* is a writer and Professor of Comparative Literature whom I greatly admire. He was born in Jerusalem in 1935 but his family were expelled from their home when Israel was declared and eventually Said settled in the USA.

Several years ago he was diagnosed as having leukaemia though he continued to lecture and tour and write about the Palestinian cause and national dispossession.

He was due to speak at the John Hewitt Summer School in County Antrim in July but was too ill to travel. And that is how several others, including the poet and writer Tom Paulin, and I were privileged to be asked to fill his slot at the last moment. The topic was 'race, cultural identity, belonging', though inevitably the discussion kept turning towards relations between unionist and nationalist and the current state of the peace process.

In my introduction I told a true story, about something that had happened to me the previous Saturday. I had been in London, only for the fourth or fifth time, having been subject to an exclusion order between 1982 and 1995. Thus, I am not too familiar with the geography of that great city. I like walking and since it was a glorious day I decided to make my way on foot from Hammersmith to Shepherds Bush.

However, my map of London was small and didn't include the area I was going to, so along the way I asked various pedestrians for help. I stopped a number of people who were English, and they gave me directions, which included landmarks like filling stations, traffic lights, a florist's and a pharmacy. At one stage I realised I had strayed past a turning I should have made and I stopped a man who happened to be Irish. I am sure he recognised my Belfast accent.

'If you go down that street,' he said, 'you'll see a pub on the left called The Orchard. Then further down you'll come to The Sun. Then after that you'll come to The Rat and Carrot, then you'll see Cobbold Road on your left.'

Perhaps he thought I needed refreshments, or perhaps they were the main things local with which he was familiar. Anyway, his pub-crawl directions were perfect. My audience laughed when I finished the story. But the point I went on to make was this: had an English person told me that story I am sure I would have been quick to take offence, would have suspected there was a subtext of racial stereotyping.

Victor Frankl, a psychiatrist who survived Auschwitz and the genocidal policies of the Nazis would make only one concession to the term 'race'. He said that there are two races of men in this world – the race of the decent man and the race of the indecent man. 'Both are found everywhere; they penetrate into all groups of society. No group consists entirely of decent or indecent people. In this sense, no group is of "pure race".'

It is difficult to resist being prejudiced and defensive, especially given the legacy of our colonial experience and of living in a partitioned, sectarian state, and given the perceived traditional attitude of the English towards the Irish. Unionism has also tended to adopt supremacist attitudes towards the native Irish, only to discover when among the people of England that they too are, ironically, seen as Paddies.

In order to survive, nationalists in the North had until the late sixties to keep their heads down and develop a thick hide. To overcome their sense of isolation and their insecurity they clung to the idea of freedom and a united Ireland. If we northerners seem slightly strange to people in the South, if we appear to have long memories and a crazy mixture of gallows humour and political severity it is because we have not experienced independence or the dubious luxury of revising and rejecting the past, but have had to rely first and foremost on our own inner and outer strengths.

We cannot escape our roots, conditioning and upbringing. Nor do we necessarily need to. Out of the ceasefires, out of the peace process and the political process nationalists and republicans have emerged full of confidence, but not triumphalistic as the anti-Agreement and some pro-Agreement unionists have alleged. If that were the case there would have been no IRA split.

It is this self-assurance, combined with a modernistic attitude, which allowed nationalists and republicans to compromise and make concessions to unionism – which unionism, seemingly, doesn't quite know how to handle.

*Edward Said died on 25 September 2003

Resting in Peace – Le Père-Lachaise

The Examiner, 8 August 2003

Foremost, there are two types of tourists: those who go away to relax and luxuriate, usually in a balmy climate, and those who go away to learn and explore. No matter where I go, or what type of holiday I embark on, even in Donegal, I get restless after three of four days and look forward to getting back to the blue skies of equatorial West Belfast above the Eiffel Mast on Black Mountain.

We went to Gran Canaria for a week a few years ago – to Playa del Ingles, and our apartment was within petrol-bombing distance of the Kasbah, the playground for youngsters with boundless energy who danced and drank till dawn. We were in bed for 10 each night and awake by six each morning. It wasn't until we hired a car and took to the mountains, away from the madness of the resorts, that the holiday became tolerable. Even so, getting home to beautiful Belfast was the best part.

So, I prefer short holidays to long ones, and pack as much in as is possible.

Last week we – my wife and I and her nephew Peter from Toronto – went to Paris for three days and walked out a pair of shoes each. Did all the usual sights: Arc de Triomphe, Moulin Rouge, Sacré Coeur, the Seine cruise, Notre Dame Cathedral, the Louvre (with the Mona Lisa looking browned off with all the attention); viewed the city from the top of the Eiffel Tower; dined in Montmartre, and drank endless cups of strong coffee at sidewalk cafés. On occasions we split up and went our separate ways and thus I spent most of Thursday, by myself, out at Le Père Lachaise, wandering through the city's largest cemetery.

I love cemeteries, not because I am morbid (though I am harmlessly melancholic), but because cemeteries speak for a people, its motley collection of individuals, from the lowliest to the highest, from the leaders to the followers, the politicians, the writers and musicians, the masses. They tell a people's history and though the briefest of details – name, date of birth and death, and sometimes an epigraph – are carved in and will fade over time from headstones, even these last words evoke a great narrative about a person's worth, their place on this earth, their legacy.

The cemetery opened in 1804 as a solution to the problem of overcrowding following the revolution of 1789. The first man to be buried here was an anonymous bell-ringer from the local police station, but several famous Parisians were re-interred in Père-Lachaise, including Molière, and it became a much-sought after resting place for the rich and famous – or the stranded, as in the case of Oscar Wilde, W.B. Yeats and Jim Morrison. Yeats died in Paris in 1939, on the same day as a Parisian refuse collector, and they were buried close together. There is a theory that the person who was re-interred in Drumcliff in Sligo never wrote a poem in his life but emptied plenty of bins.

Le Père-Lachaise covers 100 acres and I walked most of it, beginning with the grave of Rossini where I thanked him with a few prayers and found myself irreverently humming the 'William Tell', that is, 'The Lone Ranger' overture – to which I used to de-deeee-de-de-deeee-de-dee-dee-de-deee with a brush between my legs in Corby Way.

Only when I got home did I discover that the mausoleum was empty and that Rossini's body was moved to Florence in 1887 – but nobody has told the Paris Tourist Board.

Other composers buried in the grounds, and still here, I hope, include Bizet, Chopin, Dukas and Poulenc; singers Maria Callas and Edith Piaf, where fresh flowers had been laid; actors Simone Signoret, Yves Montand and Sarah Bernhardt; the dancer, Isadora Duncan; and writers from Balzac to Colette, to Marcel Proust, Gertrude Stein and the American Richard Wright, author of that brilliant novel, *A Native Son*.

The cemetery has 97 divisions and is easily navigable because each section is signed and named: something which we should insist upon for Milltown and the City Cemetery, though debate and fun will rage over what lane should be called after whom.

Soft rain fell as I made my way through the cobble-stoned avenues drawing out that universal, almost sweet, earthy odour from the trees, bushes and clay, and the scent of our dead. And then I came upon the Mur des Federes, and I stood and wondered about the dreams that died here in a nightmare.

In the Franco-German war of 1870 France was thrashed but Paris fought on and declared a 'Government of National Defence'. It lay under siege for six months until France surrendered and a pro-monarchist Assembly in Versailles, outside the capital, with Adolphe Thiers as Chief Executive, accepted an armistice. However, Paris, which had a strong revolutionary and republican tradition, rose up against the capitulation of the government and formed the Commune (municipal council). The Commune put a moratorium on unpaid war-time rents and stopped pawnshops from selling goods, made all church property state property, postponed debt obligations, and abolished interest on the debts.

Thiers, watched by German forces, bombarded the city for six weeks, which was then slowly taken, barricade-by-barricade, street-by-street in bloody battles, in which at least 30,000 people lost their lives and over 17,000 more were either executed or transported to French penal settlements overseas.

The 'Communards' made their final stand in the Pere-Lachaise cemetery. And here, at Mur des Federes, in a quiet corner, is the wall against which their leaders, 147 of them, were executed and buried.

Not far away is the grave of Thiers who died six years later.

And finally to the grave of that great genius Oscar Wilde – broken and murdered by the intolerance of society because he loved men. I am sure Wilde would enjoy the fact that the authorities no longer replace his penis and testicles, or rather those on his monument, which collectors would break off as mementoes. In his lane the trees were shedding their small, pale leaves, like a perpetual autumn. Three sides of his monument were imprinted with lipstick from the adoring kisses of many women. And on the fourth were these beautiful lines from 'The Ballad of Reading Gaol':

> And alien tears will fill for him
> Pity's long-broken urn,
> For his mourners will be outcast men,
> And outcasts always mourn.

Marwan Barghouthi – A Palestinian Hero

Andersonstown News, 6 October 2003

In a dangerous or threatening situation one or two individuals within any group will remain cool and rise above the rest who seem paralysed and incapable of action. Such individuals will exercise a focused judgement, will make decisions that may save or partly redeem a bad situation, will, in other words, show leadership (which is kin to showing courage) and in the process will become – often in opposition to their own humility – true heroes.

Similarly, throughout history, when a people finds itself in subjugation, oppressed and dispossessed – that is, facing a permanent threat which has dispirited and demoralised them – the righteousness of their cause amounts to nought in the absence of leadership, organisation and strategy.

Today, in the 21st century, right before our eyes, the Palestinian people are being destroyed by one of the cruellest and most cynical regimes in the Middle East, Israel, a state that is bankrolled by the US government. In flagrant breach of UN Resolution 242, first issued in 1967 and reaffirmed many times in the subsequent 36 years, Israel refuses to withdraw from the territories it occupied following the Six Day War. It continues to conquer, to build settlements – indeed, to build a Warsaw Wall through the West Bank, ghettoising the Palestinians and rendering impossible any viable Palestinian state.

It does this despite the fact that through superior violence and murder it has won from mainstream Palestinian groups recognition of the state of Israel. And in reaction it has spawned the phenomenon of the suicide bombers.

I watch CNN fairly regularly. I was hooked on it especially during the debacle of the Florida count in the US presidential election in 2000. CNN has incredible resources, journalists or stringers in every capital of the world and breaks news with breathtaking speed. Millions in the US watch the channel and perhaps have their political opinions influenced by what they receive.

What I noticed – and this might not be the fault of CNN but rather a regrettable feature of the quality of Palestinian representatives and/or circumstance – is that in the aftermath of a particularly violent incident or dramatic development, the Israeli spokesperson is usually in a studio. He is suave, his English is impeccable (and often delivered in a North American accent) and he is questioned courteously.

On the other hand, the Palestinian spokesperson is often interviewed on a street corner or a makeshift studio. There is distortion or atmospherics on the feed, he usually speaks in broken English (unless, of course, it is Hanan Ashrawi) and is placed on the defensive by being pressed to distance himself from Palestinian violence.

A few years ago I noticed one Palestinian spokesperson in particular who stood out in stature above many others, including Yasser Arafat and the prime minister, Abu Mazen.

That man is Marwan Barghouthi. He is articulate, confident and popular among his people.

I remember seeing him being interviewed in early August 2001 when there was a tremendous explosion on the street. A missile fired from an Israeli helicopter hit his office or his car, killing another Fatah member. Of course, since then the Israelis have murdered and assassinated several hundred alleged militants – collaterally killing children, women and men who shouldn't be out in the sun in broad daylight.

Someone who interviewed El-Barghouthi told me that after his arrest in 1982 he was on hunger strike and said that he drew inspiration from Bobby Sands and his comrades and could cite that Bobby died on May 5th 1981. In prison he mastered Hebrew from his jailors and can speak it far more eloquently than many Israelis.

He was born in 1959 to a West Bank farmer. At the age of 16 he joined Fatah and earned a master's degree in international relations at Bir Zeit university. He is married with four children. During the first intifada of 1987 he was deported by Israel. He supported the peace talks with Israel in the early 1990s, returned to the West Bank in 1994 and ran programmes for Israeli and Palestinian youth. He became secretary of the Fatah movement and was elected to the Palestinian Legislative Council of the Palestinian Authority and has spoken out against corruption within the Authority.

However, in April 2002 Israeli forces in Ramallah arrested him. He was interrogated for several months for 18 hours at a time. For three months he was allowed to sleep for only two hours at a time and then only in a chair with his hands tied. He was denied food and water, has been regularly placed in solitary confinement and denied access to his lawyers. He was charged with directing the al Aqsa Martyrs' Brigade, which is linked to Fatah and which has been responsible for many of the suicide bomb attacks, mainly against innocent Israeli citizens. He was condemned even before his trial. The Israeli Attorney-General said he was 'an engineer of all acts of killings and a thug.'

From his prison cell he played a crucial role in Palestinian dialogue and encouraged Hamas and Islamic Jihad to call a truce last June (which later broke down).

He has been tipped to replace Arafat as chair of the Palestinian Authority and Israel fears his leadership. Foreign Minister Shimon Peres remarked that if that happened, 'this will not be a positive development for Israel.'

El-Barghouthi's trial ended last Monday and judgement is expected in November. He refused to recognise the court in Tel Aviv and said that Israel's grip on the West Bank and Gaza Strip should be in the dock instead. He accused Israel of violating 30 international treaties, including the Geneva Convention and of committing war crimes against humanity.

The alleged evidence against him was confessions from 21 Palestinians, none of who appeared in court. Israel is notorious for its abuse of prisoners and has been condemned of torture by many human rights groups. During earlier court appearances Barghouthi's attempts to speak were interrupted but finally he managed to say: 'We are a people like all other people. We want freedom and a state just like the Israelis. Israel must decide: either it allows for a Palestinian state alongside it, or it becomes a state for two peoples.'

One of the three judges interrupted him and said: 'We are not historians nor government representatives. If it were in our hands we would issue an injunction ordering peace!'

To cheers from European Parliament observers El-Barghouthi replied: 'Why don't you just get up and say "I am against the occupation"!'

He said: 'I am against killing innocents. But I am proud of the resistance to Israeli occupation. To die is better than living under occupation.'

Marwan Barghouthi – a true hero to the Palestinian cause. Their Nelson Mandela.

In June 2004, Marwan Barghouthi was sentenced to five life sentences (a total of 165 years). He replied, 'this court is just a partner in the war against the Palestinian people... No matter how many [Israel] arrests and kills, they will not break our people's determination'.

Proud to be an American

Andersonstown News, 21 July 2003

In an online petition thousands of US citizens have pressed the documentary filmmaker Michael Moore to run for president of their country! He certainly is a breath of fresh air, an active conscience of the American people, and to the delight of millions the bane in the life of President George Bush.

His satirical book *Stupid White Men* had the misfortune of being due for publication on September 12th 2001, the day after the terrorist bombings on the World Trade Centre and Washington. The publishers, HarperCollins, left it lying in a warehouse, believing that its sustained attack on Bush would be perceived as being 'insensitive'. In an open letter to Bush, Moore asks him whether he's a functional illiterate, whether he's a felon and whether he is getting the necessary help for his drug and alcohol problem! In one chapter, 'A Very American Coup', Moore points out that Bush actually lost the presidential election, got fewer votes (a half a million less) than Al Gore, and that in the controversial vote in Florida 173,000 voters (many of whom were black and likely Gore supporters) were removed from the register by dubious means.

The publishers asked Moore to change the title and re-write half of the book. He refused. Then, a librarian started a campaign on the internet, criticising the publishers and they were forced to give way. When released, it went to Number 1 in about three days.

However, the book was not aired on any network television shows and over 90 per cent of the newspapers refused to review it, including the *New York Times* (on whose bestsellers' list it remained for thirty-four weeks).

Last year, Moore released his film *Bowling for Columbine* at the Cannes Festival. It has the familiar mix of his styles: confrontational, audacious and entertaining. It received a fifteen-minute standing ovation at Cannes and went on to scoop an Oscar for best documentary this year at the Academy Awards.

At Columbine High School in 1999 two pupils, armed with legally held firearms, killed twelve students and a teacher before killing themselves. Before going on their shooting spree, the two had gone bowling earlier in the day. The film is an indictment of the gun laws in the USA and the National Rifle Association in particular. Every day forty people – twelve of them children – die of gunshot wounds in the USA. But the film also examines America's foreign policy and the issue of race.

In one brilliant piece of filming, Charlton Heston, president of the NRA, is ridiculed for speaking at a rally shortly after the shooting, during which he said: 'To take my gun away from me, you'd have to prise it from out of my cold, dead hand.'

In the final scene, a stupid-looking Heston slowly and silently walks away from Moore during an interview, refusing to take responsibility for the negative side of gun use. Moore then leaves a photo against a pillar in Heston's house of Kayla Rolland, a six-year-old girl shot dead by a six-year-old boy in their first grade classroom.

At the Academy awards ceremony, in his acceptance speech, Moore again lambasted George Bush. He said of his fellow documentary nominees, including his wife Katharine Glynn: 'We like non-fiction and we live in fictitious times. We live in the time where we have fictitious election results that elect a fictitious president. We live in a time where we have a man sending us to war for fictitious reasons… We are against this war, Mr Bush. Shame on you, Mr Bush, shame on you…'

He got a standing ovation from the greater part of the audience, while others in the balcony booed. Box office returns on the film, already the highest-grossing documentary in history, were up by more than 100 percent on the Monday after Oscar night. *Stupid White Men,* already the largest non-fiction best seller of 2002, reclaimed the No. 1 slot.

Since then, Moore has stepped up his anti-war stance and regularly addresses George Bush on his website (http://www.michaelmoore.com/index.php). He needles the president over his draft dodging by referring to him as 'Lieutenant' ('the only true military rank you ever achieved… in the, um, Texas Air National Guard'). In May, Bush appeared like a five-star general on the aircraft carrier, USS Abraham Lincoln, in the Gulf and with a 'Mission Accomplished' banner fluttering in the background, announced that the war was over. Since then American troops are being killed on an almost daily basis in Iraq.

Interviewed in *The Guardian* last November Moore said of the USA: 'We're raised with the manifest destiny, the belief, that we have the right to resolve our conflicts through violence, and that we will shoot first and inspect for weapons later. That's our mentality, that's the way we're going to live our lives, that's how we're going to rule the world. And it will be our ruin if it's not addressed.'

Moore has spoken throughout the US, to audiences with an average of 2,000-3,000 per night. At one venue, 5,000 people had to be turned away.

Moore, the school dropout, with his hallmark denim jeans and baseball hat and ponderous gait, is no stupid, white man, but makes many of his co-nationals proud to be American.

In August 2003 Moore addressed a crowd of 800 people during Féile an Phobail in West Belfast, and spoke about his film Farenheit 9/11. In June 2004, shortly after its release, the film became the highest grossing documentray of all time on its first weekend of showing.

Yes, Prime Minister

The Guardian, 3 February 2004

L ord Hutton and I were once very close. I sat about ten feet from him in the witness box while he quizzed me on charges of conspiracy to murder, IRA membership and kidnapping. He eventually sentenced me to eight years in jail on the testimony of a police informer I never met.

Although in the Belfast High Court Hutton occasionally acquitted republicans and dismissed the appeals of soldiers, nationalists in general considered him a hanging judge and the guardian angel of soldiers and police officers.

I was amused at the response of sections of the media and British public opinion to last week's report when Hutton completely exonerated the British prime minister, his defence secretary and press officer from BBC allegations that the government 'sexed up' a pre-war dossier on Iraq's weapons of mass destruction (even though the Iraqi threat was sexed up, and Iraq had no weapons of mass destruction, never mind was capable of deploying such weapons within 45 minutes, as claimed by Tony Blair).

Instead, Hutton's report completely damned the BBC and has shaken that institution to its foundations. Incredibly, many of those in Britain who had closely followed the Hutton inquiry and observed the contradictions, heard the lies and saw the evasiveness of government representatives, naively expected these damning volumes of evidence to be taken into account!

Do they know anything about how the establishment works? Have they never heard of the six counties and how our poor, struggling, conscience-stricken judiciary coped with all the quandaries they faced?

What were at stake in Britain were the office of the Prime Minister (as distinct from Blair) and the judgement, integrity and morale of the British military authorities, now dug-in-deep in a quagmire in Iraq.

Lord Denning, Master of the Rolls, the third highest law lord in Britain, sat on the Privy Council with ministers of the government. They were united in one conviction: our country, right or wrong! To him the rights of Irish people in particular were subservient to the fabric of the British policing and judicial system. Denning summed this up best in his 1980 judgement when he ruled against an appeal by the Birmingham Six whose case was that they had been beaten and made false confessions.

He said: 'If the six men win, it will mean that the police were guilty of perjury; that they were guilty of violence and threats ... That was such an appalling vista that every sensible person would say, "It cannot be right that these actions should go any further".'

Our good Lord Brian Hutton has served his country well. There is an old caution that one shouldn't confuse lawyers with the clients whom they defend. However, judges almost certainly can be judged from their judgements.

Brian Hutton first made the news in 1973 when, representing the Ministry of Defence at the inquests into those killed on Bloody Sunday, he castigated the coroner, Major Hubert O'Neill, for having the temerity to suggest that the Paras had no justification for shooting the people. Hutton told him: 'It is not for you or the jury to express such wide-ranging views, particularly when a most eminent judge has spent twenty days hearing evidence and come to a very different conclusion.'

Those twenty days were a reference to the seven-week long inquiry by British Lord Chief Justice Widgery into the thirteen deaths in Derry that resulted in a historic miscarriage of justice, currently being re-examined by Lord Saville. Thirty years later, when it came to the inquiry into the death of one former weapons inspector, Dr David Kelly, the more diligent Hutton would take seven months to absolve once again those who opened fire [in Iraq] without justification.

In 1978 he was part of the team defending Britain at the Strasbourg Court against Irish government allegations that internees in 1971 were tortured. In 1981 he presided at the trial of a British soldier who ploughed at high speed into a group of people in Derry, killing two youths. Hutton advised the jury 'to consider whether you think that perhaps unconsciously some of the witnesses... had a tendency somewhat to strengthen their evidence against the army'. He suggested that the driving, while reckless, might not have been unreasonable – one of his favourite words – given the rioting and attempts to apprehend the rioters. The soldiers were acquitted.

He agreed with supergrass trials and in 1984 he sentenced ten men to some of the longest sentences ever imposed, to a total to 1001 years, on the word of a paid informer, Robert Quigley, who was granted immunity from prosecution.

In 1986 he acquitted RUC Reservist, Nigel Hegarty, who was charged with unlawfully killing John Downes at a rally outside Connolly House. When the RUC opened fire with plastic bullets on civilians at a sit-down protest John Downes picked up a small stick and was running towards two officers when Hegarty killed him from about ten feet away. Despite Hegarty offering no evidence Hutton speculated that he had acted 'probably almost instinctively' and that, given 'the stress of the moment and the obvious determination of the deceased', Hegarty's response was not unreasonable.

In the trial of two Royal Marines who had been charged with murdering Fergal Caraher in a shooting incident at Cullyhanna in 1990 he said he could not rely on the accounts given by the civilian witnesses for the defence or on those given by the accused and a fellow soldier so he acquitted the two soldiers even though he believed they were lying.

And, of course, he was involved in the Brian Nelson affair when, just a week before Nelson's trial, which would have exposed British collusion with loyalist death squads, Hutton and the trial judge, Basil Kelly, met with Prime Minister John Major. Nelson was offered a deal to plead guilty to sample charges, which he did, and served just a few years before being released.

In one episode of the BBC's series, 'Yes Prime Minister', the PM Jim Hacker is furious when someone leaks to the press that he has manipulated his Solicitor-General to suppress a political memoir, not on security grounds but because it contained a chapter about him, 'The Two Faces of Jim Hacker'. He wants the culprit found and convicted. His cabinet secretary, Sir Humphrey Appleby, rushes to set up a leak inquiry and Hacker stops him and suggests that they lean on the judge to guarantee success.

However, the wise and wily, Sir Humphrey – in this comedy from 1987, which has its mirror image in 2004 – suggests that it is better to find a judge who doesn't need to be leaned on!